CREATIVE GIRL

The Ultimate Guide for Turning Talent and Creativity into a Real Career

Katharine Sise

RUNNING PRESS
PHILADELPHIA · LONDON

JAN 1

To Dad, Mom, Meghan, Jack, and Brian.
Thank you for supporting my creativity always.

© 2010 Katharine Sise
Cover illustration © 2010 by Kristine A. Lombardi
Interior illustrations © 2010 by Corinda Cook
All rights reserved under the Pan-American and International Copyright Conventions
Printed in the United States

9   8   7   6   5   4   3   2
Digit on the right indicates the number of this printing

Library of Congress Control Number: 2010929182

ISBN 978-0-7624-3869-3

Design and interior illustrations by Corinda Cook
Cover illustration by Kristine A. Lombardi
Edited by Jennifer Kasius
Typography: Constantia, Ed Brush, Latin, and Trade Gothic

Running Press Book Publishers
2300 Chestnut Street
Philadelphia, PA 19103-4371

Visit us on the web!
www.runningpress.com

~ Contents ~

Introduction

"You're so creative."

You've heard this over and over again throughout your life. Your grandmother enthused over your fashion-forward paper doll collection, "You're so creative. What a wonderful gift!" A few years later your second grade teacher, Mrs. Darbyshire, cooed, "These watercolors are exquisite. What a creative girl you are." Then there was that ninth grade English teacher with the glass eye who called your parents—barely able to keep the emotion out of her voice—and told them she'd never read such promising writing from a fourteen-year-old. Of course, your parents nodded knowingly. They've heard this repeatedly, from those watercolors in second grade to your fifth grade performance as Rosie in *Bye Bye Birdie* (and, my God, how *did* you capture the desperation and longing of a thirty-year-old woman at age eleven?)

Welcome to your creativity. You've always had it, but now the real world is calling and it's time to make it—or break it.

When people asked me during college what I wanted to do for a living, I answered, "I want to act and write." This made well-meaning people so nervous that they couldn't help but ask about my back-up plan, as if my career was a birth control method destined to fail. I appreciate practicality as much as the next girl, but for me, the only work I've ever wanted to do was creative. Even my back-up plans were creative. After I graduated from the University of Notre Dame, I arrived in New York City with my theater degree, $239 and incredibly high hopes. I wrote short stories in the morning, auditioned in the afternoon and bartended at Tavern on the Green on the weekends. After dropping a rare and very expensive bottle of champagne on my way to deliver it to Robert De Niro's table, I realized I needed a way to fund my creative aspirations that didn't involve balancing a tray full of cocktails. So I announced my backup plan to my family and friends at my grandfather's eightieth birthday party. It went something like this:

Aunt Posie: "Would anyone like more cake?"

Me: "Yes, please."

Grandpa: "So, what are you doing for work these days?"

Me: "I've decided to support my acting habit by designing jewelry."

The reaction to this plan was like I'd said I wanted to breed unicorns. Fair enough, really: I didn't have any design experience. But I ignored the naysayers, taught myself

how to make jewelry, and launched my line in 2004. Before I knew it, major fashion magazines were covering my work and the Olsen twins were strolling around L.A. clutching Starbucks cups and wearing my jewelry. I capitalized on my previous acting training, got an agent, and started appearing on TV as a style expert, eventually co-hosting a television show on The Home Shopping Network. By the time I was in my mid-twenties, I was able to support myself creatively. I haven't looked back since.

Of course, I made a zillion mistakes along the way. The first time a magazine editor asked for images of my work, I put the jewelry on a photocopier and sent her color copies instead of taking digital pictures (I couldn't afford a camera). I mixed up a jewelry sample I designed for Target, and the piece that appeared on their website ended up being different from the one customers actually received. A necklace I designed broke ON AIR while I was chatting with the ladies from *The View*. While I was talking about my jewelry, it fell from my neck to my lap because I didn't spend enough time getting the clasp right. That glorious moment is preserved, forever, on a DVD at my parents' house.

Trust me, there are plenty more where

those came from. Everything I learned from my mistakes—not only about sturdy clasps, but the actual business and career lessons—is in this book, along with the guidance I wish I'd had then. I interviewed other creative professionals about everything they wished they'd known, too. I made it my goal to write the book my creative colleagues and I needed when we embarked on our careers.

A creative career path is winding and very different from a traditional one. This book will support you from the first moments of assessing your talent to building a financially solvent livelihood. Together, we'll debunk the starving artist cliché and become successful, self-supported artists by focusing on the financial, emotional, and spiritual fulfillment attainable in a creative life. Age doesn't matter here; you'll find guidance whether you're a college student wondering what in the world to do after graduation, a thirtysomething stay-at-home mom, or a retiree who wants to launch an interior decorating empire. This guide gives you a bird's-eye view of how to achieve the happiest creative life possible.

While you're reading, keep your mind open to the myriad options for bringing home the bacon with your creativity. You may decide to work at a creative company, freelance, or open your own business. Many of you will follow the order laid out in these pages; you'll start at a creative company and transition to freelance or a small business entrepreneurship. Some of you may work in the opposite direction—you'll start off on your own and segue into an exciting creative career with the company of your dreams.

You'll get the real story from creative girls (CGs) living life in the creative trenches. Their careers range from lipstick moguls to voice-over actors, and their positions range from interns to full-blown creative superstars. You'll discover a resounding message in each anecdote and every chapter: you *can* do this. You *can* make a career with your creativity, you *can* turn what inspires you into what pays your bills, and you *can* grin like the cat that swallowed the canary every time someone asks you what you do for a living.

The book you're holding is laid out in two parts: Part One is a welcome-to-your-creativity party where we'll figure out exactly what the heck you want to do. You'll evaluate your talent and your current job situation. If your job stinks, we'll talk about strategies for making it work before taking the leap to full-time creative girl. Because as tempting as it is to storm out of your non-creative job shouting, "Next time you'll see me, I'll be holding an Oscar!" the truth

is, you want to be financially savvy and strategic about your next move.

Part Two is your roadmap for getting where you want to go. Once you're there, we'll talk about finding emotional, spiritual, and financial fulfillment. To reach career nirvana, you have to take into account your day-to-day happiness and wellbeing. That means making money a priority, too. Financial freedom plus emotional freedom *is* freedom, and that freedom allows each creative girl the healthiest space possible to peacefully create.

You'll find numerous ideas for creating an inspired career that provides you with the ultimate in creative fulfillment. Bring your most idealistic self and approach the material with healthy curiosity. I'll discuss hundreds of practical career strategies, so the realist in you will be satisfied, but give yourself room to dream big. Resist the urge to judge your ideas. If you're not going to

make great plans for yourself, then who is?

Have a pen ready for journaling exercises. If you're on the go, scrawl ideas in the blank pages at the back of the book. Any time an urge or inspiration strikes you, jot it down. Let the material marinate, and use whatever resonates with you to move forward. Remember that wherever you are on your career path, being open, aware, and mindful will serve you. I'll give you some simple tips for meditation—it's not just for enlightened yogis, and I promise not to make you wear white—so that you can sit quietly and allow your body and intuition to give you feedback. Sometimes, after you've examined all the facts, you just need to quiet down and reflect in order to make a difficult decision.

Creative success is at your fingertips. Put your intention there, allow new adventures, and see how the world opens up for you.

Let's get started.

Creative, *adj.*

1. Having the quality or power of creating.

2. Resulting from originality of thought, expression, etc.; imaginative.

3. Originative; productive.

Creativity, *n.*

1. The state or quality of being creative.

2. The ability to transcend traditional rules, patterns,

   relationships, or the like, and to create meaningful

   new ideas, forms, methods, interpretations, etc.;

   originality, progressiveness, or imagination.

3. The process by which one utilizes creative ability.

Creative Girl, *person.*

1. A female of any age, ethnicity, or religion with creative urges.

2. A female with creative, imaginative thoughts.

3. A female who craves a life full of creative fulfillment.

Creative Girl

CHAPTER 1

The Welcome Packet

Millions of creative careers already exist.
You're going to add to that number.

Creativity is a mindset. It's a way of living, thinking, and experiencing

the world around you. Being creative manifests in your every action and decision, from who and what you love to how you want to work. Whether or not you make your living creatively, you've likely experienced an ongoing desire to create since you were a child.

When she was eight years old, actress and filmmaker Aimee Denaro thumbed through the yellow pages and dialed an advertising agency. When the receptionist picked up, she squeaked, "Hello, I was wondering if you needed any actresses?" Aimee hung up and informed her mother that she had a meeting that week at the agency. Reluctantly, her mom drove her to the meeting, where Aimee and her talent impressed the producers. She worked for the agency as a voiceover actress from eight until she graduated from high school, earning a bundle of money along the way for college.

Some CGs, like Aimee, start right away on their creative careers. Others wake up at forty-five and realize they want to make a change. This was the case for Rhonda Kave and Julie Couch. Rhonda made chocolate as a hobby for twenty years before opening her shop, Roni-Sue's Chocolates. Now, Rhonda entertains rabid media attention and a cult-like following. Julie, an interior decorator, says, "In my mid-forties, a lightbulb went off. After all of those years, I finally realized I was good enough at my hobby to turn it into a career."

Many women graduate from college and take a job they're not crazy about because it's practical. Year after year they stay in that job because it's easier than forging a new path, and because it's terrifying to walk away from a steady paycheck and benefits. They start feeling stuck and apathetic. They brush off their lingering creative dreams as impractical and idealistic, something they wanted to do when they were too young to know any better. In the course of researching for this book, I spoke with many women who claimed they hadn't yet figured out what they wanted to be when they "grew up." Others said they knew exactly what they wanted to be, but they didn't know how to get there or didn't think it was possible to pay the bills with their creativity.

I've got news for you: it *is* possible to make your living creatively. It takes talent, but above all, an unfailing work ethic and strategic planning.

Stifling Yourself is Exhausting: Let it Roar

Stifling your creativity takes a lot of energy. If you've been trying to convince yourself that career girls with Ivy League educations don't quit their hedge fund jobs to write a screenplay, think again. Just before turning thirty, Christine Hawes packed her bags and left her cushy corporate gig in Burlington, Vermont, for Los Angeles to pursue a career in costume design. Fast forward six years, and Christine is thriving as one of the industry's go-to costume stylists. Danielle Gregan left her job as an accountant at one of New York City's Big Four to work for herself as a yoga teacher. Danielle says, "At my firm, I was being promoted and making more and more money. But every day I went to work, I felt like an impostor. I walked through my office and thought, 'Is this really my life?' So I thought about how I could live a more authentic life. I'd loved yoga for years. I loved going to classes and listening to what my teacher had to say. I realized that I wanted to give that to someone else."

These CGs are everywhere. Fed up with a work life that didn't fit who they were, they decided to explore the places their creativity and entrepreneurial spirit could take them. They realized a shot at career happiness was worth it. They realized *they* were worth it.

Because what's the point of playing by someone else's rules if you're walking around feeling like Rose DeWitt Bukater in *Titanic*? As Kate Winslet told Leonardo DiCaprio on the deck of the ship, "All the while I feel like I'm screaming in the middle of a crowded room and no one even looks up." Pretending to like your non-creative life is exhausting; it drains your energy to fake it, so cut it out. Besides, your discontent will manifest in other ways, like stress, insomnia, or depression, so even if you're not quite ready to make the leap, acknowledge where you'd like to be headed. (And, if you're not sure where that is, see

Chapter 3 to get a jump-start on pinpointing your creativity.) Just vocalizing that you want something different, what you think it might be, and how you plan to achieve it will free parts of you that you've been ignoring or feeding lines like, "You can't pay the bills as an artist, so you'll have to stay in this job unless you hit the lottery."

Because that's just baloney. Creative jobs are plentiful. A screenwriter wrote the movie you saw last night. A casting director cast it. A furniture designer designed the chair you're sitting in. In his book, *A Whole New Mind*, Daniel Pink reports, "In the United States, the number of graphic designers has increased tenfold in a decade; graphic designers outnumber chemical engineers four to one. Since 1970, the United States has seen a 30 percent increase in the number of people earning a living as writers; 50 percent more are earning a living by composing or performing music. . . . More Americans today work in arts, entertainment, and design than work as lawyers, accountants, and auditors."

Recent trends confirm that a creative movement is underway. Women are opening businesses at a rate twice as fast as their male counterparts. Whether they've been laid off from their office jobs, chosen to leave them for work they're passionate about, or want more flexible careers while raising families, women are getting creative about obtaining their ideal careers. If there isn't stability in the corporate world, why not do what you love?

This isn't your grandparents' job market, where steadfast devotion was rewarded with a job for life. In this climate, we've collectively realized there isn't job security anywhere. It just may be that your best chance at a lifetime of financial security— and career satisfaction—comes from developing your own unique talents and skills and parlaying them into a self-driven career.

Start the journey by honoring the creative part of you. Write letters, write poetry, redecorate your bedroom, paint pictures, roll down the car windows, and crank up the music. Go to a new restaurant or see a movie. Paint your toenails a bright shade of fuchsia. Get lost in a book. Allow yourself to reconnect with and release that inner creative force. And *listen*. Listen to that nagging feeling that creeps in and tells you there's more out there for you. Listen to any idea that pops up and inspires you. Jot it down. Do whatever you must to quiet down and listen to what your inner creative voice is saying. Gather clues. Gain clarity about your next step.

And get ready to work it, creative girl.

From Creative Wannabe to Creative Convert

CG-in-action Kim Hoggatt works in medical device sales. I've known Kim since college, where, though she was a business major, she secretly wished she was the lead singer in her own rock band. Kim claims she can't hold a tune, but she paid attention to that inner creative voice and figured out her biggest strengths: the marketing and business sides of creativity. She brainstormed ideas for a creative venture and is currently planning the launch of Glass Slippers—not a band but a stemware accessories company.

Just because you don't paint watercolors or sing *Phantom of the Opera* at a cabaret on the weekends doesn't mean you're not cut out for a creative life. If you're feeling disgruntled with your present work and are itching to release your inner CG, take the skills you've learned elsewhere and apply them to your next career step. You're not a job title, you're a person with an amalgam of qualities and skills. So you held a manager title at your last job? Managerial skills come in handy all over the creative career map.

Entrepreneurial ventures demand both creativity and business savvy. So brainstorm ideas for your own company or partner with a designer, pastry chef, or screenwriter and get that creative business going.

Some of you may not even need to make a drastic career change; you may be able to take your unique, non-creative knowledge and apply it creatively, like CG-in-action Corey Binns. Corey was a science major in college. She says, "After I graduated, I quickly realized the science lab wasn't for me. Something was missing. I needed to find a way to use my creativity in my work." Corey took her in-depth knowledge of science and launched a successful freelance writing career. Now she writes health and science related articles for magazines like *Popular Science* and *Scientific American Mind*. She's currently at work on her first book.

These creative converts are everywhere. Take Lanesha Russell, an optician and one of the most creative girls I know. Lanesha took her training and landed a gig at Artsee, a visionary shop that sells both paintings and eyeglasses. Her job became part art dealer and part optician. Lanesha says, "Surrounded by art, my creative urge was satisfied day in and day out."

Most people on this planet don't have the luxury of choosing their work. So let's honor the choices we do have by choosing wisely, in ways that honor the creative people we truly are.

Minds Wide Open

Keep your mind open to every option this book presents you. We'll discuss options like working 9 to 5 in a creative capacity at a company, freelancing, or opening a small business. One thing is certain; creative careers have a way of surprising you. Mine did. I came to New York City to be an actress. I was such a terrible waitress that I decided to try to support my acting habit by designing a few pieces of jewelry for a local boutique. It sounded like fun. A few months later, an entire career was literally at my fingertips. I had to learn how to be a business owner on the spot.

While reading, consider this: if you happen to have a particular talent that hasn't started paying the bills yet, why not support that talent with another creative endeavor? You can waitress or work in a non-creative day job while waiting for your creative talent to financially support you . . . or you can explore other creative options for bringing home the bacon. You want to be

a tap dancer? Great. But I'll bet you have a bunch of other creative talents up your sleeve. Creativity breeds creativity and your success is like a snowball; almost always, achievement in one creative field feeds into another.

Don't misunderstand me: this doesn't mean you focus any less on your original pursuit. It means you think in an expansive (instead of restrictive) way about your creative ability. Instead of getting attached to yourself as only one thing—*I'm a sculptor*—challenge the perimeters that define your talent. When you embrace this concept, you'll be shocked at how completely boundless you are. Each creative talent is a continually evolving business and it's exciting to push your artistic limits and find unlikely avenues that stem from your original pursuit. When you're strategic about your achievements, you'll cohesively build a career.

I met CG-in-action Kimberly Rae Miller when she played Cecily to my Gwendolen in a New York City performance of *The Importance of Being Earnest*. A few years later, she began blogging about food, dieting, and lifestyle, and a Condé Nast website picked up her blog. Because of her acting training, she was comfortable on camera, so she turned her blog into a web show. That show was a hit and scored a Webby Award within a year of airing. Kim landed a topnotch TV agent and came full circle to her original pursuit: acting and on-camera work.

Most of the CGs I interviewed had multiple creative strengths, like Sarah Kuhn, an accessories editor at *Teen Vogue* who moonlights as a member of the band Left Coast. Meredith Zinner holds her own in movies like *Erin Brockovich,* but enjoys being behind the camera as a professional photographer, too. Comedienne Molly Reisner wrote a laugh-out-loud-funny novel about a sixteen-year-old aspiring comic. Arielle Fierman, a jewelry designer and holistic health counselor said, "Why not make a living with two services I love to do and strongly believe in? Having both creative outlets is ideal. And often, my client base overlaps."

The point is that you're creative. We've established that. If you want to focus all your creative energy on one goal and keep plugging away until you achieve it, that's great too. But if you're like the aforementioned CGs and me, exploring multiple creative avenues keeps life interesting. Often, when one aspect of your career is lagging, the other is flying high. This keeps you feeling productive and successful.

Your original career doesn't have to be stilted for you to pursue other goals. CG-in-action Rashida Jones is a bonafide Hollywood movie and television star. But she also loves design and genuinely understands the work involved in constructing a garment. So Rashida launched Laloo, a clothing line made with organic cotton. She put a t-shirt on me that was so comfortable I didn't take it off for days.

Movie star and CG Michelle Monaghan has starred in films like *Mission Impossible 3, The Heartbreak Kid,* and *Eagle Eye.* After nearly a decade of acting, she decided to try her hand at producing on the film *Trucker.* On a walk along a quiet street in New York City, Michelle told me she was ready to stretch herself by trying something that required an entirely different set of skills.

How do you get to where the CGs in this chapter are? Start by understanding that this is an outlook. Start seeing yourself just as you are: unlimited, boundless, and expansive. That's the truth of our creativity.

Be open to the unlikely opportunities that stem from your original pursuit. Observe how other CGs in your field have parlayed their unique skills into additional employment opportunities. The ability to shift gears and expand will serve you, so experiment and push yourself farther than you thought you could go. You never know what you might discover.

CHAPTER 2

You
Are
Here

*Take a breath,
understand the value of the present,
and create daily.*

The Present Perfect

Wherever you are on your creative path, be very, *very* present. Be mindful, aware, and open to the fact that you are exactly where you're meant to be in this moment. I know you're reading this book to learn how to translate creativity into a flourishing career. But always remember that your desire comes from a very pure place, a creative center within you that you've likely felt since you were a child. So while we'll discuss multiple career strategies, begin your journey by honoring that part of yourself. The true value in a creative life is the fulfillment of creating just for the sake of expression. I'll ask you to put your business hat on many times. But even as you're reading about garnering press or branding yourself, we'll both know that your original desire to create is at the center of every pursuit. And here's why that's so important: the truth of your creativity means there's nothing sincere or productive in the thought, "I'll be happy when I get there, or when I accomplish this."

It took me a long time to figure this out, so if you can get your mind around this concept, you're going to save yourself a lot of hassle and find the clarity you need to proceed. My entire life I've felt an overwhelming urge to imagine and produce creative work, and somewhere around age seventeen, this urge evolved into a desire to get *there*. I defined *there* as a blissful state of achievement where I'd earn an enviable living with my creative prowess. In my mind, *there* was being a fulltime writer/actress/designer who penned novels and drank champagne during Fashion Week in a swanky wine bar in Paris.

So I became restless when I felt the details of my life weren't leading me to this romanticized place. During my freshman year in college, math class was time for scrawling a short story

Instead of thinking you'll be satisfied with The Next Big Thing, think:

The present is already perfect.
There is an innate value in creating every day.

in my notebook while everyone else was doing logarithms. I spent my senior year theology class copying down lines I had to learn for a production of *Romeo and Juliet*. It's a small miracle the swimmers survived in the small town where I was lifeguarding each summer. I spent the afternoons slathering on sunscreen and daydreaming about my soon-to-be fabulous adult life as a creative girl conquering New York City.

But when I finally arrived in New York, I had a hard time appreciating each little step and accomplishment. When I landed my first theater role, I couldn't wait to land one in a better theater. When I got the next role, I told myself I'd *really* be happy when I booked my first television role. I spoke with my colleagues and realized that it wasn't just me engaging in this kind of thinking. With many creative types, there's an ever-present desire to achieve the next thing: your first painting hanging in a gallery, your first article published, or your first Off-Broadway role. Certainly, this kind of drive and determination can create great things. But the trouble with this way of thinking is that there is always that Next Big Thing that you convince yourself will be the point when you'll be satisfied or will have finally "made it." But what does this attitude imply about the creative work you're doing right now?

This way of thinking feeds off of dissatisfaction with the present. It emphasizes *lack*. Your thoughts are powerful. There's energy behind them. Whether or not you're conscious of this yet, your thoughts become your experience. Make a conscious effort to shift your inner language to reflect self-acceptance and true joy in creating in the present moment. This will open the door to the creative adventure that starts in your present place.

Creative work evolves over a lifetime and takes shape on its own schedule. So every time you want to stress about who, what, or where you should be by now, shift your thoughts by focusing on perfection of the present and the very act of creating. Honor the part of you that creates solely because that's what you love. Then, create.

I know this isn't an easy adjustment to make, but it's a worthy one. If you're thinking, *easy for you to say,* let me assure you that I've been there. After I graduated from college, my practical roommates landed great jobs and law school admissions while I stocked potato chips on the shelves of Wal-Mart for my Uncle Doug's potato chip company so I could save enough money to move to New York City. My hair smelled like snack food for three months straight. When I finally got to New York, I bartended at night and babysat an eight-year-old who thought

Guru-girl: Meditation for Newbies

If you're trying to be present and find your dissatisfaction and itchy anxieties are cropping up un-invited, sit down in a quiet spot. You might only be able to sit quietly for five minutes the first few times. So keep practicing until you can make it to ten minutes, and then twenty. Ask yourself what your anxieties are all about, and then open yourself to guidance. If you like, you can say a mantra quietly or aloud. Use whatever works for you; there's no sacred Sanskrit text needed for proper meditation. I like alternating the following three:

I am. Let go. I trust.

it was hilarious to break free and escape into the labyrinth of the subway system while I screamed, "Polly? Polly!" and chased after her.

But if I had the insight I had now back then, I would have taken a deep breath and realized that everything was unfolding as it was supposed to. I just had to keep walking through it and creating.

This book is going to give you an action plan to achieve your creative dreams, but being present must be your first priority. Do you ever hear dieters say that they'll be happy when they finally lose the weight? It's like that with career success too. If you're unable to cultivate happiness, satisfaction, and love along the way to your goal, what makes you think you'll be able to do it when you're finally there?

Author Anna Carey says, "I know I'm present when I notice the little things, when I can focus completely on what I'm doing. I'm there, creating, and fully in the moment. Sometimes, to get to that space, I focus on my own breath. After a few minutes, I can let outside stuff go and just be."

When you let the knowledge that you are exactly where you are meant to be relieve your anxieties, you'll begin to enjoy your creative process with renewed energy. This, of course, leads to higher quality work, which leads to more creative and financial success. Trust me on this one: you're already "there." Trust that where you are right now is exactly where you're supposed to be.

Keep practicing. You can keep it simple and use the above guidance. Or, find more teachings on mediation at www.tm.org and www.vipassana.com.

CHAPTER 3

Where *Is* My Creative Happy Place?

You've got options,
creative girl.

So you're creative, but you're just not sure exactly what it is you want to do. Many of you, like Aimee Denaro, the actress we met in Chapter 1, have known what you've wanted in a career for years. But for those who want more clarity, whether you're about to graduate from school or are contemplating a career change, take some time to do a little soul-searching to find your creative happy place. However you brainstorm best—with a notebook in a coffee shop, in a one-handed downward facing dog, or poolside, bouncing ideas off a close friend—get in position and answer the questions in the following pages.

When Dorothy told Glinda she didn't know where to start, the good witch smiled and replied, "Why it's always best to start at the beginning."

As a child, how did you fill your afternoons after school? I wrote stories illustrated with pastels—a subject of many family jokes because I proudly gave the messy art away as birthday and Christmas presents. Now that I make jewelry, I engage in similar gifting behavior, but with much better results.

When you were young, what creative activities were you drawn to?

_____

_____

_____

_____

_____

_____

What was it about the activities you loved as a child that made you so happy? _____

_____

_____

_____

_____

_____

Do you pour over the interior decorating exhibited in the featured homes in the lifestyle sections of the newspaper? Do you pick up baking books in Barnes & Noble? To what magazines do you subscribe?

What media (television, movies, books, websites) attracts your attention most? _____

_____

_____

_____

_____

_____

_____

Life is exciting when you're actually learning something, not just going through the motions. Take into consideration the industries and disciplines you've always found intriguing, and what aspects of your intelligence feel best when stimulated.

What are you interested in learning? What excites you about it? _____

_____

_____

_____

_____

_____

_____

What do you value most? Family/friends/time/having nice clothes/ travel/helping others? _____

_____

_____

_____

_____

_____

_____

If you could make a contribution to the world or to a group of people, what would it be? It doesn't have to be an end-world-hunger type of contribution. Boutique owners Camilla Gale and Rand Niederhoffer opened Brooklyn shop Thistle & Clover, where—in addition to retailing clothing—neighbors gather for book readings and trunk shows. Their shop has become a community gathering place where young artists feel free to show their work.

CG-in-action Caroline Moore used her musical theater training to start an arts program for children at a hospital in the Bronx.

What are the unique ways you can contribute and serve others with your talents? _____

_____

_____

_____

_____

_____

_____

Your prattling neighbor continually tells you what a great skin-care saleswoman you'd be. Your nosy aunt is always saying you should've studied architecture. Here, think about what they mean behind their endorsement. Does your neighbor see you as personable and good at relating to people? Is your aunt impressed by your attention to detail and big-picture thinking? These are qualities that successful small business owners possess.

What are people always telling you that you'd be great at? What are the qualities others see in you? _____

_____

_____

_____

_____

_____

_____

Who has what you want? I'm not talking about your rich friend Sharon who can eat twenty Big Macs without gaining an ounce. Who has what you want career-wise?

Whether you know them personally or not, which women make you stop and think, "I wish I had _that_ career." _____

_____

_____

_____

_____

_____

_____

Who do you see yourself becoming? (Not a particular person, like Cher.) Describe the best version of yourself that you'd like to see emerge. _____

_____

_____

_____

_____

_____

_____

What kind of future do you want to create for yourself? _____

_____

_____

_____

_____

_____

_____

When you're deciding what career to enter or contemplating a career switch, you must consider the lifestyle implications. Do you need to be in a big city to achieve your creative dreams? If you're raising children, what type of work hours will suit your needs?

What kind of career fits into the future you want to create? _____

_____

_____

_____

_____

_____

After you've answered these questions for yourself, ask several people who know you very well what they think you should be doing.

What kind of careers do your closest friends see you pursuing successfully?

A Creative Girl Who Quizzed Her Friends

Maurya Moran worked as an administrative assistant in corporate America. When she left her job, she asked several close friends what they thought she'd be good at. Finally, one of them cut to the chase and said, "You love celebrity magazines more than anyone I've ever met. You should work at one." A lightbulb went off over Maurya's head. She saw through her blinding love of celeb magazines to the reality that those magazines employed people. She applied to every single publication and landed happily as the publisher's assistant at *OK Magazine*. Every day, she's surrounded by her favorite friends: Britney, Rihanna and Lady Gaga.

If You're Stuck

If you get stuck on any of the above questions, sit quietly—no music, no television—for ten minutes. What comes up? Is there a feeling that surfaces or a nagging sense that there's something more you want out of your life and career? Write down these feelings. Don't censor yourself; let the words flow.

What the Heck Do My Answers Mean?

So you love flowers and baking and now you're wondering whether or not you should be a floral designer, a bakery owner, or a pastry chef who wears a corsage to work. We'll talk more about assessing your talent in Chapter 4, but let's say you know you want to use your creative talent—designing, writing, sewing, decorating, etc.—but you have no idea how to turn your talent into a career. Or maybe you're interested in one particular field—say entertainment—

but you're not aware of all the different jobs available. Get yourself to a computer and start digging. And I mean dig deep, sister. Start an Internet search on any creative skill, service, or talent you'd like to parlay into a career. Want to work in movies? Search imdb.com for a listing of who does what on a film. Want to work in books or magazines? Go to the United States occupational outlook site (www.bls.gov/oco) and type "publishing" into the search engine.

- **What variations of work are connected with this talent or service?**

- **Are there several fields you could enter, or is it a more specialized industry?**

- **What job structures are available within your desired fields: 9 to 5 employee, freelancer, or creative business owner?**

In Chapter 5, we'll plan your next career step. For now, get a feel for the variety of ways CGs work within your desired field so you understand the options. Keep going until you have notebook pages full of career possibilities. If you're researching a particular talent, say, clothing design, you'll find everything from pattern and textile designers to swimwear and eveningwear designers. If you're researching a particular field, like entertainment, you'll find everything from location scout and costume designer to actress, agent, producer, and cinematographer.

Next, research the creative types working in your desired field. From now on, any time you see a creative professional doing work you think you too might enjoy—whether you see her performing in a poetry slam, view her work in an art gallery, or see her on-stage in a modern dance performance—get online and find out more about her. These days, most established CGs have websites—even blogs—and it's easier than ever to track how the creative types you admire got where they are today.

- **What companies do these creative types work for now and what jobs did they hold in the past?**

- **Where do they sell their creative product or service? Specialty stores? Online?**

- **Check out their client list: do they sell their product or service to individuals or corporations?**

- **Do they perform one specific talent or service or do they branch out into different creative fields like the CGs profiled in Chapter 1?**

Investigating other creative types will help you come up with new career ideas and avenues to pursue. By researching jewelry designers I admired, I found great boutiques to approach with my first designs. Continue to research your market no matter where you are along your creative career path. Even if you aren't making money in your field just yet, you should still know who's who, and what's happening.

CG-in-action Caroline Moore is a singer and has performed in choirs at Carnegie Hall and the Metropolitan Opera. Her goal is to someday perform as a soloist, so she makes it her business to attend concerts and performances, read reviews, and be aware of which companies are casting roles for which she might be a good fit. She says, "I consider this to be part of my job. I have to know what music sopranos like me are performing, and at which venues they're performing it."

Being informed will serve you greatly.

Next, get local. Are there any groups for CGs doing what you want to do? Any meetings or organizations you can join? You can always find online communities, but going local means you'll have the chance to meet creative women you admire face-to-face. You might even meet a CG willing to mentor you or give you a few tips. Check out www.meetup.com to find local networking groups based on your interests.

If you're starting fresh, you need a clear understanding of what the career entails.

❋ CREATIVE TIP ❋

Attention, Multi-Talented CGs

CG-in-action Taiia Smart Young considered her two loves: music and writing, and parlayed her writing skills into a career in music journalism. She's now the managing editor at hip-hop magazine, *XXL*. Taiia says, "If you have multiple creative interests, finding a way to use each one in your workplace goes a long way toward career satisfaction."

Think outside the box while brainstorming ways to bring multiple talents into a cohesive career.

Questions for Your Creative Industry Heroine

When you get the ear of a CG whose career you'd like to emulate, treat your time together like an informational interview. Research the company she works for or her own creative business so that you're up to speed. These sample questions can get you started. Be prepared and maximize your minutes with the brilliant CG sitting across from you by writing down your own questions regarding lifestyle, requisite skills, the positives, the negatives and everything in-between.

- How did you know you wanted to work in this career?
- How did you get started?
- Did you have to obtain formal training? What kind of on-the-job training, if any, is necessary in your field?
- What is your favorite part about working in this particular creative field?
- What's your least favorite part?
- What is your day-to-day life like working in this career?
- How much of your day is spent using your creative talent?
- How much of your day is spent doing administrative work like emailing, phone calls and taking care of other business details?
- What are your hours like?
- Do they fluctuate depending on the week or project you're working on?
- How do you handle downtime?
- What is the most surprising aspect of your job that no one would know until they tried it?
- Is it easier or more difficult to be a woman working in this field?
- How long did it take you to begin making your living full-time in this field?
- Are there steps you've taken or noticed your creative colleagues have taken to achieve success in this field?
- Are there classes, certification programs or other training you recommend?
- What is your best advice for someone who wants to break into your field?

Remember to be respectful of her time. If your creative heroine seems ready to end the meeting, thank her and of course, pick up the tab. And for the love of God, remember to write her a thank you note.

Put it Out There

We'll cover networking basics and strategies in Chapter 8. Asking for introductions and favors can be nerve-wracking, but this is a great time to pick the brain of a creative girl working in the field you want to enter. Search your network for someone who knows someone who'd be willing to chat over the phone, email, or go to coffee. Social networking websites like LinkedIn.com make this easier than ever.

There's nothing like face time with a fellow CG to get the full scoop about whether your dream job is as dreamy as you think it is. It's important to get real about what a career in your desired field actually means. Find out what the day-to-day life of an actress, dancer, writer, artist, designer, or entrepreneur involves. Deciding which career lifestyle you like best is very different from deciding which talent you like best. It's not always a linear path and it's okay to experiment and adjust your course.

At 22, I started life as an aspiring actress in New York City. After four years of theater training in a cozy town in Indiana, I wasn't prepared for the business side of professional acting. I'd spent those four years continually performing: usually acting in two shows at once. When I got to New York,

I spent my days shuttling by subway from audition to audition. I still performed in small theaters, but the scheduling and business aspects of acting didn't agree with me. Turned out I just wasn't crazy about the lifestyle. In contrast, I found I love the lifestyle of a jewelry designer and writer. Though I enjoy the creative aspects of all three—acting, writing, and designing—the day-to-day lifestyle of being a designer and a writer agrees with me a thousand times more than that of an actress. I still use those on-camera skills when I host my TV show on the Home Shopping Network or host style segments for other networks, but my design work and writing occupy the majority of my creative life. Lifestyle matters; don't sacrifice your wellbeing for your art.

CHAPTER 4

Seriously, How Talented Are You?

*Face the music and
assess your talent.*

Your ability to self-evaluate and parlay your talent in a way that's financially viable will serve you well along your creative way. If you find words like *viable* distasteful when talking about your creativity, I get it. But this book is here to show you how to make a living off of your creativity. Art for art's sake is awesome, but let's figure out how to get you paid, too.

A Creative Girl Makes Creative Adjustments

Sometimes the best part of realizing you stink at something is picking yourself back up and trying it in a different way.

During early October of my junior year at Notre Dame, I'd just finished an acting class when I looked up to see my roommate, Stacy, standing in the doorway. My theater friends made her nervous with their cigarettes and dark eyeliner, and the only time she came within twenty-five yards of the theater was when attending one of my performances. Seeing her appear now out of nowhere, I assumed there was either a death in one of our families or that I was once again in hot water with Sister Annette, our dormitory rectress, a formidable nun who inspired a healthy fear of both God and premarital sex.

"Stacy?" I asked. "Is everything alright?"

She nodded and handed me a thick manila envelope. I saw the New York University return label and my stomach flip-flopped. Months before, I'd applied to the Tisch Musical Theater Conservatory's visiting students program. I tore open the packaging and scanned the form letter: I'd been accepted for the spring semester!

I bathed in the adoration showered on me by theater students and faculty and walked around campus like I ruled the school (or at least the theater department) for the duration of the fall semester. Little did I know the surprise I was in for that spring.

Within one month of studying at NYU, I realized I didn't have the musical theater chops to cut it in the professional theater world. I'm a horrific onstage dancer and my singing is subpar. Sure, I can hold a tune. After a few margaritas, I'm quite an impressive karaoke singer.

But a *Broadway* singer? Have you heard those people?

The only thing worse than having to take the stage after a classmate flawlessly belted out a high E was the discovery that jazz hands don't run in my family.

My singing and dancing failures caused much mortification and crying jags as I was forced to face my own creative limitations. But being honest with myself about what I wasn't very good at led to the greatest realization of all: I could act.

I acted circles around those musical theater students. The morning after mid-semester review, when our acting, dance, and voice teachers met and discussed each of us individually, my tap dance teacher (who'd likely contemplated leaving the teaching profession due to my inability to master a time step) strode into the classroom and stared at me. I was terrified of her. Even the good dancers were.

The entire class was silent, lacing up tap shoes and watching the two of us.

"So." She paused for dramatic effect. "I hear you're quite the actress."

She tippedy-tap-tapped her dance shoe on the floor in front of me. I took a deep breath and said, "I think I may have made a mistake by applying to the Musical Theater Conservatory and not the Acting Conservatory. But, still, I'm trying to give this my best effort."

"You are a terrible dancer. You will never work as a dancer on Broadway and I hear your voice isn't even that great." I shrugged helplessly as she continued, "But I've rarely heard a student's acting abilities so highly praised by industry professionals. Good luck with whatever you choose to do."

With that she spun on her heel and scowled at the class, "What are you all staring at? Get up, we have work to do!"

Assess Your Strengths to Navigate Your Path

You can most accurately assess your talent with a balance of self-evaluation and evaluation from others—trusted creative professionals, mentors, audience members, critical reviews, magazine articles, and other measurements of success within your respective creative industry. Later in this chapter, you'll find questions incorporating self-evaluation and outside evaluation techniques to accurately assess your talent.

Criticism is sometimes hard to stomach, but if you're truly dedicated you'll welcome it as a chance to improve. If you're going to see yourself as an artist and a business, you can't take everything personally.

When asking for an evaluation of your creative work, be aware that depending upon whom you're asking, you may have to separate their baggage (which may trickle into their advice) from their evaluation of your abilities. We're talking about talent, so be able to separate "You are very talented," from "But do you know how hard it is to make a living as a _____?" (Fill in the blank with your creative career.) Of course we creative girls realize that it's a bit harder to make a living as artists and entrepreneurs, but we plug along anyway, all the more satisfied when we achieve success.

So now, who to ask for an evaluation? If you have access to a creative professional whose work you admire and whose career you'd like to emulate, this is the person to approach. (Also see Questions for Your Creative Industry Heroine at the end of Chapter 3 for questions you might ask along the way.) If you're already employed in a creative career, you can ask a co-worker you trust or your boss for an honest evaluation of your work. A "boss" can be the choreographer of the ballet you're performing in, or a stationery shop owner who's willing to look at your hand-painted greeting card collection. Find the people whose opinions matter to you, and approach them.

You can employ this technique at any level. CG Jamie Cook completed a two year apprenticeship at Bumble and Bumble in New York City. After graduating she began working as a hairstylist at the prestigious salon, Whittemore House, and now has her own sizable client base. Still, she continues to check in with her mentor, hairstylist Michelle Snyder. Jamie tells me, "Michelle has a career I aspire to have someday. She styles hair for photo shoots, does television appearances and is interviewed for her expertise by major beauty magazines." Jamie takes the time out of her own busy day to observe Michelle working, and continues to ask Michelle to evaluate her styling work and offer an informed critique.

Be Princess Charming

Everyone loves a little bit of flattery on a dreary weekday. If your friend knows a travel writer at a magazine and offers up her contact information, let the writer know that you greatly admire her work and you'd love any advice she has on how to break into the business. Once a dialogue is started, she may be generous enough to read samples of your writing. Remember to pay it forward a few years down the road when you're the creative girl who has achieved success. (Don't fret if there isn't a CG in your network now. There will be after you put the networking plan in Chapter 8 into action.)

The Dr. Jekyll and Mr. Hyde Feedback Approach

A ninety-year-old CG shared that throughout her prolific career, she's always asked two very different people their opinions on her work. The first is a friend who loves to read her articles and short stories and thinks everything she writes is brilliant. The second is her most critical colleague, who will tear a piece apart with constructive criticism and ideas for improvement. There's productive reasoning behind balancing a dose of encouragement with criticism; you'll keep in mind that yes, you can do this, but you can always get better at it, too.

In the name of research, I decided to try this strategy out for myself. After filming a style segment, I asked my mother-in-law what she thought of my work. The first thing you should know about my mother-in-law is that she thinks every single thing I do is the absolute best she's

❋ CREATIVE TIP ❋

Get Your Feet Wet

If approaching creative professionals seems out of reach for the level you're at now, start smaller. Contact a local arts organization or apply for an internship. Taking a class with a creative professional is a surefire way to build your portfolio, gain a better understanding of the field you want to enter, and receive honest feedback.

Reality Check: How Passionate, Dedicated, and Committed Are You?

Turning your talent into a career means you must be able to do both the creative and the business aspects of the work all day, every day—especially if your career will be self-driven. You'll need the discipline to get up each morning and get to work (easier said than done). Be sure you're ready and able to commit eight or more hours per day to your creative talent and the business of making it work. I thought I loved to sing and dance, but the reality check of singing and dancing in rehearsals all day (in addition to realizing I stunk) made me reconsider what I wanted my creative life to look like.

What creative work can you see yourself doing for years on end? Consider the work you love so deeply you find yourself losing track of time while you're doing it. Prepare for a lifetime with that work. Sure, you can always make a change down the road, but take the time now to identify the aspects of your creativity you'd continue to do whether or not they made you money. Don't worry, we'll get to the green stuff, but for now, evaluate your creative desires and decide which ones you can see yourself doing all day, every day.

ever seen. And I just happen to be married to her son, who, she reminds us at most holidays, "Definitely could have had a modeling career if he hadn't gone into healthcare." (My husband, though handsome, is bald.) When I asked her what she thought about this particular segment she said, "It was just fantastic and you know, I was talking to Auntie Sue and I was telling her, Kelly Ripa wears your jewelry, why don't you see if you can do a style segment on *Live with Regis and Kelly?* And Sue agreed you'd be perfect for that program! Or, for *Rachael Ray*. She wears your jewelry too, right? I could even teach you a few recipes for the show!"

So far, my research was going swimmingly.

Then I called Dani Super, a CG who owns her own casting company and works as an acting coach.

"So I watched it," she said. "You're doing a lot of 'ummmms' in that one segment.

And you're not slowing down like we talked about; you seem to be trying to cram it all into a few sentences."

"Did you like that top I was wearing?" I asked, fishing for a compliment and hoping my mother-in-law would buzz in on call waiting.

"Your wardrobe is never the problem. Like I was saying, I think we should work on connecting to your audience and bringing your natural warmth to the table…"

I scheduled a coaching session with her for later that week. Now that I was booking on-camera work, I wanted to make sure I was at my best. As you gain momentum in your creative career, don't get too comfortable. Take the time to cultivate your talent, sharpen your abilities and *improve.*

This outlook has been key for CG-in-action Melody Thornton, a member of the Pussycat Dolls. Melody told me, "When I first became part of the group in 2003, I let myself be comfortable for about three months. And then, I started challenging myself again. I never lost sight of my big goal: to be a solo performer. So while I love doing songs like, 'Don't Cha,' they're not vocally challenging for me." (Here, Melody broke into song, which thrilled me so deeply that I had to remind myself to stay professional instead of squealing and clapping my hands.) She added, "I continue to train with singing coaches and record songs that keep pushing my talent and ability."

✳ CREATIVE TIP ✳

Befriend Constructive Critics

In the same way you'd nurture a friendship with a wildly supportive friend, nurture your relationships with mentors and constructive critics. Constructive criticism will stretch your ability and make you better. One of my favorite things about my close friendship with author Noelle Hancock is that we'll honestly tell each other when something we write stinks. Then, we'll brainstorm ways to make it better. Find a CG with whom you feel safe sharing your work and build your relationship.

Finding a Mentor

CG-in-action Eva Chen is the Beauty and Health Director at *Teen Vogue*. Eva says, "Finding a mentor is one of the best things you can do for your creative career. Surround yourself with people you're inspired by and can learn from. These people don't need to be in your exact field, rather, they can be a lighthouse for you and compass to guide you in the right direction. Make friends with colleagues at your level, but also hone in on building a relationship with people who have careers you aspire to. At a company, it can sometimes be competitive, but that makes it doubly important to find people who genuinely want to help you."

CG: How can a creative girl nurture and build a relationship with a mentor?

EC: Keep your mentor informed about what you're doing, even after you've left the company. Think of a mentor like a professional friendship: that means you don't just talk about yourself. It should be a conversation and a give and take. Ask about their life, too, and think of ways you can help them. Interns that I've mentored at *Teen Vogue* now work at other companies. Often, they'll email and let me in on a new beauty product launch or industry news I wouldn't otherwise know about. The best mentor/mentee relationships are supportive and symbiotic.

Evolve, CG

All creative girls need to continually evolve whether they're performers, writers, floral designers, chefs, business owners, or art therapists. If all else fails and you're feeling stuck in a creative rut, a class or workshop can get you back on track and sharpen your skills. Local arts programs and continuing education classes will get you out of the house (and out of your head) and into a stimulating environment. When you're led by a qualified instructor and surrounded by other creative types, you'll be inspired to reach new heights.

To help you figure out where you are now, and how you'll get where you want to go, answer the following talent assessment questions. When you're finished, create a few more questions to ask and answer with your particular creative career in mind.

Talent Assessment Questions

In my field of _____ ,
I will have to find a balance between creative talent and _____
_____ .

I think my creative talent is (circle one):

Ready to compete

Almost there!

Needs a little bit of work (thank goodness practice makes perfect!)

I'm feeling insecure and want to flush this worksheet down the toilet

I asked _____ creative professionals who know me very well, and they think my
talent is _____ .

When I asked them what I'd need to work on to make a living in this industry,
they told me _____ .

I found out that to be a _____ I must have the following training:
_____ .

If I'm honest with myself, I need to improve the following aspects of my creative
abilities: _____
_____ .

I plan to continually evolve and improve by _____
_____ .

One year from now, I want the level of my talent to be _____
_____ .

What to Do with the Feedback

Not everyone enjoys hearing gratuitous criticism, even from the most well-meaning of sources, but constructive guidance should be something you embrace. Author Anna Carey says, "Someone once taught me that good criticism feels like an arrow hitting its mark. You might even experience an *aha!* moment when someone gives you particularly valuable feedback."

Remember that hard work and perseverance go a long way. If you don't get the feedback that you were hoping for, your passion and tenacity can keep you afloat while you obtain the requisite training and experience.

If your feedback points to you becoming the next Meryl Streep, Jhumpa Lahiri, or Vivienne Westwood, fantastic! You're on your way.

Follow Your Bliss and Your Talent

If you want to make a living in a creative career, follow your talents, be open to improvements and redirections, and be smart about how to capitalize on your strengths. The art of self-evaluation will become even more important as you gain momentum. The most successful CGs continue to evaluate, evolve, and challenge themselves along their professional paths.

A Storybook Ending for a Self-Evaluating CG

CG-in-action Stacia Valle owns the New York City boutique, Dernier Cri. Before she even got started in the industry, she truthfully evaluated her creative abilities: "I knew I wouldn't be able to make it as a designer. I didn't have the right talents for getting the idea onto paper and translating that into the construction of a garment of clothing." Instead, she realized her strength was recognizing design talent in others. "I know what looks good as soon as I see it," she says. With her innate ability to predict trends and select the best pieces from different collections, it dawned on her that the perfect use of her creative talents would be to open a boutique.

CHAPTER 5

Does This Cubicle Make My Butt Look Fat? Find a More Flattering Fit

Evaluate your current situation and plan your next career move.

In this chapter, we'll evaluate your current job situation and narrow down your career choices. Assessing where you are now is vital to moving forward.

Where Are You Now?

American job satisfaction has hit an all time low, with more than 50 percent of workers reporting they're unhappy with their jobs. Are you occupying the better half?

There are some who scoff at the idea of enjoying your job. "It's a *job*. Not a *fun*," I overheard recently. Certainly, there are elements of sweat and hard work to every dream job. But there are a significant number of people who love their jobs and become positively giddy when talking about what they do for a living.

For CGs, being creative is essential for an optimal work environment and a happy life. But that doesn't mean you should waste your energy complaining about how the office should conform to your creative needs. Your accounting firm would not likely benefit from Friday afternoon modern dance classes to "free the creativity within." Don't bother trying to change your conventional work environment or your conventional coworkers. Whether or not they've found the career that best suits them isn't your worry. We're talking about what's right for you.

So here's the real question: how satisfied are you at your current job? When you roll out of bed, do you want to go to work? Maybe you hit snooze six times, but when you finally slide into your bunny slippers and make a pot of coffee, are you even a little excited? As you read that question, does a defensive voice in your head chime in with, "Oh come on, is *anyone* excited about going to work?" You don't need to be jumping out of your skin to get to the office every morning, but know that there are a significant number of people who truly love going to work, whether they work in an office or their living room. Wouldn't you like to be one of them?

Job Satisfaction Quiz

Answer the following questions on a scale of 0-10, 10 being *yes, absolutely*; **5 being** *sometimes*; **0** *being never.*

1. In the morning do you wake up, tear your lavender-scented eye mask off, and feel ready to conquer your day?

2. Does your current job engage your creativity?

3. Are you challenged?

4. Are you learning new skills and growing?

5. Do you work well within the office culture? (Culture meaning the company's policies, values, and how co-workers and management treat each other and communicate.)

6. Is your commute to and from work reasonably stress-free?

7. For the most part, do you enjoy your time at work?

8. Do you feel energized by the actual work you're doing?

9. At the end of the day, do you feel proud of the work you've completed?

10. Do you feel you're paid a fair amount for what you do?

11. Do you like your boss? (You don't have to want to go out to drinks after work with her, but do you respect her? Is she consistent and fair?)

12. Do you believe in the overall product or mission of the company?

13. Do you feel like you're making a contribution, whether it be to your company or to a larger good?

14. Do you feel you have enough decision-making responsibilities? Do you feel your opinion is valued?

15. If you won the lottery tomorrow, sure, maybe you'd quit your day job. But would you return to the same *type* of work in some capacity?

16. Are you on the career path you'd like to be on, even if this particular day job isn't ideal?

17. Are there opportunities for growth at this company?

18. Even if you're not thrilled in your current position, can you see yourself happy in another position at your current company?

19. Is your job conducive to outside creative work?

20. Is your job taking up less than forty-five hours per week, including what you take to work on at home?

Tally your points.

160–200: Good for you! You're outrageously happy. Read on for how to take your career to the next level.

100–159: Something's missing. Read on for ideas to spice up your creative life.

50–99: You're not on the verge of a complete meltdown, but you're definitely ready for something different. Read on for your creative options.

0–49: Oh boy. It's time to get out of Dodge. Read on for your exit strategy and next career move.

If you scored low, look carefully at questions 15–20. Questions 15–18 are there for you to consider whether or not there's a light at the end of your career tunnel. If you're dreadfully unhappy at a job that's not even leading you in the right direction, you need to get serious about your getaway route. Questions 19 and 20 are there for you to determine whether your day job is conducive to your outside creative work. If you make great money and have enough time and energy to work on your creative ventures outside of work hours, it may be worth it to stick it out while you get ready to launch your freelance career or small business. But if you're working such long hours and arriving home so wiped out that the only creative thoughts you can muster are whether to flip on a Lifetime movie or a *Law and Order* re-run, it's time for a change. It doesn't mean that you have to quit tomorrow. But if your score is creeping toward your shoe size, you do need to get real about your exit strategy and next career move.

What's Your Next Career Step?

Sometimes, when CGs assess their work life and realize it completely stinks, they rush into sending their résumés out and applying for every available job, reaching for anything that gets them out of their current work situation. The results can be disastrous or, ironically, can set you up for a situation similar to the one you're trying to escape. Take time now to get clear on what you do and don't want next to clarify your vision. This will make your career decision an informed one.

In a few pages, you'll complete four journal entries: the first on what you don't want, the second on any coping behaviors you might have been engaging in, the third on what you *do* want, and the fourth on creating a bigger picture of your ideal creative life. By the end of this chapter, you'll have a clear picture of your next career step.

What You Don't Want

Before we get into all of the good things that await you, take some time to think about what really isn't working in your current job or career. When you identify the patterns, situations, people, and work that make you unhappy, it's easier to avoid them in the future.

Below are the typical reasons CGs report they are dissatisfied at work. This should help you start thinking about your own situation. If any sound familiar, make sure they end up in Journal Entry #1: what you *don't* want.

Bored Out of Your Mind

After college, when I was trying to save enough money to move to New York, I worked Monday through Friday as a receptionist at a mental health clinic. (The potato-chip-stocking at Wal-Mart was my weekend gig—lucky me.) By the end of the day, I was so bored that I was ready to check myself in as a patient. At Wal-Mart, at least there was a scenery change: produce aisle, canned goods aisle, toy aisle. But sitting in that chair and scheduling people's appointments made me batty. I actually looked forward to cancellations because using the whiteout was a novelty. If you feel the same way at work, mind-numbing boredom should top your list of what isn't working. It doesn't matter how much busy work you have, or how overscheduled you are with meetings if the work itself is boring as hell.

You're meant to be challenged. That's how we grow and evolve. Studies link meaningful, thought-provoking work to longer life spans. Your work is meant to inspire and push your intellectual and artistic limits, and the first step is to know what does and doesn't get you going.

Delve into what exactly about your work life is boring you. Is it being in the same location day in and day out? Can you actually feel your IQ plummeting due to a lack of stimulating work? Do you have decision-making capability, or must you get approval from a chain of command just to go to the bathroom?

Certainly, every job has a few boring particulars; you might still have to fax and staple in your dream career. But there's a big difference between boring moments and a boring job.

Overworked and Overstressed

Job anxiety, burnout, and stress aren't feelings to take lightly; they're linked to high blood pressure, heart disease, digestive problems, trouble sleeping, emotional issues and much more. Overstressed employees are quite literally sick and tired. In 2008, CareerBuilder.com reported that 78 percent of workers felt burnout at work, and 50 percent said they feel a great deal of stress on the job. So if pure exhaustion and tension migraines are your main reasons for wanting to quit, is it the actual work that's exhausting? The environment? Unrealistic deadlines?

If you think it's the long hours you're working, really look closely as this, because you may work even longer hours if you choose to start your own creative business. Work you love is usually energizing, so I doubt you'll have the same problem as you transition into a creative career. My sister is a doctor and doesn't bat an eye at thirty-hour shifts because she loves the work. Your creative career probably won't require overnights (or putting a central line into a patient after twenty hours on your feet) but get it down on paper now if you don't think you can work more than eight hours per day.

Really delve into what drains the living daylights out of you at your current gig: what specifically stresses you out?

The Company You Keep (Your Boss or Your Coworkers Are Monkeys)

Maybe you're working with the biggest jerks on the planet, or maybe they're just so unlike you that you can't find common ground or mutual understanding. Either way, you can tell a lot about whether or not you're in the right career by the people who surround you. Your colleagues don't need to be your best friends, but you'll often find that like-minded people gravitate to the same fields.

Pay attention to where you feel truly at home.

Location, Location, Location

There are several books out there about how to escape your cubicle; I've never worked in one, so I'll let you be the judge of how pleasant or unpleasant they are. I interviewed several CGs in creative offices who didn't mind the cubicle as long as they loved the work they were doing while inside of it.

But maybe those little gray cubicles make you nuts. You want to run screaming, yank your hair out, or dump coffee on your cube-dwelling neighbor. If you think no matter what kind of work you're doing or how much you might love the work, that you are not someone who can work in a cubicle or even an office, put that in Journal Entry #1, too.

Does your job require you to make daily trips into the city when you'd really rather be in your painting studio in the country? Or maybe your job entails working in a quiet suburb when you're more of an urban creature.

What about travel? Are you doing too much, or too little? Personally, I like a hotel stay about once a month. I like the room service. I like taking a bath in a huge tub instead of scrunching up like an accordion in my apartment's four-foot version that's more like a big sink. But if you're away every week for work, do you thrive or become exhausted? Frequent flier miles or not, too much travel can be draining even for those of us with the most wanderlust.

Journal Entry #1: What You *Don't* Want

To design your creative career, you need to start with what doesn't work for you. Use the previous examples to get yourself going and elaborate on the aspects of work you plan to avoid in the future. On this list should be everything and anything you dislike: from the office culture, to specific duties you perform, to feelings like boredom. Jot down all the things you never want to do or feel again in a work environment. Add things you know you don't want, whether or not you've experienced them at work yet. Really get into the nitty-gritty of what you don't want in your ideal career—the more detailed the better.

Journal Entry #2: Coping

Now that you've gotten the rotten stuff down on paper, go deeper. Whether you're bored, overstressed, or working with jerks, how are you coping? When I worked at the mental health clinic, the only break from mind-numbing dullness was a box of candy conveniently stationed at the reception desk. I could do my duties—"Hello, welcome to P. Behavioral Health"—and reach the candy tub at the same time. I'm already a fast talker, so add a sugar high to the mix and I guarantee you I was terrifying the patients.

If you're self-medicating with chocolate stashed at your desk or too many glasses of merlot after work, journal about that as well. Your goal is a healthier, more fulfilling life. Get it all out in the open so you can work on what you want to change.

The prompts below will help you get started.

What do you reach for when you're stressed or bored? Wine, potato chips, chocolate, cigarettes, remote control? _____

_____

_____

_____

_____

_____

What behaviors would you like to change? _____

_____

_____

_____

_____

_____

_____

How do you see yourself changing? _____
_____
_____
_____
_____
_____

What does a life free of those things look like? What does it feel like?
_____
_____
_____
_____
_____
_____

If you weren't engaging in your not-so-good behavior, what would you be doing? Meaning, what would you have time to do if you weren't zoning out and eating potato chips in front of the television? What would you free yourself to accomplish? _____
_____
_____
_____
_____
_____
_____
_____
_____
_____
_____
_____
_____

Journal Entry #3: What You Do Want

Think of your career as a piece (or two) of red velvet cake: the actual work (acting, writing, singing, designing, dancing, creating) is the cake and the job details (your ideal work environment) are the icing. You need both to make it ideal. Consider both aspects as you journal.

a) The Cake. (The actual work.)

When do you feel the most inspired and in the zone? What creative work—painting, drawing, cooking, singing, crafting, writing, sculpting—has you so enraptured that you lose track of time?

b) The Icing. (The details.)

After journaling about the actual work, journal about your ideal working environment. Go back to internships, summer jobs, or volunteer work you've done in the past.

If you get stuck, return to Journal Entry #1. Take any item where you wrote, say, *too much travel,* and write down what amount of travel would be right for you.

Your happiness is in the details, so dig deep and get it all out in the space provided. Feel free to add details you haven't yet experienced in a work environment. If you've only experienced satisfying teamwork during your Wednesday night softball league, you can still list that below. If you want a flexible work schedule because your job lacks this, jot that down, too. If you're just graduating, pull from prior work, school, and life experience. Think of this entry as your career wish list. Check out the questions on the following page to make sure you've covered the basics.

- Do you like interacting with customers and clients?

- Do you like the social aspects of an office?

- Do you like your office space?

- Do you like having a boss to report to? And if you don't like your actual boss or office space, what about the bigger picture—are you someone who likes the structure of having a boss or an office to go to each day?

- Do you like a steady paycheck? (Who doesn't? But would you be freaking out if your pay was more sporadic? If you don't think you're someone who could handle the emotional and fiscal issues of inconsistent pay—even if the potential was there to make more than you're currently making—steady paycheck should be on your list of what you want in an ideal work situation.)

- Are you happy with the amount of money you're making?

- Do you like working with your hands?

- Do you prize organization?

- Do you like working in a group or working solo?

- Do you want to manage people or be managed?

- What is your ideal commute?

- What are your ideal hours?

- How much flexibility do you need?

- Do you want to make your own schedule?

What details and work specifics combine to create your ideal environment? _____

_____

_____

_____

_____

_____

_____

_____

_____

_____

_____

_____

_____

To Each Her Own

While I was workshopping this section in my writer's group, CG Allison Gaudet Yarrow asked, "Who doesn't want to make their own schedule?" Noelle Hancock, author of *My Year With Eleanor* piped in, "I don't. I really don't. I have to schedule myself every day and I wish someone would do it for me, to actually lay out how it is I should structure my day." Noelle found the best solution for this was to ask her editor to give her strict deadlines. We wrote our books at the same time, but while my manuscript was due in one big chunk eleven months after I signed the contract, Noelle had pages due to her editor every two weeks. This part of the process is about figuring out how you create best. What's right for *you* when it comes to scheduling yourself and structuring your day?

Your Next Step

As you read over your journal entries, what job ideas mesh with your ideal work lifestyle? You might not get everything you want right away, but there are career choices you can make that will jive with your lifestyle preferences and the realities of the marketplace. Even if there's one clear career choice for you—say, video game animator or casting director—you'll still narrow down your job choice based on the work aspects you've identified as the best fit for you.

Let's say your journal entries make it clear you thrive in an environment with structure and deadlines. So you decide your next step is to work at a full-time creative job. Now, go further: are you going to narrow your search to only include creative companies? Or will you go for creative positions in corporate America, too? Some creative girls thrive on being the artsy type in a corporate environment. One graphic designer told me, "I like having my tattoos on display while the vice president walks by in pearls. The pay is great and I get to do what I love—design—each and every day."

Other CGs say they do their best work in a thoroughly creative environment. CG-in-action Allison Kave worked for years as an art gallery director and currently works as the studio manager for artist Kelley Walker. Allison says, "Certainly, there are non-creative aspects to my job, but for the most part, I'm surrounded by artists, art, and creativity day in and day out. I'm involved in the creation and curation of artwork, and the installation of shows. I have a voice and a role in the creative process, which is very satisfying for me."

Let's say you love to write and want to be a full-time writer. There are various types of writing careers—from novelists to fashion journalists—and within each subset there are even further breakdowns based on job structure. If you've assessed your talent and decided your writing is best suited for magazine and article writing, think about what structure works for you. Do you want to work on staff for a single magazine or contribute to multiple publications as a freelancer?

CG-in-action Jamie Rosen is the beauty and health editor at *W* magazine. For Jamie, having an office to go to each day helps keep her at her most productive when it comes to writing. The staff position also allows her the flexibility to edit other stories and plan a section in the magazine each month. She wisely took her personality type into consideration when she made this decision.

Jamie says, "Writing can be very solitary, so it's nice to balance what can feel like a very lonely career path with something that's unbelievably collaborative."

CG-in-action Dani Super is a casting director. Instead of working full-time for one television network or production company, Dani chooses to freelance. She says, "Being my own boss outweighs the freelance uncertainty factor. The pay is more sporadic, and I have to be my business's bookkeeper and financial planner, but I get to take on all kinds of different theater, film, and television projects. I get to choose when and what I want to work on. And I'm constantly meeting new people with each new project, which makes work feel exciting, like the first day of school."

Some of you may have a bag of tricks you'd like to apply to an entrepreneurial adventure. Your journal entries likely point to the small business structure. So, how does your ideal creative life as a She.E.O. look to you? Do you see yourself at the head of your own company's boardroom giving orders in a Chanel suit, or quietly toiling away in a studio wearing jeans and a t-shirt?

I never fantasized about an office or a staff of employees. Certainly, there are people who help me with the business aspects of my career, like my agents, but day-to-day, it's just me creating solo in my living room or at a coffee shop.

CG-in-action Poppy King is the owner of the cosmetics company Lipstick Queen. Poppy says, "While visualizing, I always imagined myself leading a group of people. And now, I love being in the boardroom and presenting new ideas."

Location Station

CG-in-action Brinn Daniels is a wedding videographer. She loves traveling to the locales of the weddings she shoots. "I'm never bored," she tells me. "I'm constantly meeting new people and traveling to new places." And as far as the morale and "coworkers" of her work environment, she says, "I have a job where I'm with people on the happiest day of their lives. How great is that?"

Journal Entry #4:
Envision Your Ideal Creative Life

Now that you're clear on what you do and don't want in a creative career, you can ascertain where you're most likely to find the ideal workplace. Your structure and lifestyle preferences plus your talent equals a perfect career fit.

As you're journaling, keep in mind your previous lists and expand on your "things you do want" list to get a bigger picture. Let's say you wrote "flexibility" as something you'd like in your next venture. Expand on that; journal about what this flexibility might actually look and feel like. When would you arrive at work each day? When would you leave? What are the best parts about your flexible work situation—is it picking up your children each day from school? Or being able to put your hours in at midnight when you're most creative?

If you wrote that you love the social aspect of work, now journal about how that translates to your ideal environment. Are you interacting with coworkers, your own customers, or both? Are you managing a staff? Are you meeting new people every day? Create a picture of how the ideal social environment looks to you.

Let's say you wrote, "I want to be my own boss." Are you taking on numerous projects as an independent contractor, or are you opening your own business with a storefront?

What about location? If not in a cubicle, are you on set wherever the movie/photography shoot/commercial job takes you? Are you in a coffee shop? An artist's studio? In your home? On the road?

As you write this list, dream big. Free yourself by remembering that no one else needs to read it. Get down on paper anything and everything you imagine for yourself. Nothing is too out of reach. Let's say you write: *I open my own coffee shop and there's a little section where I also sell paintings by local artists and hold book readings with guest authors,* and a little voice pipes up with, "Oh come on, that's just ridiculous." Silence that voice by reminding yourself that all is possible; you can create anything and everything you desire. You *will* have to work hard and make sacrifices. Later on, we'll discuss practical approaches to achieving your goals. But while you're journaling, remember that *everything is possible.*

I'm going to show you a condensed version of my own wild list so you can see how expansive, detailed and ballsy yours can be. If you don't dream big for yourself, who will?

_____

_____

_____

_____

_____

_____

_____

_____

_____

_____

_____

_____

_____

_____

_____

_____

_____

_____

_____

_____

_____

_____

_____

_____

_____

_____

_____

_____

_____

_____

_____

My Creative Life

In my ideal creative life, I write two books a year. Some days, I write from home, and some days, I'll go to a coffee shop. I want to write a bestseller at some point during my thirties. I go to lunch with my literary agent once every few months to discuss my books. I leave the business side of things to him so that I can focus purely on writing.

My jewelry line remains in boutiques and I keep doing press to maintain visibility. I continue collaborating with outlets like Target and the Home Shopping Network, while maintaining collections in smaller boutiques.

I film television segments about once a month, enjoying the travel and collaborative aspects. Within the next year, I pitch a television show to a network like Bravo or Oxygen.

Location: Unless I'm traveling to film, I work at home. The dog sits next to me. I wake up at 7:30 and check emails for a little while and drink coffee. I start writing around 9 am and write until 3 pm. From 3 until 6, I work on jewelry.

After seeing my list, do you feel free to let go and dream big? I hope so. I have practical to-dos along with the goals of pitching a television show and writing a bestseller in my thirties! Most people would say that's pretty unattainable. But you're the one who makes plans for you. Not even the most dedicated agent, manager, or career cheerleader can do it for you. So be expansive: you can create anything.

Your Next Move

Now that you have a clear picture of the type of career you'd like, Part 2 provides the road map to your next step. But some of you may need to build more experience before transitioning. Or you may prefer to save cash or garner clients first, in order to try making a go of it as a freelancer or small business owner. For these CGs, let's talk about making over your current job so that you actually have the time to do these things. The next chapter provides job makeover strategies and a survival guide for those of you dangerously close to super-gluing your boss's toupee to his Power Point presentation.

CHAPTER 6

Can't Quit Your Stink-o Job Just Yet?

*Job makeover strategies
and interim survival guide*

Sometimes, making the switch to the career of your dreams isn't an all-at-once proposition. If you can't quit your job because of financial reasons, let's try making over your current job so that you can get going on your creative work while still bringing home a paycheck. Part of being a successful CG is being able to come up with creative solutions. If a full makeover isn't in the cards yet, put the interim survival guide into action.

With hard work and perseverance, the time will come for you and your dream creative career. It's just going to take some planning and strategy.

Day Job Makeover

If your day job isn't stimulating you creatively and isn't allowing time for outside creative endeavors—but you're not financially ready to quit—it's time for a job makeover. And I don't mean inspirational kitten posters and a cactus for your cubicle. We're going to explore how you can make your day job mesh with your creative goals. The idea is to bring your work and life into balance and gain hours during the week so you'll have the time and energy to achieve these goals. Freeing up extra hours will allow you to take on freelance projects and build a client list, develop a portfolio, or get moving on your small business plans. It's tough to audition, paint, or gain creative experience while working 60 to 80 hours a week at a law firm. What can you do to change that?

We'll also explore the option of transitioning within your company to a more creative position. If you'd like to stay with your current company, this section will help you brainstorm the creative ways your employers can still send you a paycheck.

Let's get started on the makeover.

Flex Work

Flex work is an umbrella term for all flexible work options, including flexible work hours, part-time, telecommuting, and job sharing. Silence your inner skeptic—the Families and Work Institute's 2008 National Study of Employers found that 79 percent of companies offer some form of flexible work. Today's workers value flexibility for many reasons, such as pursuing outside interests, raising a family, or achieving a work-life balance that improves their physical and mental health. If your company doesn't provide flexible work options, it may take your well-planned proposal to get them up to speed in the flex work revolution.

While you're reading the options outlined below, think about what your ideal creative schedule would be. This way, even if your current employer turns down your flexible work

Hold Your Horses, CG

Before telling your boss to stick data entry where the sun doesn't shine, let's get you in good financial shape. Before you strike out on your own as a freelancer or business owner, financial advisors recommend you have an emergency fund saved to cover at least one year. This includes one year's worth of expenses (rent, health insurance, groceries) and fun money (shopping, chardonnay, travel). I know this is a buzzkill, since going about life and work as usual until you've saved enough could take an excruciatingly long time. So shorten the transition into full-time-creative-girl status by obtaining freelance clients while you're still employed at your current job. There's also the possibility of outside financing, which we'll cover in Chapter 13.

It can be a real thrill to start making money creatively. But don't get so intoxicated with your new creative mogul self that you quit your day job before you're financially ready. Once you have your creative goals in place, with an actual plan in mind, think of your day job as a means to save your pennies to get where you want to go.

proposal, you'll know what you want if you decide to search out new employment. In the meantime, let's see if your job can accommodate a flex work makeover; flexible work hours, part-time, telecommuting, or job sharing could be a fantastic way to free up hours in your week for your creative endeavors while still collecting a paycheck.

Flexible Work Hours

Companies are increasingly open to this idea; the trick is to present reasons why this would benefit your company and not just you.

Flexible hours can mean squeezing your forty-hour workweek into four ten-hour days. In this case, your fifth day could be devoted entirely to your creative projects.

Or, maybe you find your creative juices are flowing from 7 am until 11 am and this time block is best for you to work on your novel. Perhaps you could work at your day job from 12 to 8 instead of 9 to 5. Again, it's necessary to prepare a detailed proposal outlining why this will also benefit your company. An East Coast company, for example, could find a great benefit in having an employee who is reachable after hours for clients in different time zones.

Part-time

When you sit down and do the math, you may realize that though you're not financially ready to completely quit your day job, you can afford to downsize to a part-time or reduced-work schedule. Investigate your company's policy regarding salary

❋ CREATIVE TIP ❋

Propose

You know the details of your job better than anyone else. You're the one who knows how these flex options could work with your position. But if you want to be extra thorough, check out www.workoptions.com to download a flexible work proposal for around thirty dollars.

and benefits; some may be willing to pay 80 percent of your current salary for you to work four days a week, 60 percent if you work three days, and so on. Or you might work hourly instead of being salaried—just make sure your benefits will stay in place. If this hasn't been done in the history of your company, your proposal must be extremely thorough.

Keep in mind that there will be bumps while you're transitioning. Other full-time workers may resent you, and some bosses will continue to heap the same amount of work on you. It may take weeks—or even months—for everyone to become used to the setup. The point of your reduced workload is for you to *move forward* on your creative endeavors. So as soon as you leave the office, leave office drama and worries behind. After all, you have creative goals to meet.

Telecommuting

Telecommuters complete their work from a home office, and a surprising number of jobs are well suited for this setup. For the CG who wants more time to work on her outside creative goals, telecommuting cuts the crap—commuting time, business lunches, hectic office distractions, and even getting dressed in the morning. With focus, a telecommuter is able to complete her workload more efficiently, freeing up extra hours each week.

If you're going to telecommute, refer to Chapter 11 to make sure you're cut out for the work-from-home lifestyle. Many companies provide telecommuting employees with equipment like laptops and fax machines. Some may pay for your phone and Internet. Make sure you and your company

CREATIVE TIP

Communicate and Set Boundaries

With many different flex work options, you can imagine how boundaries could easily get blurred. You'll have to be firm and enforce limits during this time so that you don't end up with the same workload for less pay.

agree on an expense policy before setting up your home office.

CG-in-action Sarah Menkes works in advertising and event marketing for the Marine Corps. She says, "At my previous job, I commuted through midtown Manhattan and I felt like a part of a massive herd of cattle. I could actually feel my blood pressure rising in Grand Central Station." When she took the job with the Marine Corps, she negotiated a telecommuting schedule where she works two days in the office and three days from home. "I feel much more productive when I work from home," she said. "There are no distractions, no one stopping by your desk to bother you. Instead of wasting time on the Internet, I actually work straight through the day so I can be done by four o'clock. And I'm happier. I eat healthier because I'm cooking for myself instead of grabbing something on the run. I go to the gym either on my lunch break or at the end of the workday because I'm not drained from a long commute. As soon as my work is finished, I'm free to do what I like, and I'm a much more productive employee because of it." Sarah is passionate about cooking and uses the extra time she gains experimenting with new recipes and writing her cooking blog.

Almost every telecommuter I spoke with raved about how much more productive they were on the days they worked from home. They also bragged about what they were able to do in their spare time. This was music to *my* ears—but be careful not to create envy among your cube-dwelling coworkers. Now that you have a sweet deal, it's probably best not to mention the day you got so much done you quit at 2 pm and went to the pool to work on the illustrations for your graphic novel. Keep the good stuff to yourself or brag to your mom instead. Let your coworkers and bosses believe you're working as many hours as they are. And stay at the top of your game; you don't want to be the person who slacked off and gave flexible work options a bad name.

Job Sharing

This setup is just what the name implies; the responsibilities of one full-time position are shared between two people. Job sharing takes extremely thorough planning and communication between you and your partner in crime. It only works with two employees who are true team players, so do your best to pair with someone who doesn't get territorial over work and can share the load evenly. You can either find your own job share partner outside of the company (in this case, you should offer to help interview and train the employee so that it's less work for your company), or you can find a candidate within the company.

Consider sharing with a more junior level employee at your company who wants to take on some of the less challenging aspects of your job. You're likely to find a junior candidate who would jump at the chance for more responsibilities and a bump in salary. To simplify: let's say there are ten tasks to be completed. Currently, you have five and the junior employee has five. In the job sharing scenario, you give away two tasks. Now, the junior level has seven tasks, and you have three. The ten tasks still get done. Propose to decrease your salary more than you increase the junior employee's salary. When your bosses do the math, they'll see that they gain money while the same job gets done.

Proposing Flex Work Options

The reason most people don't get a flexible work schedule is because they're afraid to

Flex Workers with Benefits

As a general rule, if a company offers benefits to part-time employees, job-sharing employees will also be allowed benefits. If not—and if you're not married to a bringing-home-the-benefits type of guy or girl—consider job sharing with an employee who is married to that person so you can get full benefits. Everybody wins. If this isn't an option, include in your proposal a suggested way to split two employees' benefits so that they equal the cost of one full-time employee.

ask. You know your bosses and place of employment best, so use your judgment on how to most effectively broach the topic. Schedule a meeting with your boss to discuss the idea face-to-face. Start the conversation by letting her know how committed you are to your work. Be armed with a proposal that details how you plan to make your flexible work arrangement work for both you and your company. This proposal absolutely, positively has to cover how this arrangement will benefit your company. Brainstorm every angle and present your case logically, thinking through counterarguments ahead of time.

Your boss will likely express concerns, and you should be willing to negotiate. If you're coming up against a lot of resistance, offer a trial basis of three months so that you and your manager can both evaluate whether the arrangement is working.

Always keep in mind why you obtained a flexible work schedule in the first place: to get moving on your creative endeavors. Whether you're writing an album, finishing a collection of poetry, gathering freelance clients or in the preliminary stages of opening a small business, get motivated and start working. Create a schedule to devote the hours you've gained to your creative goals, and stick to it.

Transitioning Within the Company to a More Creative Position

Even the least creative companies employ creative types in some capacity. Copywriters, editors, graphic designers, art directors, and many other positions may be available at your current company. Explore all the possibilities for you to be creatively fulfilled while your employer continues to send you a paycheck. When a company knows you personally, you're at a big advantage for switching departments and jobs entirely. Because they know you're a smart employee with a great work ethic, they're more likely to let you switch from the production department to the art and design department, even if your design résumé is a bit lean.

If you're nervous about what your company's reaction will be, then start small. Ask to take on a creative project outside your normal duties. You'll get bonus points for doing the extra work, and if you do an excellent job, they'll come back to you again for a similar task.

While I was in college, I worked at NBC Sports as a runner, which is basically a paid intern. I got coffee for the on-air talent and did anything to make sure they were comfortable. (Now that I'm the on-air talent, I sometimes get confused when I hear my co-host ask for a latte—I momentarily think I should go and fetch it.)

While I was employed at NBC, I traveled to The Gravity Games in Providence, Rhode Island. I was prepared for two weeks of manual labor and coffee runs, but when we had our production meeting at the beginning of the week, I asked the production manager if the set designer would need some extra help. The production manager agreed, and I was assigned to assist her. The set designer was happy to share the creative efforts; we got along well, and by the end of the first few days she gave me all kinds of artistic freedom with the design of the set.

I went on buying trips around Providence to find odd objects that would help our overall set concept—a 1980s living room—and had a glimpse into what set design was all about. The set designer left in the middle of the first week, leaving me in charge of the set for the remaining time. It was the most creative responsibility I'd ever had up to that point, and it was thrilling. All because I asked for some extra work.

Jump at the chance to take on any extra creative responsibility; you'll not only be more fulfilled at your day job, but you'll have additional creative experience for your résumé. Find inventive ways to take on projects outside of your comfort zone. Remember, there's no harm in asking. CG-in-action Jenna Yankun worked as a sales girl at a high-end boutique. After a few months, she asked the owner if she could

✿ CREATIVE TIP ✿

Get Social

Do you have access to a creative type within your company? Take an art director or graphic designer out to lunch. Of course, use discretion. Don't gripe about your current position. Just let the person know you're interested in finding out more about his or her work.

assist her on buying appointments. Her boss said yes, and Jenna began accompanying her to the clothing showrooms. Jenna assisted in every way needed, whether taking notes, snapping digital pictures of clothing, or holding her boss's iced coffee. She did such a fantastic job—offering her opinion on the clothing when asked—that within months, her title switched from sales girl to assistant buyer. She told me, "My boss began to see me as a valuable second set of eyes when selecting the clothes and accessories we sold in the boutique." Jenna turned a retail job into much more, and one year later, parlayed her experience into a buying job at online retailer Gilt Groupe.

Approaching Your Employer

If you're planning to approach your employer about a flexible schedule or a more creative position, your recent work performance should make Oprah look like a slacker. If you're unsure, step back and evaluate how valuable you are to your company. When was the last time you were praised for your work? Have you been focusing on the tasks at hand, or daydreaming about a more creative life? If you've been dissatisfied lately, you may have been a grumpier, lazier version of yourself. If that's the case, take two months to get your game face back on before approaching your boss. Even for those of you on your best work behavior, you're probably going to feel a little nervous about suggesting changes. Try to remember that the worst thing your higher-ups can say is *no*.

It's your decision whether or not to clue in your employer as to why you want a flexible work schedule. I spoke with several employees and employers and the responses to this question were all over the map; in the end, it boils down to your relationship with your company and your bosses. Some employers advised to keep the proposal strictly business. One boss from the land of corporate America said, "Keep your proposal focused on how this schedule could work well for the company. I don't want to hear about your side business because it makes me think you're going to be distracted and only partly committed to your job."

Other employers I spoke with believe honesty is the best policy, and a few claimed that it creates more positive feelings when an employee wants to reduce their time in the office due to an outside pursuit. One television executive said, "If they let me know they want to reduce hours for a creative project, it's not that they dislike being in the office, it's because they have an outside interest they want to pursue." Proceed with caution: I'm sure even the most encouraging employers would get a little suspicious if an employee proposed telecommuting because she wanted to work on her screenplay. It would be natural to worry that you'll be writing your screenplay while you should be working. I'm not suggesting you lie, but use your judgment. An answer like, "I'd like a better work-life balance," or, "I'd like to spend the hour I'd be commuting with my children instead," will serve you better than, "I'm starting my own business and hope to be the heck out of this office within a year."

An exception to this rule is if you're still going to be putting in equal face time in the office, just with different hours—say, four ten-hour days and Fridays off, or 11 to 7 instead of 9 to 5. In this case, you have more room to give a reason such as, "I'd like to take a web design class that's offered at 9 am on weekdays."

Your proposal will focus on how your schedule will benefit the company, but you should still have an answer prepared when your employer asks why you're interested in a flexible schedule. With any luck, your job makeover will be a raging success. It's my hope that you'll achieve a Zen-tastic work-life balance that would make a Buddhist monk jealous. More importantly, I hope the makeover allows you time to create outside of work and prepare for your next career move.

If a makeover just can't happen, read on for your survival guide. You *can* get to creative career nirvana; the second part of this book is your roadmap.

Interim Survival Guide

You'd rather be the clown in a rodeo Monday through Friday than go to your job. I get it. Your job is makeover-resistant, your boss is change-retardant, and you know you need to leave it A.S.A.P., but you can't ditch this one until you find another one. Here's your game plan for surviving the job that makes undergoing oral surgery sound like fun.

Part 1:
Exit Strategy

You're now your own Creative Career Coach. Feel free to tuck a whistle underneath the blouse of your business suit.

Finding Another Job
Is Your Job

Get on it. Send out at least three résumés per week. In the next section, we'll review all the skills you'll need for networking, résumé writing, interviewing, and job-searching while employed.

Smart Girls
Set Goals

Make a list of the things you want to accomplish during the week. This list should include the tasks at your current job, as well as all the things you plan to do to track down your next job, gather freelance clients, or start writing your small business plan. When you hate your day job, it becomes even more important to work on your art or creative business ideas so you don't fall into a depressed slump.

Be Good to Yourself

The period before your exit may be tough.

You have to devote energy to your current work while searching for new work and still dedicate time to your creative pursuits.

Treat yourself kindly while planning your escape from job hell. Watch your language; how are you talking to yourself? Curb the self-deprecating inner monologues and remarks. When you're going through a tough time, talk to yourself the way you would a close friend. When I catch myself saying something not-so-nice I think, *I'm kind to everyone else, shouldn't I be just as kind to myself?* Especially now, you deserve your own kindness and compassion.

Greener pastures await you; take good care of yourself until you get there.

Pimp Out
Your Mornings

Go to bed thirty minutes earlier and get up thirty minutes earlier. Making your mornings truly your own goes a long way toward creating a day more in line with what you want. You'll feel more in control of each day from the get-go. Meditate, do Pilates, or stop by your favorite coffee shop with a book (or, even better, a creative project) and sip a caramel latte.

Creative moms, I know your schedules are extra-crazed and mornings might not be doable. Check out Appendix C for tips.

Part II: Activate

If you want to get to job heaven, be prepared to work for it. This starts from the moment you chose a profession. Every step along the way, whether it's practicing, researching, studying, performing, auditioning, designing, or creating, you'll immerse yourself in your life as an artist. Job dissatisfaction runs rampant, but that doesn't mean you're immobilized or helpless. If you're unhappy at a job that doesn't fulfill you, and you don't yet feel you can leave because of financial reasons, that doesn't mean you can't move forward on your creative life.

Discipline

Here's the part where I give you some tough love. Because no one's stopping you from writing your novel, oil painting for hours outside of work, or taking a night class on a creative skill you'd like to improve. I know you're tired when you get home from work. So take a brisk walk or grab a cappuccino. Do not sit on the couch and zone out in front of the TV. This is where the creative *I wish* types are separated from the creative *I will* types.

If you haven't been earning money yet in the field you want to pursue—or haven't earned enough to do it full time—you need to work even harder to cultivate your talent and pursue your creative venture. The best way to become a full-time creative girl is to behave as if you already are one.

If you're an actor, your hands should be on every monologue book in the library. Are your comedic and dramatic monologues rehearsed to perfection and performance ready? If you're a writer, get writing. Seriously, finish that novel. What's stopping you? (If you have a terrible case of writer's block or a problem with procrastination, we'll deal with those creative hurdles in Chapter 18.) The bottom line is this: whether you're a painter, designer, crafter, or candlestick maker, get to work. Devoting yourself to your craft ensures you're at the top of your game. If you want to start a business with your creative services, start building your client list one client at a time. Work on weekends. Be proactive. Don't half-ass anything. Start now.

Allison Kave, the studio manager you met in Chapter 5, works Monday through Friday from 10-7. In addition to her full-time job, Allison is launching her pie company, First Prize Pies. Every weekday, she bakes pies in the wee hours of morning before going in to work at 10. She also works weekends. Allison says, "I went into this understanding that when you start a new business, you'll work these type of hours. Working to start a creative company I can call my own is worth every minute."

Information Overload

The Internet ensures that an overwhelming amount of information is right at your fingertips. I'm always surprised when people say things like, "You're writing a book? I want to write a book so badly, but I don't know how." There's endless information out there on how to get where you want to go in every creative career. We're lucky to live in the Information Age. Use this to your advantage.

So that I was clear on the business side of publishing, I went to the bookstore and bought several guides about how to write a proposal for a nonfiction book. I went on the Internet and researched which literary agents sold which types of books. You can do the same version of this no matter what your creative interests are. Research is important throughout every stage of your creative career, in both the artistic and business sides of your profession.

Study and Meet Others Who Do What You Want to Do

Remember that list of local CGs you brain-stormed in Chapter 3? Is there a way for you to view their work, listen to them lecture, or watch them perform? I'll bet you can find a mailing list for their public events. Is there a creative woman in your network that you could shadow as she runs her business? When you open yourself up to learn, you'll be surprised at how many women enter your path with something to teach you. A year ago, I read a book called *Lessons of a Lipstick Queen,* an encouraging guide for entrepreneurs written by Poppy King, the CG you met in the previous chapter. I did some research and found out she was doing a book reading at a nearby boutique. I attended the reading, and when Poppy's fans dispersed I approached her. We started talking and immediately clicked. Within twenty minutes, we'd planned a lunch date and Poppy offered to read my proposal for this book. After reading, she recommended I speak with her literary agent. I met with several agents, but in the end, it was the agent Poppy introduced me to that was the perfect match. That agent sold this book. I never would have found him if I hadn't made the effort to meet a CG who was doing what I wanted to be doing. So put yourself out there. You never know who'll you meet and how they'll influence your creative journey unless you do.

Take a Class

You can complain about your job during happy hour drinks with coworkers and friends, or you can get your butt to class. CG-in-action and recent college graduate Sara Polsky works at a job she's not so crazy about. Instead of drowning her sorrows in after-work margaritas, she took an evening young-adult fiction writing workshop taught by YA author Micol Ostow. When her first twelve weeks of class ended, she signed up for another twelve. Sara told me, "I knew that fiction writing was where I wanted to go. There wasn't time for me to work on my passion project during the day, so I had to make time at night. Taking the class made me feel proactive, like I was taking charge of my career instead of just sitting around and moping. And being surrounded by a community of people interested in the same things I am was really satisfying, especially because that wasn't the case at my day job."

It doesn't matter where you live; if you're in a one-stoplight town, research online classes

In the Meantime

Do remember to keep up the good work at work even if you hate it. You don't want to burn your bridges—you may need a recommendation from the same boss you currently want to tell to eat your pencil shavings. If you need to use a few of your allotted vacation days so you don't go postal on one of your coworkers, do it. Come back rested and ready to put in your best work until you've found the next job. Think about the achievements you can accomplish in this job as talking points for future interviews.

Some CGs even find inspiration for their creative work from their non-creative jobs. Writer/director Daryn Strauss drew from her experience as a paralegal at an investment company and created the critically acclaimed satirical drama web series *Downsized*. Daryn says, "I observed everything happening around me—it was a time of uncertainty when everyone feared for their job security. I was able to tell that story by having lived inside the corporate world." *Downsized* was selected as one of YouTube's Top 10 Made-for-the-Web shows in 2010.

offered by resources like mediabistro.com. Your company may reimburse you for classes if they're related to your job. Your employer may even offer training courses of its own. They're probably geared to specific technical proficiencies—instead of advanced doll-making or cake decorating—but take advantage of this resource to make yourself an even more attractive candidate for the job you *really* want.

And If Your Job Becomes Truly Unbearable . . .

If your job causes you too much despair and doesn't allow you time to work on your creative projects, it may be time to consider a new day (or night) job in the interim. If you can't transition into a creative career immediately, there are options to tide you over in the meantime so you can still pay your rent *and* move forward on your creative goals. The work that will support your creativity is a highly personal choice. Some CGs prefer waiting tables or bartending because they can leave at the end of the day with a maximum amount of money per hour. This frees up the rest of their week for writing, auditioning, running their online creative business, or taking classes. Plus, you can leave work *at* work. There are no deadlines, emergency Monday morning meetings, and no boss pushing you to sell more of a product you don't believe in. On the flip side, there are picky eaters who send food back, drunken patrons, and swollen ankles after six hours on your feet. These are jobs you take solely for the schedule and the paycheck.

During my bartending stint at Tavern on the Green, I worked three days a week from 4:30 in the afternoon until midnight (an example of both reduced hours and flexible work hours). This left my entire day free for writing, auditioning, and taking classes. It was my priority to have the morning and early afternoon hours—the hours when I was the most present and focused—free for my own work, instead of devoting those hours to another job. Some of you might feel panicked at the idea of ditching your conventional job for a bartending gig. It's not for everyone, but if your job is making you miserable and getting in your creative way, there are plenty of non-traditional jobs out there that can accommodate your desired schedule.

A word to the CGs who are currently waitressing or bartending: I've been there, I've done it, and there are certain careers, like acting, where a late afternoon/evening job is essential, since auditions are held during the day. If I'd taken a 9 to 5 office job, I never would have been able to create the career I have for myself now. And when your creative talent starts paying the bills, you'll have great perspective and major gratitude. You'll also forever be a generous tipper.

The other option is employment (part-time or full-time) at a job in the field you want to enter, even if it means taking a position that is entry level or close to it. This is often a very smart move. You'll gain insight into the inner workings of your creative field while garnering contacts that can be useful in the future. When CG-in-action Sara Mann embarked on her singing career, she made coffee and bagels at a recording studio. She said to me, "I was strategic about where I put myself. The way I saw it, I could either make coffee at Starbucks or make coffee at a recording studio." She was surrounded by high-profile creatives who have since influenced her career. She now tours with Miley Cyrus as a backup singer and released a debut album titled *The End of You.*

This strategy is not just for those in tran-

sition. Many established CGs continue to work in another aspect of their career—like a casting director who teaches an acting class or an editor who teaches a writing class. This helps them network, maintain visibility, and keep their skills sharp.

CG-in-action Caroline Westbrook is a singer who works during the morning hours as a private school music teacher. She's gone the waitressing route before, but now prefers to supplement her performing income within the music education industry. "I love being surrounded by other teachers who are also working professionals," she says, "I'm immersed in music all day, whether teaching lessons during the morning or performing at night."

While I was acting, I often worked as a reader at Playwrights Horizons, an Off-Broadway theater in New York City. (The reader is the actor who reads opposite the role being cast.) I read with each actor auditioning, and when that actor left the room I was privy to the conversation that took place between the producer, director, playwright, and casting director. Having a front row seat to this inside information was invaluable. I learned which details about each actor and performance the group liked and disliked, and what part of each audition worked for and against the actor.

My own audition technique improved dramatically because I had this inside view of the casting room.

Part of this process is figuring out what works for you and makes you the happiest and the most creatively fulfilled. *So here's what doesn't work*: staying at a job you hate that doesn't allow enough time for your creative endeavors. You have options to support your creative work, whether you decide on a job makeover, a day or night job that pays the bills and gives you enough time to create, or a completely new creative career. Commit to achieving creative satisfaction, and get ready for the adventure that awaits you.

CHAPTER 7

The Fear Chart

*You're about to quit your job,
change careers, or start a business.
Get ready to face your fears.*

"Life shrinks or expands
in proportion to one's courage."

—Anaïs Nin

You've decided that you're ready to take the leap into Creative Girl Life. And it probably involves several of the following things: quitting your job (if you haven't already), changing your life, changing your hair, telling your parents, telling your spouse, telling your friends, and a whole list of scary that goes on and on. If you've decided it's time to look for new work, change careers, or open your combo horticulture-and-art therapy business, you're going to experience a few night sweats. This chapter gives you the fear chart: your new weapon for overcoming fear.

Leaving Your Job and Changing Careers

Hardly anyone likes change, and this is your career we're talking about. Embrace the uncertainty; it's an unavoidable component on the path to where you want to go. I know this is way easier said than done, so let's look these fears right in the eye. Remember, fear and anxiety are related to the fight-or-flight response we've had since we were cavewomen. Fight-or-flight was a very useful response back when food was scarce and we were sharing a jungle with predators. But now, fear and anxiety can really get in the way of making progress toward your goals. You don't need to ignore your anxiety; allow your fears to surface and address them with actual facts and solutions.

THE FEAR CHART

There are two energies on this planet: fear and love. Fear contracts, love expands. Her Holiness Sai Maa Lakshmi Devi teaches to think of fear and love as two plants—you're always watering one of them with your thoughts. All thoughts fall into one category—fear or love—so which plant are you choosing to water and grow?

Now that you've been given this information, it's too late to ignore it. Your thoughts create, so pay attention. We're going to work on a method for replacing fear-based thoughts with truthful, enlightened thinking. If you apply it, your entire outlook, mood, and way of moving through the world will change. This method becomes easier the more you practice. If you commit to this work, it becomes a learned habit, and when fear-based thinking starts, you'll know how to handle it.

The following exercise will help put your fear in perspective—and come up with solutions for conquering it. We're going to make four lists. In the first column, you'll make a list of every single thing that scares you. Delve into every fear, no matter how shallow or ridiculous. Reflect on the emotion behind each fear. In the second column, write what you know to be the truth behind the fear. If aspects of this fear are actually based in truth, write that down, too. In the third column, write what is in your control and how you can take action to reduce this fear. In the fourth column, replace the fear-based thought with a thought that carries a higher energy (a thought with a *higher energy* is a fancy way of saying *a more love-based thought or feeling*).

I wrote out one of my fears as a sample; this fear was a huge one for me about a year ago, a few months before selling this book.

COLUMN ONE: The Fear

I'm afraid that I will spend a year writing a book proposal and no publishing house will want to buy it. I'm especially afraid because I like writing so much and I could fall flat on my face and be hugely disappointed. I'm afraid that if I do fail, everyone will think I wasted my time. I'm afraid everyone will think I should have just stuck with jewelry and TV and been happy. Why, *why* did I have to tell all of my friends and family about this book? I should have just kept it to myself.

COLUMN TWO: The Truth

I have nothing to lose by trying this. Even if my book doesn't sell, my life is exactly the same as it was before I tried this. My friends and family are supportive of me. Trying this is important to me, no matter what the outcome is. I'm proud that I gave it a chance.

COLUMN THREE: What I Can Do

I can try to find the best literary agent possible for the selling part of the process. I can make sure I've done my research on the creative career market. I can take classes and work on revisions to ensure my writing is in top shape. I can send my work to trusted colleagues, friends, and teachers to get constructive feedback.

COLUMN FOUR: The Love-Based Thought I Choose Over Fear

My life is an adventure. I'm excited to take this chance and see where it takes me.

Now, you try.

❋ CREATIVE TIP ❋

Calm the Mind *and* the Body

Fear is often stored in the body as well as the mind, so if you're coming up against fear and resistance, check out Mary Sise's book, *The Energy of Belief*. (Yes, she's my mom, so I'm a little partial). Or read *Energy Medicine: Balancing Your Body's Energies for Optimal Health, Joy, and Vitality* by Donna Eden and David Feinstein. These energy medicine practitioners can teach you movements to calm the body and move through any fears that block you.

THE FEAR CHART

The Fear	The Truth

What I Can Do

_____
_____
_____
_____
_____
_____
_____
_____
_____
_____
_____
_____
_____
_____
_____
_____
_____
_____
_____
_____
_____
_____
_____
_____
_____

The Love-Based
Thought I Choose Over Fear

_____
_____
_____
_____
_____
_____
_____
_____
_____
_____
_____
_____
_____
_____
_____
_____
_____
_____
_____
_____
_____
_____
_____
_____
_____

The What Will People Think Fear

This fear is so pervasive and crippling that it needs its own section.

The reality is that most of us care at least a little bit about what others think. And people *will* react to you announcing that you're planning to change careers from an investment banker to a photographer, or an accountant to a pastry shop owner. If you're changing careers or starting a business, some friends and family won't be ready to see you change. Several of them will find it unsettling and uncomfortable, usually for one of the reasons below.

The Debbie Downer Effect

There are people who create a web of negativity everywhere they go. A few of these folks might be in your life right now. They gripe about mean bosses, corporate bureaucracy, lack of money, lousy first dates and dimwitted husbands. When you're trying to make a big life change, these are often the people who make underhanded remarks to "bring you back down to reality." And that place may be their reality. But it doesn't have to be yours.

If you realize a relationship or friendship was built around complaining and mutual suffering, try to transition it into something positive by communicating what you need. If that doesn't work, it may be time to cut the cord. You'll need all the positivity and support you can get.

Metaphoric Mirror Girl

You're holding up a shiny mirror and it's making people uncomfortable. Some people will take your dissatisfaction and desire to change as a reflection on their own lives. Your coworker suddenly thinks, "If this job isn't good enough for her, what does that mean about me?" or, "I've always wanted to be an artist, too, but it's just unrealistic." You can't control how your actions affect the way someone else thinks about themselves. Would you keep on an extra thirty pounds because you don't want to make your friend feel bad about her extra thirty pounds?

I didn't think so.

You're Climbing Out of the Box People Liked You In

If you've always been the good daughter, the girlfriend who doesn't make waves, or the practical spouse, the new choices you're making might confuse those who love you. They may respond by not taking you seriously at first. Spouses, boyfriends, and parents might say something like, "Sure, I'd love to quit *my* day job, too." So open up a dialogue about what they'd like to be doing differently—career or otherwise. Then, assure him or her that you're not going to do anything rash or quit your job in a huff and blow all your savings on a get-rich-quick scheme. You're exploring your options and together, you'll come up with a plan.

The Fear of Saying Goodbye to Status: Low Woman on the Totem Pole

This is another big fear that may have reared its ugly head on your chart. If your business card boasts a cushy managerial title at Corporate Soul Sucking, Ltd., it may be hard to wean yourself off status, expense accounts, four interns, and an administrative assistant to boss around. Are you ready to take a job in the lower rungs of your new career, or pinch pennies while you start from scratch opening your new business? Or rather, is your ego ready?

If you're contemplating a career change, you've most likely experienced the fear of taking a pay cut. Being treated like the newbie can be even harder to stomach than the money. Prepare yourself for workplace culture shock. Remind yourself that regret—especially a lifetime of it—is far worse than any temporary pay cut or ego blow. The shot at true career happiness is worth swallowing your pride, at least for the time being.

When Christine Hawes—the CG we met in Chapter 1—ditched her successful marketing gig to pursue a career in costume design, she had to start all over again. She ran errands around Los Angeles picking up and dropping off clothes and fabric and worked fourteen-hour days.

Christine says, "I worked my way up and in the end, it was worth it. I was pursuing what I loved, learning on the job and feeling stimulated every day."

Swimming in the Deep End

Accept that you're afraid, and go forward. Taking action is a necessary part of becoming the creative success you want to be.

CG-in-action Caroline Wright told me, "The saying 'fake it till you make it' is one of my favorites." We were sitting outside on the veranda of her bed-and-breakfast in Durban, South Africa. Caroline is an interior designer and had a successful business in Johannesburg when her husband was relocated to Durban for work. She still flies to Johannesburg for her design work, but decided to open a bed-and-breakfast while in Durban. Caroline said, "At first, I was terrified. I had no experience with this type of work. But I finally took a deep breath and told myself that I'd already acquired all the business skills I'd need to open the bed-and breakfast from my years of running an interior design business. It was worth it for me to try something new, even if it flopped." Caroline forged ahead and now manages two very different small businesses. She says, "Having your life in little boxes is very uninspiring at the end of the day. As long as you're swimming in the deep end, celebrate it, because that's when you're learning."

So get out of your comfort zone. Hardly anything exciting ever happens there.

Blowing the Taco Stand the Right Way

You've completed the fear chart and you're ready to face your boss. Before you shout "Peace out!" to your higher-ups and hop over that cubicle wall like a subway turnstile, take a step back and remember that it's important to leave any job on good terms. Besides the obvious reasons— acting like a jerk is unenlightened and inconsiderate—you never know when your boss's sister might know an editor at *Marie Claire* who wants to write a story on your new lingerie line.

Always tell your direct supervisor and higher-ups first. Don't let them hear the information through the employee grape-vine. Schedule a meeting with your boss and thank her for all she's taught you, and explain that it's now time for you to move on. Let your boss know your plans; there's always the chance your company may counteroffer by hiring you in a new capacity as a freelance writer, web designer, or another position more geared toward your creative ambitions.

Give plenty of notice; two weeks is the bare minimum. A month is ideal. Offer to train your replacement. Every industry is different; some employers will tell you to pack up your desk and leave the moment you quit. If that's the case, at least you've done the right thing and offered to stay longer.

Once you've given your resignation, finish your work. Don't behave as if you're one foot out the door. Don't fall into the trap of badmouthing the company; often, other dissatisfied employees will approach you to gripe, since you're the one who "got out." Do not align yourselves with them; your higher-ups will sense this and you want to leave on a positive note. You never know when your paths will cross, or when you'll want to use this company as a reference, so remain a model employee until your very last second on the job.

Many creative girls find it harder to say goodbye to a boss they respect creatively, especially if they're leaving to start their own business in the same field. CG-in-action Wendy Levey worked for two years as an assistant to Lori Goldstein, one of the top fashion stylists in the world. When Wendy decided to start her own styling business, she approached Lori honestly, letting her know that her time spent working as her assistant was invaluable. She told her boss she would stay on for three more months, and would help hire and train the next stylist who would take her place. She gave the same consideration to her first boss, Evyan Metzner. Wendy says, "This may seem excessive, but if you're working with someone you deeply respect as a mentor and will see time and time again, it's worth it."

One of the many positives to working within your desired creative career are the connections you make while employed. However, any self-respecting creative girl who leaves a job to go freelance never steals her boss's clients. If you're starting your own P.R. company, remember this is not an episode of *Sex and the City*, and you are not to steal a client list from the real life equivalent of Samantha Jones.

Certainly, while employed by your boss, you likely developed wonderful relationships with a variety of clients. There may be instances where it's appropriate for you to work on a smaller project for one of these clients. (Wendy Levey styles the fashion lookbooks for one of the bigger fashion houses while her former boss still styles the runway shows.) But don't insert a memory drive into the computer and snatch clients for your own business. It's not ethical, and you always want to treat coworkers, bosses, and clients the way you'd like to be treated.

Get Ready for Part 2

Creativity lends itself to all kinds of job structures. Don't become so obsessed with making the exact right step that you paralyze yourself from moving forward. Your creative life isn't set in stone by a single action or choice; you can always change your mind and change your course. Let's take CG Wendy Levey from the previous page. Wendy left her full-time job as a stylist's assistant to start her own freelance styling business. She freelanced successfully for several years, styling pages in magazines like *British Vogue* and *Nylon*. Six months ago, she decided she was ready for a change. She applied for and landed the position of Associate Creative Director at the powerhouse fashion company RACHEL Rachel Roy. Wendy's back to working full-time for someone else, using the years of styling experience she gained as a freelancer in her new position.

There's crossover on the majority of creative career paths, so keep your mind open to the choices explored in Part 2 as present and future possibilities. If you choose a full-time creative job, it's likely you'll find freelance work on the side. As I was researching this book, I couldn't get over the amount of CGs who worked during the day at creative jobs and moonlighted as business owners. Your creative path may take all sorts of twists, turns, and detours, but now that you've decided what it is you do and don't want, you'll be the one navigating the roadmap. There will always be surprises, but setting goals and making plans means you'll have a better chance of creating your ideal life instead of being a bystander or leaving it to chance.

Your career adventure is about to begin, so brew some coffee, creative girl, we're just getting started.

Get Where You Want to Go

CHAPTER 8

The 9 to 5 Creative Girl

*Polish your résumé, write a cover letter,
network like a superstar, and find your dream job.*

Full-time creative girls employed by a company work every day in their desired fields while bringing home a steady paycheck. If this sounds like something you'd dig, read on for strategies to network like a superstar and find your dream job. The next few chapters will prepare you for nailing the interview, negotiating your salary, and excelling in your new position.

Finding the Jobs

The Internet has made it easier than ever to track down job opportunities. Remember the industry-specific sites you researched in Chapter 3? Check those for job boards that post openings, or sign up to receive email newsletters with job listings. But remember, the majority of jobs aren't advertised. So look up contact info for the HR department of companies for which you'd like to work. Pick up the phone and inquire about employment opportunities for someone with your qualifications. You have nothing to lose by dialing a company you'd love to work for and asking about the possibilities.

Refer back to the list you made of CGs you admire. Take a chance and email one. I receive emails all the time from fashion students and other creative types looking for work and asking if I'm hiring. I hold onto résumés that look great and pass them along to creative friends who are looking for assistants. So be resourceful and bold as you search for job leads; you never know what doors might open.

Get Online

In addition to the major job sites like Monster and Career Builder, check out job listings on sites like www.creativepro.com, www.24seventalent.com, www.simplyhired.com, and www.careerjournal.com (the *Wall Street Journal*'s career site, filled with job searching tips). Visit www.jobkite.com, a job board focused on positions available at smaller companies.

When you dig deeper, you'll find websites particular to your industry with job listings, like www.gag.org, the website for the Graphic Artists Guild, or Publishers Lunch, a free daily email newsletter that reports news and job openings in the publishing industry: www.publishers marketplace.com/lunch/subscribe.html.

To find a great job, you have to put yourself out there. No one likes asking for favors, but to get where you want to go, you may have to suck it up and ask for introductions and possible job leads. Remember that everyone's been in this position. Down the road, you'll be the one to lend a helping hand and connect others to their dream jobs. For now, open your mouth and ask family, friends and colleagues about their networks and possible contacts for you.

An online network is a powerful tool. Websites like LinkedIn.com prove how massive a network can become with just two or three degrees of separation. But face-to-face time is crucial, too. So get yourself to industry events and surround yourself with likeminded creative types. Be bold and show up by yourself. Or, if that sounds too nerve-wracking, grab a pal and offer to treat her to a pre-event dinner.

Network Like a Superstar

Networking doesn't have to be a slimy term that conjures images of exchanging business cards after stilted conversation (though it isn't a bad idea to have a card with your contact info handy). Becoming a master networker is easier than you think. We'll cover networking here so you're armed on your job search, but know that mastering this ability will serve you at every step of your creative career. Creative careers aren't like corporate jobs where there's a more obvious and logical ladder to climb. Starting a network of people with similar goals will help you discover how others are making their way in the creative world.

Think of networking like having a conversation. You're opening lines of communication and allowing a potential relationship to form. It doesn't have to be scary, forced, or inauthentic. And it doesn't have to take place at the business equivalent of a singles bar. You can strike up a conversation anywhere you go. I chatted up Melody Thornton (without knowing she was a member of the Pussycat Dolls) in an airport bathroom because I really liked her sunglasses. We got to talking, exchanged information, and she gave an interview quote for this book. As with everything else, openness serves you; you never know who you're standing in line with at the movies or sitting next to on a bus. Maybe that person works in your dream field or is married to, roommates with, or the dog-walker of someone who does.

The first step to becoming a master networker is to open yourself up to meeting new people. It's that simple. So try it in a way that feels genuine to you. Always be your authentic self, and don't oversell it. You're someone who's looking to get to know a new person who may or may not become a friend or business contact.

❋ CREATIVE TIP ❋

Get Social

Check out local interest-based events at www.upcoming.yahoo.com. Find local interest-based networking groups at www.meetup.com. Wannabe fashion writers and editors should check out www.ed2010.com, an innovative networking community with chapters in cities and college campuses across the country.

Networking Events

When you attend a networking event, know what you're looking for and how someone can actually help you. This way, if you're asked directly, you won't be fumbling around for an answer. Be specific about what your qualifications are and what you're looking to do next. Even though you'll have these answers prepared, remember that this is still a conversation. So don't stress about what you're going to say next. Instead, *listen*. When you hear what the person has to say, you can respond and allow conversation to meander and flow naturally.

While conversing, ask open-ended questions. These are questions that can't be answered with a single word. Instead of "How long have you been working at the company?" ask "How did you get your start at the company?"

Join a Networking Group

If you choose to join a group, see if you can visit on a trial basis so you can check out the atmosphere and members. Do they seem supportive of each other's endeavors, or are they overly competitive?

✳ CREATIVE TIP ✳

Get a Move On It

If someone offers you contact information for a potential job lead or new client, honor their generosity by following up on their referrals in a timely manner (within a week is preferable). That way, you'll be fresh in their mind, so if the referral calls to check up on you, the person who referred you won't scratch her head and say, "Claire *who*?"

Social networks emphasize different things, so don't join a network that focuses on matchmaking if you're there to make business contacts. Visit a bunch of groups and choose a network of people based on your career goals and whether their group mentality vibes with yours. If money's tight, see if you can volunteer at an organization in lieu of paying a membership fee.

Networking is about building relationships that go both ways and help all parties. So be on the lookout for how you can help those with whom who network. If you're a former editorial assistant at a cookbook publishing house looking to get into magazine editing, be on the lookout for someone who needs a leg up in the book publishing world or who might benefit from some of your chef contacts. We all help each other get where we want to go.

Join a Special Interest Group or Start Your Own

If you're looking for a specific group—say, a writer's group, an indie filmmaker society, a papermaking club—and you can't find one, why not start your own? Contact CGs you've met through classes and workshops and see if you can drum up enough interest to start a group. Jewelry designer Andrea Montgomery started a monthly group for female entrepreneurs in her Texas hometown. Andrea told me, "At every meeting, one member presents on an aspect of entrepreneurial life: say, marketing strategies or health insurance for employees. It's empowering to meet with a group of women who are all dealing with the same issues. We can work through roadblocks together and help each other brainstorm ways to make our businesses stronger."

The more people you meet with your interests, the better the chances you have to hear about or secure a job interview for a position you otherwise wouldn't have access to. People rarely get places without the help of others. Sure, you can make your own luck. But we live in a world where people with connections get further. So get out there and connect.

Scam Alert:
If It Sounds Too Good To Be True . . .

Before we get into résumés and interviews, let's deal with the looming reality of job scams. And I don't just mean the ones on the Internet.

When I was in my senior year of college, I went to an audition held in the middle of Indiana for an independent film. As I was leaving the audition, a pretty blond girl followed me outside, handed me a business card and said, "My modeling agent thinks you're really

Using a Recruiter to Find a Job

A recruiter—also called a headhunter or staffing firm—is paid by a company looking to fill a position. (You do *not* pay them.) Because a recruiter makes a commission—usually, a percentage of your first year's salary—it can be tricky when it comes time for salary negotiation. If a position caps at $80,000 and the company didn't budget for the recruiter, you might be offered a lower salary because of the fee going to your recruiting firm. Then again, you might never have found the position without the aid of the recruiter. Some companies rely heavily on recruiters and may not post job listings where you're searching for them. CareerBuilder.com reported 37 percent of companies used at least one recruiter to fill a position in 2007.

If you choose to work with a recruiter, make sure you're extremely specific about what you're looking for, including actual job details, location and salary. Keep the dialogue open and explain your reasons for switching jobs so that you don't end up in a situation similar to the one you're currently in.

Ask friends for references or check out www.i-recruit.com for to find a recruiter based on specialty and location.

beautiful and wants you to call him."

"Who, me?" I gasped, thrilled that someone recognized my unconventional, Kate Moss-like potential. "Thanks so much! I'll call him right away."

Eager to unleash my inner supermodel, I dialed the agency that afternoon, spoke to the modeling agent and made an appointment to visit his office. Later that week, my boyfriend drove me to the address provided, and as we pulled into the driveway, I saw that the office was actually a ramshackle home.

How peculiar, I thought.

We went inside and were greeted by a teenager. "Hi," she chirped. "Come on in and meet Roger. Do you mind taking off your shoes?"

"Sure," I said, worried about tetanus, but ready to sacrifice anything for my career on the catwalk.

Roger was sitting at a table next to another young girl who he later introduced as his assistant. "Hello there," he said, "sit on down and I'll tell you a little bit about the agency."

We sat.

After a few minutes, it became very clear that something wasn't quite right. Maybe it was the way the three girls nodded and smiled like insane hand puppets, or maybe

it was the girl who sauntered upstairs in a bikini, dripping wet, followed by a man with a dinky handheld camera.

At the sound of their footsteps Roger exclaimed, "See, I've got the photographer right downstairs ready for you!"

Or, maybe it was the fact that Roger was blind. Blind, as in he couldn't actually see what I looked like. When this became clear to me, I excused myself to use to the bathroom. Roger's assistant trailed after me and asked if I'd like some water.

I abandoned my manners and asked, "So, Roger's blind?"

"Yes." She nodded solemnly. "He was kicked in the head by a donkey a few years back."

"How then," I whispered, "did he see me at the audition?"

"Oh," she smiled, "Roger just has a sense for these kinds of things."

My boyfriend and I got out of there and laughed the entire way home. But when I look back, it wouldn't have been so funny if I'd been by myself in that house. Scams like this happen all the time—though usually in a more subtle manner. Two years after Roger, I found myself in a refined version of the same scam. This one involved a photographer that you had to pay on the spot, after the "modeling agents" gushed about your potential. These scams follow a similar format and almost all involve money that needs to be handed over for photography, training, or other vague startup fees. If you're moving to a big city to become an actress, singer, model, or dancer, keep your eyes open and be overly cautious. If something doesn't smell right, it probably isn't. I wouldn't mention these stories if almost every single one of my acting and modeling friends didn't have their own tale about something similar happening to them. And sadly, some of them got swept up in the moment and forked over the cash because they were so excited that an agent saw potential in them.

If an agency is legit, you will never, *ever* have to pay *any* amount of money to get started with them. Agents make their money from commission, meaning when they book you for a project, they negotiate your pay for you and then take a percentage. Normal commission standards are 10 percent for film, television, theater, and commercial agents, 15 percent for managers, and 15 percent for literary agents.

Research your industry so that you're aware of what standard practices are, and what falls under the category of complete baloney. If you're unsure, and an agency is asking you to get photos (which you will,

of course, need) mention that you'll get the photos with a different photographer and see if they're still interested. This way, you avoid a kickback scheme. Any time you're asked to hand over money on the spot, head for the door.

The Internet has made scamming even easier. While job searching, CG Maurya Moran showed up for an interview she found on a reputable job board for a marketing position. The interviewers told Maurya they wanted to see how her people skills were out in the field. She showed up at an address that turned out to be a gas station. The "interview" consisted of locating gas station customers whose car windshields had cracks and offering to fix the windshield with a product the company was hawking. When Maurya realized what she'd signed up for, she got the heck out of dodge. She later Googled the company and found all kinds of complaints listed. Now she uses the Internet to her advantage to research a company if she's unsure. You do the same, okay? If you haven't heard of the company, do a Google search and plug in the name at The Better Business Bureau: www.bbb.org. If a company isn't listed, that's not a red flag. Many legit companies don't pay to be listed, but the ones who've had complaints registered against them will appear.

It can be tempting when you see jobs listed online that promise money to be made working from home. Watch out for language like: Work From Home! Make thousands while you sleep! 15K a month!

Don't accept a job without an interview. Don't give out financial information. Don't give out information that could make you a victim of identity theft (your social security card, birth certificate, driver's license, passport) until you're sure the company is legit.

Be smart, and don't put yourself in a compromising situation. If you answer job or audition notices and show up to a not-very-professional looking office space and your stomach gets a funny feeling, hightail it out of there and ask to interview at a coffee shop. Or show up the next day with your most muscular guy friend. Who cares if you look overly cautious? Better safe than sorry.

Job Searching While Still Employed

One blogger at the *New York Daily News* left her résumé in the copier. Her boss returned it to her. Yikes.

If you're living paycheck to paycheck or have limited savings, finding a job before quitting your current one is vital. It's financially prudent to keep a steady stream of income before jumping ship, but searching while employed is a delicate situation. You need to be hyper-aware of keeping your search private. Many companies monitor email use, so don't use your company email while job searching. Use a personal account. (A gmail account is free to set up.) And don't leave your email open for a passersby to view. Ditto for job sites.

When you do get the interview, try to set it up for 8 am so you can be at work by nine. Post-interview, don't show up wearing a business suit to your current job if you typically roll in with bed-head and leggings. Don't blab to coworkers about your job search (unless you're asking a trusted coworker for a referral).

The same goes for CGs starting to freelance and taking on outside gigs. See the sidebar for one CG's cautionary tale.

Toeing the Line:
Taking on Outside Work While Employed at your 9 to 5

CG-in-action Christa Bourg is an author and book packager. Years ago, when she was first starting her business, the lines blurred as she tried to juggle her freelance projects with her day job.

Christa says, "My boss knew I did freelance work outside of my day job and, in fact, it was even in my contract that I could. But one day, while she was out of the office, I was working on a proposal for a freelance project. I printed it and promptly went home for the weekend, leaving it in the printer for my boss to find on Monday morning. She was rightly annoyed with me. She never really seemed to trust me as much after that. Several months later, after 9/11, when it seemed like everyone in any media industry in New York was being laid off, she asked me to downgrade to part-time. I was pretty sure that that incident was a big part of the reason.

"At the time I thought she was overreacting. It wasn't like I had let my work go unfinished. But now that I've been in a position to hire and supervise people myself, I completely understand why she felt betrayed. She gave me a lot of latitude and never looked over my shoulder and I took advantage of that by using company time and resources for my own ends. For all she knew, I was working on freelance projects every time she left the office. I wasn't, but it was my responsibility to make that clear to her. When you're juggling multiple jobs, it's easy to let the lines blur, but it's absolutely your responsibility to make sure you're being fair to everyone who is paying you."

Submitting Yourself: Polish Your Résumé

A résumé should include:

- **Contact information**
- **Target Job Title**
- **Career objective**
- **Career Summary and Relevant Qualifications**
- **Technical proficiency**
- **Employment history**
- **Education**

There are variations on résumé structures, especially within creative fields. Temps can check out www.cehandbook.com for résumé pointers. For additional guidance, you'll find entire books dedicated to résumé-writing in the career section of your local bookstore. Ask CGs in your field if you can look at their résumés and portfolios to be sure yours is standard for the industry.

The following headings will get you started, but know that you can use your creativity as long as the information is clearly presented. You can try an interesting graphic that runs vertically along the right side and lists your contact info. If you're an artist, create a logo with

❈ CREATIVE TIP ❈

Get Artsy

Check out www.webdesignerdepot.com and search "résumés" for some seriously creative examples. Find all kinds of valuable job-hunting information and sample creative résumés at jobmob.co.il.

your contact information up top. Author Anna Carey uses a graphic that makes each letter of the title sections stand out like individual typewriter keys. As long as you include the information described below, feel free to showcase your creativity. Show your finished résumé to friends to be sure the pertinent information is easily located.

Contact information: List your name, phone number, address, and email address. I'm sure this goes without saying, but your email address must be professional. Brittneyluvsyou4eva@aol.com isn't acceptable. A simple brittney.smith@gmail.com will do, or even better, brittney@brittneysmith.com if you have your own website with career-appropriate information.

Target Job Title: List the job you're applying for. This allows your résumé to stand out to the employer in database searches. It also gives the reader a focus point for viewing your application.

Career Objective: This part is optional. But if you're just out of school or making a career switch, including a career objective lets the interviewer know exactly what you're looking to do next, which may not be obvious from your prior work experience. It

should be one to three sentences stating your background and future job goals, such as:

> "Public relations specialist with four years experience in fashion publicity, media, and branding. Looking to use my understanding of the fashion market in a design and trend forecasting capacity."

> "Recent college graduate with a degree in film and television. Looking for an entry-level position in film production."

> "Recent graduate from the Fashion Institute of Technology with an extensive design portfolio. Seeking a position in a costume design department."

Career Summary and Relevant Qualifications: Employers scan résumés quickly; including this section makes it clear right away that you're qualified for the position they're hiring. You can change this section each time you send out a new résumé and tailor it to the job you're applying for and the target job title.

Focus on Transferable Skills

If you're making a career switch, your résumé should now focus on the career skills you've acquired that will come in handy in your new creative field and make you the perfect candidate. It's okay to use volunteer work on your résumé, and you may have an easier time finding transferable creative skills there. Transferable skills can include leadership, managerial, customer-service, communication, and organizational or interpersonal skills. You're focusing on skills, achievements, and personal qualities that make you eligible for this job.

Technical proficiency: This is where you list your computer and relevant technological skills. If you've been out of the workforce raising a family or living off your inheritance in the Virgin Islands, your résumé should include recent courses you've taken to keep yourself tech-savvy (if they're applicable to the position).

Employment History: List your past jobs, including your title, your employer, and the dates you worked there. Include your job responsibilities, achievements, and contributions made to your company. Use action verbs to give this section a kick in the pants and show what an active, creative contributor you were in your previous positions. Talk about the way you trimmed costs, garnered clients or raised the productivity of the office. If your goal is to transition from hospital administration to party planning, focus on contributions like, "I organized a fundraiser for 500 guests which raised 1.2 million dollars."

Education: List the university's name and date you graduated, your major and degree earned. If you haven't yet graduated from your college or masters program, you can write: Currently attending ABC University, M.F.A. Lighting Design, expected graduation May 2013. You can also include professional education if you've taken courses and accrued expertise in a relevant area.

And if Your Résumé Doesn't Recommend You?

Lack of experience has to be dealt with smartly, and without lying. Morality aside, employers can check the validity of dates, salary, and job responsibilities with one phone call to prior employers. Even if you're not found out before getting hired, little white lies have a way of coming to the surface and can present problems down the road. I interviewed a filmmaker who took a job as a casting assistant in Los Angeles just after graduating with her Film and Television degree. She said, "One of my college classmates ended up at an audition where I was working with the casting director. After the classmate left the audition, my boss and I were looking over her résumé and I was shocked to see the college roles she'd listed, since she'd never actually played them. The biggest irony was that she'd listed a role that I myself had played!"

Needless to say, they didn't hire her.

Don't lie, don't exaggerate. The world is too small, and it's bad karma anyway. Instead, beef up previous jobs you've had with the reasons why they've made you an all-around wonderful employee. You worked at a coffee shop? I bet your customer service skills are extraordinary. There are all kinds of assets and proficiencies you've gained along the way that make you valuable to a company. Employers understand that there will be on-the-job training necessary during your first months. The editors at CareerBuilder report that 78 percent of hiring managers say they're willing to recruit workers who don't have the requisite experience in their particular industry or field and will provide the training and certifications needed. So don't let that stop you from sending your résumé.

Consider coming up with projects you could do for free for friends and family so that they can be added to your résumé. Design a few websites, do the floral design for your sister's wedding, plan an event for a friend's birthday, or offer to decorate three of your friends' homes. Take pictures of your work. If the job you're applying for requires a portfolio, you'll have to do this anyway, but even if that isn't the case, get yourself some quick experience so you have relevant work to put down on your résumé. Plus, these examples of your creativity-in-action make for great topics to discuss in your interview.

Carrie Solomon
WWW.CARRIESOLOMON.COM   CARRIE@CARRIESOLOMON.COM   646 234 5115

WORK EXPERIENCE

BLOOMBERG L.P., NY	Designer, Global Corporate Branding and ID	July 2009 - present Senior design and creative direction of corporate visual systems, global corporate premiums and user experiences; consultation on product ideation and production, interior design and wayfinding; development of visual system towards the repositioning of the company's overall brand promise; overall branding development for company collateral and partnership identities
	Art Director	November 2008 - July 2009 Leadership and management of a team of nine print, motion and interactive designers in the NY division of creative services; collaboration with account reps and business managers in teams ranging from sales, to product, to philanthropy and with our dedicated sustainability group
	Senior Designer	October 2006 - November 2008 Print and motion design, art direction, product conceptualization, print production, branding and sustainability initiatives
SCHOOL OF VISUAL ARTS, NY	Curator	January 2005 - March 2005 *Thesis+ Exhibition* - Research, organization, writing, design and installation of retrospective of five years of socially beneficial thesis projects at SVA
	Curatorial Assistant	January 2005 - May 2005 *Object of My Obsession Exhibition* - Management of staff of students for production, budgeting and design of exhibition
STUDIO DROR, NY	Senior Graphic Designer/Intern	June 2005 - September 2005 Graphic design, corporate identity, product design internship
COMEDY CENTRAL, NY	Motion Graphics Designer	January 2005 - June 2005 Freelance, off-air creative
WISE ELEPHANT, NY	Lead Designer	September 2003 - September 2004 Print and web designer, production, account management

EDUCATION
MFA Design, School of Visual Arts, New York, 2006
BA Philosophy, Bard College, New York, 1998

PRESS AND AWARDS

2010	Type Directors Club Winner American In-House Design Award, Graphic Design USA for Design and Art Direction
2008	American In-House Design Award, Graphic Design USA for Design
2007	Photo District News Annual Featured Website - www.jodyake.com Core77 LightObjects Competition -Notable Entry for the Ante Shade HOW Magazine online, Top 10 Website - www. janellelynch.net
2006	Interior Design Magazine online, Designwire, "Bright Young Things," June 2006 Design*sponge, May 4, 2006
2005	HOW Magazine online, Top 10 Website: carriesolomon.com

EXHIBITIONS

2010	*Lift, Hold, Roll*, The Future Perfect, Brooklyn, NY
2007	International Gift Fair, A+:The Young Designers' Platform at Accent on Design, NY
2006	*Fanstastic Routes*, The Lab at Roger Smith Hotel and Galerie Galou, NY *Depicting Design*, Brooklyn Arts Council, NY *SPARK: SVA MFA Designer as Author*, Visual Arts Gallery, NY
2005	*Object of My Obsession*, SVA Gallery, NY The Affordable Art Fair, David Allen Gallery, NY
2004	*Compositions in Hi-Fi*, David Allen Gallery, NY *Look Closer*, AG Gallery, NY
2003	*Group Show*, Table Space Gallery, Philadelphia, PA

Your References

The key thing here is to pick a reference who can set you apart from other job applicants. So don't pick someone who barely knows you. Always ask ahead of time to be sure the person is willing and able to give you a superb recommendation. You can make that easier (and more successful) by sending an email with some of the things you'd like mentioned. So that the person doesn't feel micromanaged, phrase your email like this: "Because this company is looking for a highly innovative arts coordinator, I'd love you to talk about the time I orchestrated the musical acts for our company's fundraiser."

If you're unsure how a person will speak about you, test them out. Have a friend of yours call and ask the person for a reference on you. Why not? A poorly picked reference can easily cost you the job, so be very sure of your choice.

If you want to include a reference from your current job but you don't want your current employers knowing you've got one foot out the door, choose a colleague who you're absolutely sure will keep your job search confidential.

The Cover Letter

You'll need a cover letter for every single résumé you send to potential employers. These suckers are tricky; you have to get to the point in three short paragraphs while letting the employer know who you are and why you're the perfect candidate for the job.

Type your full name and contact information on the top left of the page, just in case your cover letter gets separated from your résumé. In your introductory paragraph, state the title of the position and the reasons you're qualified for the job. If the job listing asked for specific qualifications, now is the time to mention the ones you possess. Be specific; give them every reason to pick up the phone and call you in for an interview. If you lack a skill, don't draw attention to it. Don't write, "I know I've been working as a paralegal for a few years, but you can't imagine how many music magazines I've read during that time. I'm completely up on the music scene, and I'm ready to write the indie rock band profiles for your magazine." Get the interview with the skills you *do* have.

Under no circumstances should you send out cover letters that aren't personalized or addressed to a specific person.

It looks lazy, and it's unlikely you'll get called. So cover your bases, and find out the name of the HR person.

Think of your cover letter as the part of your application that makes you stand out from the competition. Don't shy away from flattery; go ahead and write a sentence or two about

Sample Cover Letter

Textile designer Leah Quinaz shares the cover letter she sent for an art director position at MarthaStewart.com. Her cover letter is concise and professional. Leah makes it clear what position she's applying for and the reasons she should be considered.

Dear Danielle,

I am writing in regards to the Assistant Art Director position available. I am a textile/graphic artist based in Brooklyn. I have designed prints and graphics for companies such as Brooklyn Industries, Loomstate, and Scoop NYC. In the Spring of 2009, I helped launch the Loomstate for Target campaign with original artwork for Earth Day awareness.

I've had extensive experience with layouts at each company I've worked for, creating ads, store signage, and look books. I'm hoping to take this experience and apply it toward art direction.

My résumé is attached. For a sample of my work you can visit my website: www.leahvanessa.com

I look forward to hearing from you.

Sincerely,
Leah Quinaz

why you want to work at the company. For example: "I admire your company's innovative marketing work; I especially enjoyed the Internet campaigns you created for X product" or, "I'm aware that your company donates 10 percent of its sales to arts education, and I'd be proud to call myself part of your team."

The more you know about the company, the more your application seems targeted and informed.

Use animated language that makes your reader sit up and pay attention. Target what the employer needs while showing your creativity and personality.

If writing isn't one of your strong suits, get your cover letter into the hands of friends who are more grammatically inclined and have them edit it for you. Check out the old standby *The Elements of Style* by Strunk and White. You can view sample cover letters and résumés (and search for all kinds of career information) on sites like monster.com, jobstar.org, and careerbuilder.com.

Follow Up, Creative Girl, Follow Up

Don't assume that just emailing your résumé will get you in the door. If you don't get called in for an interview, follow up with another letter and résumé. Mention that you applied online, and try to include something new in this cover letter. When CG-in-action Sara Polsky applied for an editorial position at Perseus, she followed up her initial résumé submission two weeks later with a cover letter saying she'd just been interviewed for this book, an upcoming publication with Perseus. Get creative and come up with something to say that catches the attention of hiring managers.

If more than a few weeks have passed, go ahead and call the person hiring and inquire if the job is still open. Draw the line, of course, at persistently emailing and calling. One phone call and two emails will do.

A Temporary Solution

If you're having a hard time getting called in for interviews or transitioning directly into a creative position, you can try applying for a non-creative position at a creative company with the goal of transitioning into a creative department. You can often do exactly what you're doing now, but at a creative company. This option is a half-step, certainly, but if you're dying to get out of your current job, and don't have the creative experience just yet or haven't had luck transitioning, this career move is a quick fix to quench your thirst for the creative on a day-to-day basis. The idea here is that once inside the company, you can transition into a more creative position. Even if you're working as the company's lawyer or receptionist, being surrounded by creative energy during the daytime will fuel you to work on your creative projects when you get home. And think of how fun it will be to trade those business suits you've been sporting for a more relaxed ensemble of denim and chandelier earrings at your new creative place of employment.

CG-in-action Jenny Feldman is a senior writer at *Glamour*. Jenny advises, "Just get your foot in the door. Once you're there, you can worry about figuring out exactly what you want to do."

If you're just out of school and don't yet have a skill set, this is definitely an option to consider. Entry-level positions may be heavy on the administrative, but, again, your plan is to set yourself up for that future transition into a creative position. You can often judge the possibility of your transition by being up-front in your interview. Obviously, you can't say, "I'd like a complete job switch in about one year from now from editorial assistant to creative director, so how does that look for me?" But you can ask about movement within the company, and do your best to gauge how the company promotes from within (and whether your timeframe is realistic).

CG-in-action Irina Gonzalez works as the international assistant at *InStyle Magazine*. Her ultimate goal is to work in a more creative capacity on the editorial side of the magazine. Irina decided that taking a job at her ideal creative company—even if not in the ideal position—would put her on the right track to where she wants to go. She told me, "When I started as an assistant, I did a lot of administrative work. But after a year at the magazine, I'm given much more responsibility and my creative muscles are being flexed. My role has grown to include managing creative projects. I've started doing publicist approvals for stories that are done exclusively for *InStyle*. And I get to attend more meetings which has increased my involvement in the magazine and the international editions as a whole."

CHAPTER 9

I Want
You to
Want Me

*Nail the interview and
negotiate the job offer.*

The Interview

It's inevitable that you'll be nervous during your interview at a new company; the best way to keep your nerves in check is to prepare. You can do this by researching the company and predicting the type of questions you'll be asked. Research everything from the company's mission statement to last year's annual report. Get onto their website and find press releases and news bulletins. Know what products they sell, how they advertise, who their clientele is, and the demographic of their target audience. Plug the company's name into Google to find what other people have to say about them (although you might not want to bring up the bad reviews of the company's new fall collection you read on fashionista.com).

CG-in-action Jane Lauder is the Senior Vice President and General Manager of Origins. Jane told me, "I was recently blown away by an interviewee who conducted research among her friends on an Origins product. She came into the interview with insights and ideas for our company. That impressed me more than twenty-five years of industry experience ever could."

Search your alumni network and see if you can find a contact within the company. Ask if he or she can set aside a few minutes for a phone call so you can find out more about the company's hierarchy and recent news.

It's very likely your interviewer is going to ask you the following questions. If you're someone who clams up when nerves strike, write down your responses to these questions ahead of time. Try a mock interview with a friend standing in for the interviewer. At the very least, practice saying your answers out loud.

What are your weaknesses?

This is a bit of a trick question. Certainly, you can't mention things that make you undesirable. You can't say you're not detail-oriented if you're interviewing to be a copyeditor. And the kleptomaniac phase you went through in college shouldn't be mentioned, even if your therapist says you're in recovery.

Nor do you want to shrug this question off by giving a vague and generic answer like, "I'm too hard on myself." What you *can* do is list a weakness that you've made big strides

No Blubbering Allowed

When you're asked a question, you should be able to give an answer in under sixty seconds. You don't need to set a stopwatch, but don't go on and on because you're nervous. Don't be afraid of silences; you don't have to fill the space with chatter. Your interviewer will need some silence so that he or she can let whatever you just said sink in and form a follow-up question.

improving. Something like, "I used to hate public speaking, and I even got nervous when speaking in front of a group at work. So I signed up for a debate class that involved speaking and debating in front of a large group of people. From that class, I learned that thorough preparation allows me to handle public speaking much more confidently."

Look at your résumé with a critical eye. Anticipate what an employer may see as a weakness or gap. This way, if an employer says, "I'm concerned about your lack of . . ." you'll already have an answer prepared with the proactive steps you're taking to address that concern.

What are your strengths and your biggest accomplishments?

My biggest accomplishment is saving my little brother from choking on a mozzarella stick at Jim Dandy's Ice Cream Parlor when I was thirteen, but that's not the kind of accomplishment you blurt out in your job interview. Don't mention the time you helped deliver a baby in the backseat of a cab or that you were crowned Montana's Rodeo Princess in 1995. Do mention how proud you are that you increased ad sales pages for the last magazine you worked at, or that you choreographed a music video for a local rock band. Maybe you directed a play in your hometown or started a recycling program in your college dormitory. Give an accomplishment that lets your interviewer know creative and organizational strengths that are relevant to the position for which you're interviewing.

When asked about your strengths, don't be too general or you risk sounding like a fifth-grader. Instead of saying, "I'm a great leader," say, "I'm comfortable taking leadership of projects and delegating tasks. At my last job casting an independent film, I cast the main characters in Los Angeles, but assembled a team and delegated the remaining casting duties in Vancouver, where the film was shot."

Instead of, "I'm a people person," say, "I work well brainstorming and collaborating as part of a team. I like bouncing ideas around in a group setting; I think the best marketing campaigns are developed this way." Then give an example of a time you used these strengths with a successful outcome.

It doesn't matter if you've just graduated from college. The interviewer knows you just graduated (it's on your résumé). Pull from your previous work, school, and volunteer experiences to discuss your strengths and accomplishments, and use examples to illustrate in the same manner as above. If you worked your way through college, bring this to the interviewer's attention; it takes serious organization, hard work, and the ability to multitask to pull this off. If you've been out of the workforce raising a family, use an example from the school board you served on or a committee you co-chaired. Moms are the ultimate multitaskers; you can pull all kinds of examples of how you've balanced your family life with your creative work. The interviewer wants to get to know you: your strengths, skills, and the qualities you bring to the table.

Why did you leave your last job?

Proceed with caution. No matter how bad it was, under no circumstances should you badmouth your previous job during your interview. Even if you're bonding with the woman interviewing you, bite your tongue at the urge to tell her how lame your last boss was and how she didn't appreciate the time you got creative and spontaneously painted a mural on her cubicle. This will scare any potential employer; it's clear you'll have no problem badmouthing their company, too, when you eventually leave. It makes you look unattractive. Don't do it.

You should, however, anticipate what your old boss is going to say about you when the new company calls for a reference. If you're worried something negative might be mentioned, take this time to put a positive spin on the situation: "My former employer wanted to take the company more mainstream, which meant less creative involvement for me. We just realized that we'd grown as much as we could with each other and it was time to move on."

If you were laid off because of downsizing, be honest. Of course, if you had an awful break up with your previous company, do not include them as a reference.

If the interviewer really pushes you to talk about your previous place of work and why you're leaving, you can mention one or two things that didn't work as long as you also list several positives. And choose carefully what you mention as negative. It's okay to say, "At my last job, I didn't leave work most nights until after ten o'clock, and I often came in on weekends. Even though I enjoyed my work, I started feeling exhausted and wasn't able to spend time with my friends and family." It's not okay to say, "All of my coworkers hated me!" or, "I really had a hard time with how strict they were about office conduct, especially the policy about interoffice dating. And is smoking in the bathroom really that big of a deal?"

If you're wondering whether or not you should mention something, don't. If they really press you, say a variation on one of the following that makes sense for your situation:

"I loved the work, but the company was very large, and I'd really like to work at a smaller company with more opportunities for growth."

"While I loved my coworkers and my boss, there was a lot of data entry and administrative work, and I'm looking to do something more creative. It sounds like the position you're hiring balances office work with the chance to be creative out in the field."

"I enjoyed my time at *X Company*, but I'm realizing I'd like to take what I learned there and apply it to a different line of work that I find more exciting. A job like this one is where I see myself in the future."

Go ahead and reflect on past work experience, but stay positive. And feel free to ask why the previous employee left the position for which you're now interviewing.

So, why do you want to work here?

This is where your research will come in handy. If you're asked this question, use it as a chance to get specific and show how well you understand the company and its agenda. Instead of an earnest, "Because I love music/dance/art/fashion," comment on what it is specifically about this company that will make you excited and proud to work there.

When CG-in-action Jules McNally interviewed at the New York City Ballet, she mentioned her love of dance and experience as a dancer, but focused on her organizational and event planning ability, since that's what the job required.

Mention classes or informational interviews you've secured to find out more about the industry. Let your passion shine while you explain the reasons you think you're a great fit for the company.

Do you have any questions about the position or the company?

You'll come across as an amateur if you don't have any questions for your interviewer. And you don't want to pass up this opportunity to find out more about a place where you might spend years working. An interview is a time for both you and the company to decide if you're right for each other. It's not a one-way street. You're looking for a job that will suit you and provide a great environment for your creativity, skills, and personality. You're looking for a company whose values are in line with your own.

If you've researched thoroughly, you've already come up with a few intelligent questions about the company and what will be expected of you. Use this interview question to show you've done your homework and are genuinely interested to find out more about the company and your potential position there. Even if it's not asked of you, ask the questions you've come up with anyway.

I've listed some ideas to get you started on the next page.

A Few More Interview Tips (I'm Serious About Getting You This Job)

Calm your nerves even more by leaving yourself plenty of time to get to the interview. Leave enough time for the train to break down or to get stuck in unusually bad traffic.

Questions to Ask Your Interviewer

- What kind of strengths and skills are you looking for in the person that will fill this job?

- What will my responsibilities be?

- Will I be working directly with clients?

- Will most of my work be done solo or in a team?

- What kind of results do you want me to produce?

- What will my day-to-day work and schedule look like?

- What would a typical week look like in terms of workload and hours?

- What personality traits/abilities are needed to succeed in a position like this?

- What kind of challenges might I face in this job?

- What is the atmosphere of the office? (This question is a great way to get a candid answer about the stress level of the office, and hopefully to hear positives about the office spirit and high levels of camaraderie and collaboration. You can also ask, "What is the corporate culture like here?")

- Where does the department fit into the organizational structure of the company?

- What has the department accomplished over the past few years?

- What upcoming projects or products is the company most excited about?

- What is the future the company envisions?

- How have other employees advanced within the company after doing great work in this position?

- Does the company provide training or workshops for an employee to acquire new skills?

Certainly, don't keep asking questions just to hear yourself talk. When you've gotten the information you'd like, thank the interviewer for her time. If the interviewer is looking at her clock or seems ready to end the meeting, you can end your questions by asking when you should expect to hear back from her.

By having questions ready, you'll show your genuine interest and intelligence, and you'll learn a lot from her answers. You wouldn't just date someone because he or she wanted to date you. This company has to want you, but you have to want them too.

Don't bring rushed, frazzled energy into the interview. You should arrive a few minutes early, but not more than ten minutes.

Always keep in mind that you got the interview in the first place because the employer saw the correct skill set on your résumé. So take a deep breath and relax. You're already qualified to be there, now let the interviewer see how great you'd be to work with each day. In every audition and interview situation, remind yourself that the people sitting across the desk or behind the camera actually want to hire you. They're not hoping you bomb the interview. In fact, it makes their lives easier for you to be the perfect candidate. CG-in-action Mele Nagler is a casting director who has cast televisions shows like *Brotherhood* and *Gossip Girl* along with Broadway theater. Mele says, "Remember, we're rooting for you. This isn't *American Idol* where it makes good TV for you to be terrible. If you can wrap your head around the fact that the person behind the table wants you to be great, you'll have an easier time letting go of your anxiety."

Remember to smile during your interview; no one wants to work with a grouch. Don't fidget. Don't sit with your arms crossed over your chest. Do sit slightly forward in your chair and make positive expressions to show you're engaged and interested. It sounds simple, but a firm handshake and eye contact go a long way. Don't wear a ton of perfume (ever, but especially in an interview or work situation).

Creative types sometimes think, "I'm going to wow them with my off-the-wall uniqueness and creative outlook." But at the end of the day, the interviewer is looking for someone who will represent the company well, so be aware of how you're presenting yourself. Don't go on and on about your sixth sense or your cats. If you want to convey this information in a context that makes sense for the interview, let the interviewer know you have an innate ability to predict trends and find buzz-worthy items to write about. Be prepared with relevant examples. Don't misunderstand me; I'll bet your individuality is one of the best things about you, and if you can't make it work in an office full of people, you might be better suited to opening up your own business. But if you want to work for a company, leave the Friday night séance invitations at home, unless you're going for an interview at a Wiccan bookstore.

Clothes Make the Woman

The way you dress for the interview says a lot about you to potential employers. This can be trickier with creative jobs because the work environment will often be more casual once you're actually employed there. If you're unsure about the company's aesthetic, play it safe by going business casual for the interview. Of course, you'll have to use your judgment; if you're interviewing for a position as an illustrator in a lofted office space in Seattle, you shouldn't show up in a business suit from Talbots looking like you're ready to argue a law case. Ditto for fashion positions: whether you're interviewing to be a fashion writer, a designer, an editor, an editorial assistant, you have more room to dress the part. See the sidebar on the opposite page for more tips.

A Final Piece of Interview, Audition, Performance, and Whenever-You're-Scared Advice: Fake it Till You Make It

This piece of advice applies to all of us at different points in our careers. I can't tell you how many times I heard this outlook echoed among the creative women I interviewed this year.

There's a fine line here, so it depends on how comfortable you are. When I auditioned to be a host on the Home Shopping Network, I told the producers I could handle an ear piece and teleprompter (notice, I didn't lie and say I had experience when I didn't). *How hard could it really be?* I thought. I chanced it and read a teleprompter for the first time on live television, while a producer shouted instructions through an earpiece.

Luckily, I made it through that one with flying colors, but I've pushed my limits a *little* too far before. Like the time I really, *really* wanted to do some on-air commentary for a webcast during the Gravity Games in Providence. The only catch was that the on-air host had to have

The Fashion Interview

It's your own *The Devil Wears Prada* moment, and you want to be prepared.

Fashion stylist Wendy Levey gives her tips for a successful fashion interview outfit.

"I think the most common mistake people make is wearing something designer or expensive, for no other reason than it is designer or expensive. In a creative position, the interviewer is looking for creativity, and what better vehicle than your own person and its vestments to show it off?

"It's fine if you want to wear a label, but make sure you're wearing it because it's special and also appropriate to the event. (No sheer slip dresses, no matter how gorgeous, and anything too dressy looks forced.) Choose a piece that is interesting and you feel defines you and your aesthetic. If you love colored tights, wear them. If you love platform shoes, wear them. If you like pulling your hair up in a bun with lots of tiny braids, do that, so long as your hair is clean and it doesn't look like you just rolled out of bed (or kindergarten). The important thing is to let your personality come through, as so many creative people wind up making things they themselves like and want to wear. Interesting jewelry, an unexpected way of wearing a scarf, a bag you bought at a tiny market on some faraway vacation can give you a chic edge. The interviewer is not looking to see what is already out there, but what you can help create so the company can put something of its own out there. A Prada bag is nice, but a bag you embroidered yourself is better.

"No matter how artsy, creative, or unexpected your look, remember that some things hold true for all interviews. This means your shoes can be vintage, but flapping soles aren't acceptable. Your bag can be a two-dollar number from a street vendor in Bali, but should not have holes in it. No tops with trailing bits of yarn you meant to cut off the last six times you wore it. Wrinkles, unless part of the design, look unprofessional.

"In addition to creativity, the employer is looking for competence, and at the end of the day, fashion is a business just like any other. If they are offering you a position with responsibility they want to make sure you are a reliable person who will work well within their company, so dress accordingly."

experience in extreme sports. I recalled my high school athletic accomplishments and thought, *How hard can extreme sports really be?* I was confident that a knack for swimming and lacrosse would translate into extreme sports prowess.

My little white lie caught up with me a few days into the job when I was asked to ride a dirt bike off a jump. Never one to back down from a challenge, down the ramp I went as the bike hurtled faster and faster beneath me. I flew up the slope and into the air, completely out of control. Since I had no idea how to point the nose of the bike back down again while in mid-air, I crashed at the top of the jump, tried to stand back up but was so dizzy I tripped over the bike and tumbled down the ramp of the second jump. I escaped with minor scrapes and bruises, the main damage done to my pride.

There's a fine line between taking a risk and being foolish, but nearly every woman I spoke with had a ballsy story about starting a new business, interviewing for her dream job, or convincing her first client. There was always some point along the way where she decided she'd do whatever it took to get her where she wanted to go. You'll never find out your true potential unless you *try*.

Always come from a place of yes and inspire confidence. An interview is not the time to be humble. This is a company looking to invest a large amount of money in your talent and ability. Don't think it's coy to act awestruck that this big company wants to hire little ol' you. That kind of behavior won't cut it in the creative business world. You'll need this confidence throughout your creative career: the first time you name your prices out loud to a client, the first time you go on-air for a television interview, the first time you close a business deal or give a presentation. Take ownership of your creative ability and know your worth. Embody confidence and enthusiasm.

Sometimes, when I know I'm completely out of my league, I think of it as an adventure. Last week, I went on an audition for an on-air wardrobe stylist gig for TJ Maxx. It paid big bucks and everyone there had way more styling experience than I did. The casting director actually looked at my résumé and said, "Um, I'm not going to pass this onto TJ Maxx. We're looking for real stylists, not actresses with styling experience."

A split second after the warm welcome, she turned on the camera and began taping my audition. She'd basically just told me I was too underqualified to even be in the room. But so what? This isn't heart surgery. What was the worst thing that could happen? I have my health, my family, and my dog. Getting a job is just gravy compared to those things. So I winged it. Smiled huge and pretended I was the most confident and capable stylist TJ Maxx would ever meet.

Your career is an adventure. An interview or audition is a step along that adventure. Don't waste time doubting yourself. Your doubts and fears only have power over you when you give power to them. Every time a voice pops in your head telling you that you can't possibly do something, it's just a part of you that's fearful. Let that part surface and explain why she's so afraid. Often, when you define the worst possible outcome for trying something new, it's not so scary after all.

Because really, what's the worst thing that could happen in that interview room? You say something stupid? No one's perfect. It probably wasn't even as stupid as you thought. And if it was, you won't say it at the next interview. I once choked on live television. Literally, not metaphorically. On a cough drop. I had to run off-screen and throw up into a garbage can. My microphone was still on so you could hear the hacking as I ran off-camera. Your interview won't be on live television. So I promise, if you choke, it *will* be okay.

Relaxation Preparation

In the days leading up to your interview or audition, change your language. My mom taught me this trick when I was eight years old and I've been using it ever since: whenever you want to think or say, "I'm nervous . . . " or, "I'm scared . . . ," change your words to, "I'm excited." So, "I'm nervous about this interview," becomes, "I'm excited about this interview." Remember, your words and your thoughts create your experience.

The night before any interview/audition/performance, lie in bed and breathe deeply. Starting at the tips of your toes and working to the top of your head, tighten each muscle group as you inhale and hold for ten seconds. Then release as you exhale, feeling tension leave your body.

Take some time to visualize how you want your big moment to go. See yourself performing well and feeling excited about your possibilities.

Remember, it's all right to have a little bit of nerves on the day of something important. They'll keep you sharp and on your toes.

Salary: How the Heck Do I Know What I'm Worth?

Don't sell yourself short, creative girl. Determining your worth is tricky, and creative types—women in particular—often have a harder time naming the price they're really worth. When determining your salary, take into account your education, prior work experience, your proficiency and skill level, and the market value of the job. If you're transitioning into a spanking new field, be realistic about the amount of experience you have and the salary you can command. Do take into account the transferable skills you've learned at prior jobs.

In general, if an interviewer asks for the salary you're expecting, proceed with caution. You don't want to blurt, "How about $60,000?" if the position is more likely to pay $75,000. Hold off on discussing salary until you've been offered a job. Even then, you want the company to throw out the first number. You can sidetrack the interviewer by asking, "Could we talk more about the job first so I understand the responsibilities? I'd be able to answer the salary question with more information."

If the interviewer pushes you, you'll need to know a salary range to quote. The best way to phrase your quote is to say, "I've done the research on similar positions and found the range for my position to be from 65K to 75K."

❋ CREATIVE TIP ❋

Send a Thank-You Note

According to CareerBuilder, 15 percent of hiring managers said they wouldn't hire someone who failed to send a post-interview thank-you note. 32 percent said they would think less of the person. Add those percentages together and you've got 47 percent of hiring managers who would think less of a person or outright eliminate them. 47 percent! Write the thank-you note. A thank-you email is better than nothing, but a handwritten note is your best bet.

Keep in Touch

If your interview goes well but doesn't end with an offer, keep in touch with your HR contact at the company. CG Libby Golden's first interview at HarperCollins didn't result in a job. But she kept in touch with the HR department and was called in again to interview for the next open position. You can send an email every month with relevant career information—from a newsworthy accomplishment to an industry seminar you attended.

There are a few numbers you need to figure out before any monetary conversations take place. The first is the salary range you're worth. The most straightforward Internet salary calculator I've found is www.indeed.com/salary. You plug in any job along with the city you're working in to get an instant salary average. With creative jobs, it can be difficult to determine an average for the position you're considering. Continue researching; Google your job title and the word "salary" and see what else you can dig up. You can also try www.salary.com, www.jobstar.org, or the salary service provided by CareerBuilder, www.CBSalary.com. The trusty Bureau of Labor Statistics, www.bls.gov, is a great starting point for any job questions, including salary.

Check out trade associations or ask around within your network. With a little finesse it's possible to politely gather information about salary without flat out asking your creative colleagues what they bring home each month. Try phrasing your inquiry like this: "I'm trying to research salaries for X position I'm interviewing for at X company, but I'm coming up with conflicting information. Do you think X to X amount of money sounds about right if the company asks me what I'm expecting for a salary range?"

Compensation for creative work is less straightforward. We CGs are all in the same boat, so some of your colleagues or friends may be happy to share their financial experience if it will help you make a decision. But be discreet and wait until the information is volunteered.

Once you have a salary range you feel comfortable with (the one you'll quote in an interview) you need to decide upon the rock bottom number you won't go below. Certainly, money isn't everything, and factors like a great company culture, flexibility, and potential for upward movement within the company are all good reasons to take a job. You may fall in love with a small company with tons of potential for you to grow as they do. There's a lot of pride in starting somewhere small and helping it soar.

If you're escaping from corporate hell, it may be well worth it for you to take a reduced salary to join the love fest that awaits you at Small Creative Inc. But you have to be able to pay your bills. Creative girls need to know their bottom line whether applying for full-time creative jobs, starting a business, or becoming a freelancer. Take the time to track your expenses for at least one month, preferably two or three. I'd even recommend this exercise for those of you already bringing home the creative bacon. When I recorded my expenses (I'm embarrassed to admit I had no idea how much I spent on food each month) I discovered an obscene amount of cash supplied an out-of-control takeout sushi habit. So I spent a weekend reading online and teaching myself how to make my own California rolls. (Sorry, Miyagi Sushi, I know you're a small business too).

Multiply your monthly expenses (food, rent, mortgage payments, etc.) by twelve to get a yearly total. The guesswork comes when you add in all the unpredictable expenses that crop up each year, like gifts, weddings, and unavoidable travel. Do your best (and always *over*estimate) what you think your monthly expenditures will be for those items. Once you have a number, figure out what you'd have to make to live paycheck to paycheck (don't forget to factor in what you'll pay to the government in your tax bracket). Since paycheck-to-paycheck isn't the ideal way to financially exist, add an additional number that is your goal amount to save each year. Now you have a salary range (paycheck-to-paycheck to money-saver-extraordinaire) and you know your rock bottom salary. When you go into an interview, you won't get caught up in the moment and accept an offer that doesn't cut it.

Of course, don't mention your rock bottom number when you quote a salary range to a potential employer—I'd rather you not live off canned tuna for a year. But you need to have the number in mind so that you know the lowest you'll go, even for your dream job. When the employer hears your salary range, you're going to hear a variation on, "Great. That sounds in line with the position, so I'll get the paperwork started," or, "I'm sorry, that number is much too high."

You can ask, "What number did you have in mind?"

If the employer offers a number you deem too low, it's time to negotiate. Certainly, you can express your enthusiasm at the offer of this creative job, but if the salary is lower than you expected, ask for time to think it over. Often, you can break up the job offer discussion into two separate conversations. The first can be to go over exactly what will be expected of you in your new position, and the second can be to negotiate your salary and benefits.

Salary.com lists the following five steps as guidelines in salary negotiation.

1. Agree on a benchmark job.

2. Agree on your proficiency and performance level.

3. Agree on the market value of the job.

4. Agree on where your salary should fall.

5. Agree on what performance is necessary for future salary increases.

Here's what this means for you:

Step 1: **Agree on a job title. For example: Junior level graphic designer.**

Step 2: **Agree on your skill level.**

Step 3: **Agree on what a junior level graphic designer at your skill level makes in your area. Graphic designers in Omaha are paid very differently than graphic designers in San Francisco.**

Step 4: **Agree on a salary range.**

Step 5: **Agree on what you can do for future promotions or salary increases. Find out what it takes to be promoted to senior graphic designer and see a bump in compensation at this particular company.**

Tips for Successful Negotiating

No matter what, don't get emotional. Even though you really, *really* want this job, this is still business. Keep your attitude professional. Keep your body language open: don't cross your arms or pout. Don't talk about how much you need to earn in order to pay your rent or chip away at student loans. Do talk about the market research you've done on relative salaries in your field. Do talk about how you're going to earn the salary you're requesting. Remember, a negotiation is a time to communicate fairly and realistically. Be aware that every company has different amounts of flexibility when it comes to negotiation. Smaller companies traditionally have more room to play around with numbers.

If the number comes back well below your rock bottom, and there doesn't seem to be any room to negotiate, you can say, "I'm very interested and excited about this position, but I won't be able to accept less than $XX,000."

At that point, you're not going to take a job that means going into debt, so lay it out for them. The only exception to this rule is if you're so passionate about this job that you're willing to work

Get Over the Idea That Talking About Money is Unladylike

In *60 Seconds and You're Hired*, Robin Ryan writes, "Women still make 23 percent less than men . . . Much of this discrepancy is due to the fact that men often try to negotiate their salary, whereas women typically accept the original offer as given."

The editors at CareerBuilder reported that 60 percent of hiring managers will offer a higher salary if asked.

Television agent Tracy Weiss says, "Neophyte women in the business world take first offers because they don't know how to set clear cut boundaries about their financial worth. Just getting an opportunity isn't always enough; at some point in your career, you have to stop accepting what's offered and place a value on your services. I've found that many people—myself included early in my career—simply listen to what the person in the power position has to say and accept the dollar amount offered. Those new to negotiations are just happy to say yes to get the deal done and make the awkward part go away."

For more of Tracy's negotiation pointers, see Chapter 16.

a second job on the nights or weekends, or majorly cut down your expenses by getting a roommate or moving back in with your parents. (Hello, Mom and Dad!)

While negotiating your salary, make sure you fully understand the payment structure. Will you be offered bonuses, or is your salary the full compensation? If there are bonuses involved, are they based on your performance or how the company as a whole performs each year?

Before accepting the offer, make sure you're clear about paid vacation time, retirement, and health insurance. Get the full story about the benefits this salary includes. For example, the company may pay for you to get a graduate degree or provide stock options. There may be an on-site daycare or a gym membership included. Do they have a 401K? Do they offer dental insurance? Know exactly what you're getting yourself into and factor in anything not included (like health insurance) into your monthly expenditures so you know what you can afford to accept.

Remember, performance evaluations and salary negotiations are a recurrent process. If you're not thrilled with your starting salary, ask the employer when your first evaluation will be. Make sure you know exactly what is expected of you to secure a promotion and salary increase. Every performance evaluation is a chance for you to negotiate salary, bonuses, stock options, and benefits, so get in touch with your inner negotiator. Do your best to ditch the fear of coming across as overly aggressive; your higher-ups will respect you for knowing your own worth. I'm not talking about insisting on a salary raise every five months or making ridiculous demands, but the truth is that if you're in a job for over a year and you haven't had a conversation about your progress and a salary raise, you're not being proactive.

✻ CREATIVE TIP ✻

Be in Control of Your Cash

Check out www.mint.com. This site is a fabulous, free tool for budgeting and money management. While you're at it, read *On My Own Two Feet: A Modern Girl's Guide to Personal Finance* by Manish Thakor and Sharon Kedar.

CHAPTER 10

You Got the Job: Now, Work It

The keys to getting promotions and more creative control

If you're reading this book,

you don't just want to stay in your new job, you want to excel: to move up the ladder with promotions and raises and become an indispensable part of a company you care about.

So if more creative control sounds like something that interests you, follow the steps below to thrive in life at the office.

Give Your Attitude a Makeover

You're not just punching the clock anymore. Whether you're an art director, copywriter, production assistant, set designer, fashion editor, or online video producer, this is the start of your creative career. I'm sure you've read generalities like "approach your job with dedication and commitment," or similar advice that's easy to gloss over while reading a career or self-help book. You may think, *yeah, of course, I get it*. But do you really put the advice into action?

To succeed, you must value the company's needs along with your own. In your previous job, maybe you thought of work as a chore, a necessary evil, or something that got in the way of what you really wanted to be doing during the day. Now that you've found a creative job, abandon that attitude. That time in your life is over, so reframe your thinking.

Start by immersing yourself in your work with renewed energy. Ask yourself: how will I contribute to this company so that it operates at its smoothest, so that it grows and achieves great things? Treat the company like a partner; the more loyal you are, the more "big picture" thinking you do, the more your company values you. You may not plan on staying there forever, but behave as though you do. How would your work change if you were going to work for this company until retirement? Put those changes into action. Think long-term; how will the creative project you're working on now affect the company during the next few years? Verbalize those questions. Employers will sense your commitment and treat you differently than an employee who clearly thinks of the job as a way to pass the hours between nine and five.

Ask for more work. When you're done with a project, don't sit around looking at your Facebook account. Let your boss know you're finished and ask what else you can do.

Be willing to learn new information and acquire fresh skills. Welcome the challenge when you're presented with a difficult project; it means your employer thinks you're capable of completing it. Ask pointed, informed questions about anything for which you need further clarification.

These little adjustments to your attitude and work ethic make you exponentially more valuable. You'll not only notice more frequent raises and creative control; your attitude shift will spill over into other aspects of your life and you'll likely find yourself

happier overall. Never underestimate the ability work has to bring you great satisfaction. For some people, work is just work. But for most CGs, it's much more. Having it all means a full life: health, family, friends, love, spirituality, and meaningful work. The majority of your day will be spent at this job. Make each minute count.

Avoid Personal Problems with Coworkers

Many creative girls love drama, naturally. But there isn't time for this in an office. So figure out the best ways to avoid petty problems with coworkers. Creative disagreements are fine. I'm talking about how annoying it is for everyone else in the office when two coworkers can't get along. The most valuable employees are able to get along well with others.

Remember, this is work. Not a social club. Whatever you need to do to keep work professional, do it. If you tend toward melodrama, avoid socializing with work friends in order to keep your personal life out of the office. Don't date your boss. Don't share intimate information with people you don't trust. Make office gossip beneath you by refusing to engage in it. There will likely be coworkers who love to gossip, but they'll give up on stopping by your desk if you appear disinterested.

Gossip is poisonous. When you participate, it breeds negative energy in *you*, so avoid it both in and out of the office. When someone tries to gossip with me about someone else, I say, "Oh, that's too bad. I'll send some good thoughts their way." This inevitably freaks out the person who was trying to gossip, and he or she backs off. Do it a few times, and the office chatterbox will learn to look elsewhere when she wants to dish.

When you're a diplomatic and cooperative worker who gets along with employees, you'll find yourself placed into leadership positions more frequently. Your boss trusts that you'll be able to delegate fairly and manage others. If you can't get along with others, it won't matter how smart or creatively talented you are.

Speaking of your smarts and talent: there's a fine line between being a creative genius and trying to prove to everyone that you're a creative genius. Being a team player means encouraging others to share their ideas. It means valuing other opinions. Don't be a hot shot and use your creative energy to show people up. This generates a restricted environment that stunts creativity. A collaborative, expansive workplace starts with you, so adjust your attitude and behavior to reflect your openness to alternate viewpoints. Almost always, the best creative work is born from collaboration.

Ask yourself, is this office a better place when I'm in the room?

Get to Know Your Boss and Coworkers

You don't have to be a pest or try to become best friends, but it's important to have a relationship with your boss even if she's in charge of sixty employees. Keep her updated on the great creative work you're doing. You can employ this strategy however feels most natural. You can send a weekly email with updates on the work you've completed or the status of your projects. If you have pertinent and valuable information to share, you can schedule a meeting with her.

The same goes for other coworkers.

Networking doesn't stop when you land the job. Grab lunch or coffee with higher-ups or coworkers you admire. Find out how they arrived at the level they're at now. Ask what recommendations they have for you.

Being on good terms with your boss and coworkers ensures you'll have maximum support when the opportunity for a promotion comes your way.

If your supervisor has criticism for you or your work, don't get defensive (unless she has misinformation you need to correct). Instead, accept constructive feedback and apply it going forward.

Know Your Industry and Your Company

Creativity as a career means immersing yourself into the industry. It's not about creating in a vacuum. Do research on the Internet, read trade magazines, and stay up to date on the innovations and newsworthy items in your field so that you're informed enough to participate in work dialogue and offer intelligent input. Research your company and find out what other people have to say about it; sometimes, that's the easiest way to find out about your company's shortcomings.

When you consider your company's shortcomings, you're on your way to becoming a big-picture thinker who solves problems. It doesn't matter if you're an entry-level employee; when you're in the know about your industry and company you're able to be a more active contributor. You'll be in sync with your company's goals. You'll see beyond your job. You'll see what the competition is doing. Your natural inventiveness will be stimulated and new ideas will flow. Employers love employees who are always on their toes and thinking about creative solutions and approaches. Being informed guarantees you'll take a great interest in your work. You'll see your job as an adventure and yourself as an energetic participant.

Know What Makes You Different

Look around your office. What skill, talent, or expertise do you possess that can make you the go-to creative girl for certain projects? If you don't have a skill that makes you stand out, is there something missing from the talent pool at work that you could learn? Think of your office like a mini-market and find ways to stand out among your peers. Learning to think this way will serve you well if you choose to transition to life as a freelancer or business owner in a few years.

If you can bring something unique to the table, even among a slew of employees who all perform a similar job, your value to the company increases exponentially.

Know What Is Expected of You and Make Good on Your Promises

This is a big one. You need to ascertain your job responsibilities in order to perform them properly. Get clear on your duties by communicating with your boss and coworkers. Know what is expected of you both inside and outside the office. For example, are you expected to be reachable evenings and weekends for emails and phone calls?

Then, do what you say you will. Start by living up to what you promised in your interview. Meet your deadlines. Get to the office on time (or early). Don't act as though your work is beneath you, instead, become a team player who realizes there will be some non-scintillating grunt work mixed in with the creative stuff.

Think Like Your Clients, and Sell, Baby, Sell

If your job involves selling a creative product or service to a client, get excited about it. Selling is like a dance where you charm your partner with your knowledge and enthusiasm. Anticipate their questions or concerns before they arise so that you're prepared with a solution. If you're not naturally thrilled about the product—or can't help but think about the ways you could

Creative Girl as Corporate Hire

When I met Carrie Solomon, an art director and graphic designer at Bloomberg, she described being the artistic type at a corporate company like being a black sheep on a very fancy farm. Here, Carrie shares her thoughts on taking her creativity corporate.

Carrie: I received my MFA from the School of Visual Arts. The program was called "The Designer as Author and Entrepreneur." The program encouraged the designer to be the owner of an idea or product, and in charge of everything from conceptualizing to the marketing of that product.

CG: So what made you decide to work for a corporation instead of for yourself?

Carrie: Financially, freelancing was just too scary for me. And I don't have the self-discipline; I need someone to give me a deadline. So I chose a company that's very corporate but also values design and innovation. At Bloomberg, if you want to create a new product or implement a new idea, you're given the freedom to try it. That's pretty cool for a creative type, to be able to see one of your ideas through to creation and have the support of a company behind you.

CG: How is your life different than your freelance colleagues?

Carrie: At a company, you feel more secure about your next paycheck, but there are things you sacrifice for that security, too. You have to get used to being creative within set hours. You have to be able to push yourself and be creative when you don't feel like it. That's not an easy adjustment, and it can change something within you when you're forced to work within specific parameters. It takes a certain willingness to find your voice when you're working in-house and it's not all creative all the time. You have to carve out your niche and be able to deal with structure.

CG: Any tips for creative girls entering a corporate environment?

Carrie: **To thrive as a creative type in a corporate environment, it's key to find a connection to the company you're working for and feel ownership over your projects.**

With regard to working in a corporate environment, I think a real strong sense of self and a high level of confidence is crucial. Designers by nature have to contend with rejection, along with being questioned quite regularly. We are constantly being asked to defend our choices and points of view. For me, in an environment with so many alpha personalities, and in an industry that is often dominated by men, that confidence has to become even stronger, yet remain couched in intelligence and preparedness. I was recently advised by a very senior manager to not be afraid to ask questions, as this is also a sign that one is confident—not afraid to appear weak—and this allows that person (in this case, me) to learn more.

For me, working in a corporate environment, I always find myself questioning if I'm in it for the money, or if I am really learning something. It can sometimes be hard to separate happiness from a paycheck, but it's crucial to remain objective and be sure that creativity and learning are still a large part of the job. Otherwise, your creativity can become a victim of your fear of losing security, or routine, and that ultimately results in boredom and regret.

make it better—focus on what *is* strong about it. If you're really feeling uninspired, remind yourself that someone out there needs, wants, and will love that silly product, so work on connecting with *that* client.

Many creative types dislike the selling part of creativity. So use your time at a company to practice and become comfortable with your inner salesgirl. Learn to cultivate great interpersonal relationships with the clients for whom you work. These skills will help you greatly in a few years if you decide to sell your product or service in a freelance or small business structure.

Nip the Negativity

It's easy to complain about a boss, an unrealistic deadline, or whatever aspect of work you're not crazy about. But negativity breeds negativity, so don't get caught in the spiral. Instead, be proactive. Look for ways to solve the problem. Figure out how you can work around or improve the particulars of your work life.

Especially in this job climate, employers are looking for competent, confident em-
ployees who breed positivity in an office environment. Besides, you won't make any headway griping to a coworker. If the problem calls for action, then take it. If you're just complaining to complain, figure out why you're behaving that way. With what are you dissatisfied? Is it work, or another area of your life? Whenever a pattern of negativity arises, deal with it. Meditate, do yoga, or exercise. Talk to someone outside of work. Think of your emotions like clues. Don't ignore them. Figure out what they're all about.

Time Management

Great time management comes with learning to prioritize. At a creative job, you'll find that some assignments will be more creatively stimulating than others. Instead of jumping at the ones you're inspired to do (while shoving aside the anxiety-producing tasks for later), make a list of the three most important tasks you'd like to complete that day, or that workweek (depending on the size of your tasks). Give each one your full attention while you're working on it. Don't stress about other projects or incessantly check email while you're working on your present task.

If you're having trouble knowing which tasks to prioritize, ask a boss or trusted coworker.

Get Great at All Kinds of New Things

Jump at the chance to take on work that stretches you, cultivates new skills, and makes you more valuable. Learning a new specialty or taking on a project outside of your comfort zone beefs up your résumé. What you can learn in an office (while being paid to do so) is invaluable; think outside the box about the myriad of new skills, clients, and projects you can acquire, so that if you do move on to another company or go the freelance or small business route, you'll be all the more prepared.

Dany Levy is the founder and creator of DailyCandy. Dany told me, "Working for a company is one of the most important things you can do before starting your own

business. You'll learn about office politics, structure, and different work personalities: what works and what doesn't. I don't think DailyCandy would have succeeded if I hadn't had the company experience. I had to do the grunt work and learn."

You met Eva Chen, *Teen Vogue's* Beauty and Health Director, in Chapter 3. Eva says, "Seek out opportunities. Don't ever say, 'That's not my job.' Make *everything* your job."

Jen Ford, the Fashion News Director at *Lucky*, agrees. Jen says, "It doesn't matter that there's a 'director' in my job title. I still have to keep learning and growing professionally. Wherever you are on your career path, make yourself as valuable to your company as possible. Have your unique specialty, *and* become as skilled in as many areas as you can."

While on someone else's dime, stretch yourself and learn everything imaginable from your place of work. Profit and loss statements may bore the hell out of you, but they'll be necessary if you decide to open your own company in a few years. The pitch meetings you go to now for your company's plastic sports figurines will teach you skills for future pitch meetings for your own creative product.

Every time you speak in a group setting

you have an opportunity. A small project can turn into a great way to gain visibility if you do it in an innovative way that gets people's attention. Become a master at delivery and creative presentation. Check out *Presentation Zen: Simple Ideas on Presentation Design and Delivery* by Garr Reynolds.

If you're looking to become a more confident public speaker, check out toastmasters.org.

Ask for a Review

Some companies schedule these on a regular basis, every six months or every year. If reviews are more sporadic (or nonexistent) it's up to you to make sure you get the feedback you need to perform well. A review is the most straightforward way to find out how you're doing: how your company perceives you and how you can improve. Refer back to the negotiating section when the time comes to ask for a raise.

Be Fair, Honest, and Ethical

Your personal integrity is everything. Enough said.

Following the above advice helps make you a top-notch employee and puts you on the receiving end of more exciting projects with greater creative control. But I think you'll find that really diving into your work and being the best at what you do is its own reward.

If you decide to work for a company, I'd like to propose a way for you to think about your employment. In the same way that a freelancer would, think of this company as a client you work for; you will only continue to work for this client as long as both of your needs are being met, and as long as the relationship is symbiotic and beneficial. Be an active, motivated participant in your career, the same way you would be as a freelancer who pounds the pavement to get clients, or a hungry small business owner who continually innovates to stay relevant. Do not get too comfortable doing the same tasks over and over. Push yourself, and look for opportunities to take on new projects and build your creative skill set to keep you as marketable as possible for the future.

Graphic designer Carrie Solomon says, "I maintain a constant focus on what I want to be in the future. It changes, but if I have that focus and I can use what I have in my current work environment to get there, then I know I'm still on the right track. I continually reevaluate what I want in my career and make sure I'm in the right place now to get where I want to go in the future."

CHAPTER 11

Self-Employed Wonder Girl

*Do you have what it takes
to work for yourself?*

"This new epidemic of self-employment is being driven by an increasing awareness that we can all create our own big break . . . Thoughtful people are seeking fresh options—options that honor their creativity, add meaning and purpose to their lives, and allow them to go as far as their imaginations will permit."

—*Barbara J. Winter,*
Making a Living Without a Job: Winning Ways for Creating Work That You Love

The Self-Employed CG

So you want to work for yourself. You've got an idea, talent, or skill that you want to parlay into a business. Whether you want to open an art gallery or freelance as a makeup artist, for many creative types, there's nothing sweeter than being your own head honchette. When you work for yourself, you go to bed each night with the satisfaction of an entire day spent working to achieve your own ambitions.

There's overlap in the small business owner and freelancer categories (both are business-owning entrepreneurs), and the following guidance is pertinent to both forms of self-employment. In the reference section, you'll find ideas for further reading on both subjects.

A freelancer is defined as any self-employed person who takes on various projects and isn't committed to a single employer. Many freelancers consider themselves small business owners; the product they're selling is the creative service they offer. Not all business owners set up a storefront or place of business; many do business on the road or at their kitchen table. Creative work is particularly conducive to the freelance and small business structure, and your creativity can be translated into self-employment in a variety of forms. With gumption, a savvy plan for a knockout idea and an unfailing work ethic, you're well on your way to opening a successful creative venture.

The Good News First

Opening your own business is your chance to turn creativity, inventiveness and inspiration into a profitable livelihood. The work is challenging, exhilarating, and endlessly rewarding. Sometimes, the amount of new tasks and responsibilities is overwhelming, but when you work for yourself, you can guarantee you'll never feel stagnated or bored out of your tree. Simply put, it's nothing short of amazing not to have to answer to anyone else. You won't have to grovel for a raise or a promotion; in fact, you'll actually promote yourself by upping your rates, which we'll talk about in Chapter 16. Just imagine the dinner parties you can throw for yourself each time you self-promote or reward yourself with Employee of the Month.

Whether you freelance or run a business, you're still working for other people in some regard. I have jewelry clients who order custom pieces that need to be done in specific ways by specific dates. When I do television gigs, I can't go on-air and swear or stick my tongue out or I'll never be hired again. Still, you're in charge of what projects and clients to take, what work that entails, and a zillion other little decisions you wouldn't have had

control over if you were working for a boss. You get to create your ideal, impeccably feng shuied working environment. Everything you've ever dreamed "work" could look like can now be your reality.

When you're the boss, your schedule is in your control. Certainly, you'll be working long hours when starting your business or freelance career, especially in the first few years and maybe always. But when you work for yourself, you can often fit your work hours into your life. If you like to sleep in until ten o'clock, your boutique may open for business from noon until eight. If you want to pick up your children from school and be there to help them with their homework, you might work from seven o'clock until three, and fit in an extra hour or two after they go to sleep. It's easier to schedule work around doctor's appointments, childcare, and other priorities, instead of the other way around.

And Now for the Bad News

Now that you've heard the good stuff, there are, ahem, some not so great things about being your own boss. When you work for a company, it's not your money on the line. Sure, if you mess up, you could be fired.

But the amount of time, thought, money, and creativity invested in your own business is an entirely different ball game. And it can be scary.

As a creative business owner, you're almost always thinking about money; in fact, you're almost always thinking about everything having to do with your business. This takes some getting used to. Stacia Valle, the boutique owner we met in Chapter 4, says, "For me, having a store is like an umbilical cord. Even when it's technically my day off, I have to be available for any problems that arise and ready to drop whatever I'm doing. And even in the best financial times, I think about my business's finances morning, noon, and night."

Some CGs are great at turning off their work radar as soon as they close their store, turn off their computer, or shut the door of their home office. But for the most part, when you own your own business, its welfare is always at the front of your mind. On the first day of a weeklong meditation retreat in Vail, I waited until everyone's eyes were closed and they were chanting "Om" before checking my Blackberry. When we vacationed in Belize, my husband shook his head in disbelief when I brought my laptop to an ocean-side hammock to field emails from Target over a mix-up in

jewelry product photos. His mouth dropped when I asked the front desk to print out eighty pages of edits so I could work on some fiction I'd brought along. I slunk back to our hotel room with my eighty pages, apologized, and we negotiated a three-hours-of-work-allowed-per-day rule that coincided with the three-hour nap he took each afternoon.

Most of the small business owners I interviewed engage in the exact same working behavior. Surely, we have to work toward balance (I forced myself to leave my Black-Berry in the hotel room for the duration of the meditation retreat). But be aware that this kind of all-consuming obsessing can be a drawback of self-employment.

Get Ready to Be Your Own Boss

There is a perfect storm of elements for starting your own business or striking out on your own as a freelancer. Here's a checklist to get you in shape for self-employed-creative-girl status. Check those that presently apply to you. Keep this list handy (rip it out and post it on your bathroom mirror if you like) and actively work toward the items you're not able to check off yet. It's okay if you're missing a few, but if you're missing more than five or six, you may want to reconsider your timing. When you've checked off nearly all of them, you're well on your way to establishing a creative empire.

The SHE.E.O Checklist

☐ **You trust your intuition and your ability to make tough decisions.** It's your business and your livelihood. Are you ready to tame your inner-waffler? Are you ready to step into your role as a woman in charge of her own enterprise?

☐ **You've saved enough money to weather the sporadic pay that accompanies working for yourself during the first few years (and sometimes, longer).** Experts recommend having enough money saved to cover your expenses for at least one full year. You'll need these savings, outside financing, or plenty of paying jobs already lined up before striking out on your own.

We'll discuss financing options in Chapter 13. And even if you don't have the money saved or jobs lined up, you can still start your business or freelance career on the side. You could keep working part-time or try any of the other flex options we discussed in Chapter 6 to help you transition. At the very least, there are evenings and weekends. Use your free time to start planning and collecting clients.

Check your credit rating and see where you stand. You're entitled to a free annual credit report at www.annualcreditreport.com. Credit scores are available for an additional fee.

Your credit rating must be in tip-top shape and remain that way. Take the time now to whittle down credit cards. It's easier said than done, so find yourself a financial planner who can strategize with you and keep him or her around when your business is up and running. Ask other small business owners for recommendations, or search "financial planners" at www.fpanet.org. There may be free financial planning services available at your bank. Check out the nonprofit

Money Management International—www.moneymanagement.org—where you can increase your financial knowledge and consolidate your debt.

☐ **You'll be able to handle the emotional ups and downs of sporadic work.** You won't be popping anti-anxiety meds or having a nervous breakdown at the first sign of financial trouble. Instead, you'll troubleshoot and formulate a plan of action. You'll be prepared for both good and bad months. Know that there will be slow months. If you're prepared, you can use these periods to do clerical work for your business, get up-to-date on new software, take a course, get certified in a new service, or use the time wisely in whatever way you see fit.

☐ **Financially speaking, you're ready to trim the fat.** If need be, you're willing to curb your spending to balance out the bad months. You're ready and willing to sacrifice expenditures like vacations, a new spring wardrobe, or a fancy car (because you want this career more).

When you open your business, give some thought to where you want to spend your dollars. The end may have come for splurging on new shoes that are *to die for* but cost a frighteningly high fraction of your rent. Trust me, your creative career looks better on you than four-inch stilettos any day. The plan is for you to get to a rock star financial place. But initially, you'd better be willing to sacrifice financially. If you're not willing—or can't imagine sacrificing without becoming resentful—it may be best to stay at a creative job with a steady paycheck. For those of you ready to forgo a few material niceties in order to get your creative career going, it will certainly be well worth it in the end. Really, would you rather be decked in an expensive outfit and bored as heck in your cubicle, or rocking flip-flops from the dollar store while penning a screenplay?

Good, that's what I thought. So trim the fat, creative girl, trim the fat.

☐ **You're gaining visibility as an expert in your field.** Your experience and know-how are top notch and you're well regarded as a creative talent. If you're not yet well-known in your industry, actively work toward upping your visibility by networking and putting in the time and energy to develop your reputation.

☐ **You've done the research on your market.** You must go into your venture knowing your market inside and out. Doing market research guides you from tweaking your original idea to understanding your customer base and knowing how to reach them. Later, we'll discuss how to research and position yourself in the market, so don't fret; you'll be ready to check this box after completing those exercises.

☐ **In general, you understand what it takes to open your own business and understand the individual business model that will best serve you.** If you're not there yet, this is something you can educate yourself on through classes and books. We'll go further into detail in the next few chapters.

☐ **If your business will require employees, you're a natural leader or have learned to be one.** You're able to delegate without micromanaging. You enjoy mentoring employees and believe you can create a healthy, fair working environment that mirrors your values and encourages those who work for you to do their best.

☐ **If you'll be working daily with clients and customers, you're a people person.** Owning a business that provides a service requires serious people skills. There's no way around it. You'll deal with all kinds of situations. What happens the first time a customer sends back the paella dish for which your restaurant is famous? Or when you have to negotiate a rate for the extra services a client assumed were included in your initial rate quote? What about the first time a customer wants a refund for an item of clothing and your boutique has an exchange-only policy? Are you able to communicate what you want and need? Do you know when to say no? Do you have patience with people?

☐ **You're comfortable selling yourself.** Check this box if you're ready to promote yourself and your business. This means everything from opening your mouth and telling anyone who will listen what you do for a living, to cold-calling potential clients and introducing yourself. Eventually, you may have a PR person or an agent who does this for you, but in the meantime, you have to be willing to put yourself out there.

Before opening her own business, Zonobia Washington worked as a freelance fashion stylist for magazines like *Vogue, Essence, O,* and *Elle Accessories.* She says, "You have to be okay selling yourself to the people you meet. I had to be comfortable enough to say to new people, 'Would you like to see my styling book?'"

☐ **You're able to put on a business hat.** Most of us wish we could spend all day doing right-brained activities like painting, writing, acting, and designing. But if you want to work for yourself, you have to understand how a business works and wrap your head around things like sales tax and Excel spreadsheets. Creative girls have varying degrees of business savvy, but

Abigail Lorick

Abigail Lorick is the designer behind the clothing line Lorick (and Lorick is the ghost-designer behind fictional designer Eleanor Waldorf on *Gossip Girl*—everything you see in Eleanor's shop or trotting down the runway is designed by Abigail). Abigail says, "It's unbelievable just how much business goes into designing my fashion line. I have to understand everything from accounting and forming an LLC to converting sales estimates into production orders and making sure that production ships on time from India. Just remember that in the beginning, while you're working crazy hours, you still have to remember to take time to nurture the creative being that you are. For me, that's meditation. You have to find what's right for you so that you stay balanced while your mind is swimming with business matters."

it's inexcusable to think you can work for yourself and not learn the business side of your creativity. It's naïve to think, "I just want to create. I'm not really a business person." Certainly, you can hire people to do some of the business aspects of your career. My agents negotiate my contracts and help me with all sorts of business matters. I have an accountant who does my taxes. But I have to understand the elements that create the bottom line. Unless you want to hire a stage mom, keep your business wits about you. Polish your organizational skills to keep great records. Think strategically and embrace your new role.

☐ **You're confident in your abilities.** From the moment you quote a rate to a new client to your interview on *The Today Show*, confidence in your abilities is crucial. If you don't think your new cookbook, architecture business, or bridal salon is amazing, why would anyone else?

Plus, the more confident you are, the more you'll rouse confidence in your employees and other women wanting to work for themselves.

☐ **You're fearless about trying new things and thrive on variety, not routine.** I doubt variety will be a problem, since most creative types are stimulated by new people, scenarios, and opportunities. When you work as a business owner or freelancer, you'll get to experience a smorgasbord of new clients and creative projects. One day you're rifling through patterns in a fabric store and

---

❊ CREATIVE TIP ❊

Business Education for the Price of a Paperback

If you're serious about opening your own business or are already running one, check out *The Business Side of Creativity* by Cameron S. Foote, and *The Small Business Start-Up Kit* by Peri H. Pakroo.

the next day you're doing an interview for a local radio station or negotiating a contract with a new vendor. Do you thrive on learning new things or do you get overwhelmed and shrink back in the face of scary new challenges?

If you're a shrinker, you can still check this box if you're ready to face your fears. Make Chapter 7's Fear Chart your friend and banish fear-based thinking once and for all.

☐ **You're willing to take responsibility for the good, the bad, and the ugly.** Being your own boss means there's no one to pass the buck to. You're responsible for everything. If an employee of yours messes up, you're the one who has to sweep up the mess. And if you're the one who's been wronged—say, a vendor is late with a payment—are you willing to call the vendor and confront the problem?

☐ **You're willing to seek guidance.** Don't be shy about asking for guidance from other business owners; most are happy to answer questions and share their experiences and opinions. If you have the extra cash, you could bring in another business owner as a consultant. You can pay a one-time consulting fee or pay them by the hour to help with your business plan, or to oversee the business in the first month of operations. A board of advisors is another great option to consider.

☐ **You're tireless and beyond motivated.** You're able to accomplish work without deadlines or a boss breathing down your neck. You're able to structure your workday and self-impose deadlines and work efficiently.

You're willing to work long hours and twenty days straight if that's what your new business requires. When CG-in-action Rhonda Kave opened her chocolate shop, Roni-Sue's Chocolates, she worked seven days a week during her first year in business. Of course, she took a few mini-vacations to clear her head, but her norm was Monday through Sunday.

☐ **If your business requires you to work from home, you're sure that you're cut out for the lifestyle.** Read the following section to find out whether or not you're ready to check this box.

Working from Home: Can You Handle It?

Before we go further in the *You As Your Own Boss* category, let's find out if you're cut out for the work-at-home lifestyle. It's a big change from office life.

Depending on what type of freelance work you take on or business you open, you may be out in the field in a variety of locations. Many jobs involve creating in a collaborative work environment like a movie set, an architectural office, or behind the register at your own business, interacting with your employees and customers alike.

But many freelancers and small business owners run the show from their living rooms. Writing this book has taken place in complete and utter solitude (unless you count my Bernese Mountain Dog, Greta).

Working from home in a messy ponytail and fuzzy socks is a swell life, but it's also a little lonely. Some personality types are just plain better at it than others. If you're going to be working from home, there are two main things to consider. The first is your loneliness factor. Are you okay being alone . . . with yourself . . . and your thoughts? Are you able to spend long stretches of time by yourself without human interaction? If you're working in solitude, from home or in your own studio, it can be easy to get the blues. As free as creative types like to be, the majority benefit from a schedule and at least some human interaction. Working from home means there's no more office politics, but there's also no office chatter, and you may start missing that sweaty bald guy from accounting who regaled you with bad jokes every time you went to the watercooler.

The second question to ask yourself is if you'll be able to motivate and schedule yourself without a boss looking over your shoulder or anyone supervising your workday. Working from home offers a ton of perks. You can work in sweatpants (I'm in them right now) and enjoy incredible flexibility with your schedule. You can wear Crest White Strips whenever you feel like it, and take a fifteen-minute break to dance around your living room. But at the end of the day, you still have to get your work done. You have to be able to schedule yourself and set limits and agendas.

Zonobia Washington, the stylist we talked to earlier in this chapter, and her partner, Ruthie Schulder, co-own Little Bird, a teen wardrobe styling company. Zonobia thrives on being in charge of her schedule. She says, "I know exactly what I need to get done and I want to go at my own pace, which is very fast. I like being able to forge ahead and not have to wait to get something approved by a boss." Her partner, Ruthie, sometimes misses having a boss to delegate tasks. Ruthie says, "I love having my own business, but when three o'clock rolls around, sometimes I wish there was someone else telling me what to do next."

It boils down to personal preference. And of course, there will be some days that you just aren't feeling it. But you'd better be able to get yourself back on track without someone checking on you. Before you jump headfirst into a work from home situation, consider your loneliness factor and your ability to motivate and structure yourself. If you're worried these factors might be a problem, but still plan to work from home, there are solutions like shared studio space and weekly volunteer work. We'll talk about how to combat loneliness and procrastination in the final chapter.

If The She.E.O. Checklist Is Giving You Hives...

If you're just not sure that you're ready to open your own business, a good option is to

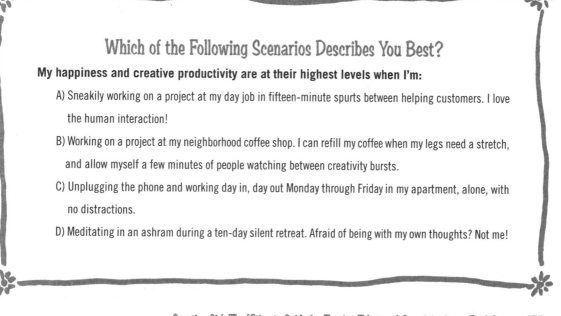

Which of the Following Scenarios Describes You Best?

My happiness and creative productivity are at their highest levels when I'm:

A) Sneakily working on a project at my day job in fifteen-minute spurts between helping customers. I love the human interaction!

B) Working on a project at my neighborhood coffee shop. I can refill my coffee when my legs need a stretch, and allow myself a few minutes of people watching between creativity bursts.

C) Unplugging the phone and working day in, day out Monday through Friday in my apartment, alone, with no distractions.

D) Meditating in an ashram during a ten-day silent retreat. Afraid of being with my own thoughts? Not me!

The Plunge into Full-time Self-Employment

Becki Singer is a freelance writer and marketing consultant. She specializes in public relations and business development for creative companies. Below, she shares her story of how she knew it was time to take the plunge into full-time self-employed creative status.

Becki: In terms of making the leap and committing to full-time freelance, I'm not sure you ever "know." It's very much a leap off a bridge, and a terrifying one at that. But it's one you have to take if you're serious about being independent. I think it's incredibly rare to be able to build up enough freelance work to feel solid about going full-time until you're able to actually stop working your day job and solidly commit to finding clients of your own, marketing yourself, and making a real go of being a freelance/independent professional. You need some kind of force pushing you to step outside your boundaries and comfort zones to market yourself and build a client base that will sustain you. At least for most people, that safety net your paycheck provides will keep you from doing those crazy things you might otherwise do to get clients . . . and those are usually the tricks that turn out to be genius. Now that I'm a full-time freelancer, I don't let a single opportunity go by. If I'm shopping in a boutique, I guarantee I won't leave without at least mentioning what I do, and odds are, I'll leave a business card. Sure, that takes some guts, and it was absolutely terrifying at first—I am not a saleswoman at heart.

CG: What does it take to be a full-time freelancer?

Becki: At first, it takes guts. Leaving a sure thing with your paid job, committing to relying totally on your expertise and abilities in order to pay your rent, being convinced you can develop and maintain a client base . . . these are definitely gutsy things to undertake. Just know that eventually, your comfort zone will expand, and you won't believe you were ever scared of dropping a business card to a total stranger.

CG: What lessons have you learned as a freelancer?

Becki: Especially in the beginning, I think one of the hardest lessons I've learned is that being self-employed doesn't mean you only do the work you want to do. I've learned that offering a wider scope of service is what keeps my business moving, and keeps me being able to do the parts of the job that I really love.

work six months at a business similar to the one you want to open. Just don't be the creepy creative girl who works at a high-tech gadget boutique and then opens up a similar shop down the block six months later. No one likes that girl.

Let the owner know that you're interested in starting a similar business, and that you'd love to work for a certain amount of time before opening your business one town over (or across the river in a land far, far away) from her business. Make it clear that you'll respect her territory and proprietary information. Most business owners will be happy to have an enthusiastic helping hand. Just be sure you're on the same page about the time you'd like to commit and your ultimate career motive.

If you choose to work for another small business before opening your own, you'll learn the ropes, and you'll learn what works (and what doesn't), all while bringing home a paycheck.

If the reasons behind your hives are a deep aversion to organization and left-brain thinking, you could seek out a business partner who can handle those aspects of the venture. You can also take a class to hone your skills or check out mentoring organizations like www.score.org, a free counseling service for small businesses.

If the reasons behind your anxiety are financial, remember that one of the best parts about being an entrepreneur is that you can start out by doing it on the side, while still collecting a regular paycheck from your employer. Many CGs choose to work this way, or they negotiate a part-time schedule so that they can have a steady paycheck even after they could technically afford to go out on their own. If you've realized loneliness is a factor for you, part-time office girl and part-time freelance girl makes for a more balanced life.

Moonlighting as a freelancer or business owner is an invaluable way to do market research and build a client list. It's the best way to get going on your creative business while still enjoying the perks of a part-time or full-time job. When there are too many clients for you to handle while working at your day job or you're feeling financially ready and able, you'll know it's time to go out on your own. In the meantime, you'll gain expertise and insight into the inner-workings of your new industry. You'll grow and nurture your business at your own pace until you're ready to take it full-time.

CHAPTER 12

Birth the Creative Baby

*Get started as a freelancer
or entrepreneur.*

You've got the qualifications and you're ready to work for yourself. Prepare for the ride of your life. There's nothing like starting your own business or striking out on your own as a freelancer. There's not a single thing I've done yet that has taught me more about myself, my values, and my abilities.

First things first: clear your schedule. Especially if you're still working a day job and planning to start your business on the side, it's time to pare your responsibilities to a minimum. Any responsibilities you can delegate or get rid of, do. You'll need as much mental energy as possible. Don't volunteer to make eighty kibble cupcakes for your dog's daycare. Don't take on the job of throwing a bridal shower for your friend Debbie Sue and her forty closest friends. As your business takes off, you'll likely enjoy a more flexible schedule somewhere down the road. At that point, you'll be the go-to girl for those cupcakes. But for now, clear your plate so you have the time and energy to put toward starting your business.

In this chapter, we'll explore the warm and fuzzy fundamentals: your vision and intentions, your business strengths and weaknesses, your big idea, what you're selling, and why you're selling it. In the following chapters, we'll get into the nitty-gritty of a business plan and the daily ins and outs of running a freelance or small business.

Your Vision and Intentions

For CGs, our businesses are an extension of ourselves and reflect who we are as creators. So what's your vision? What are your intentions for your new life as a business owner? What are your reasons for starting your business or freelance career? Is it about making more money? Is it for more freedom? Is it to experience creative fulfillment in your everyday work? Don't second-guess your vision if it's different from other business owners. It's okay to want something out of the ordinary, or to prioritize values in your own unique way. You can start with these questions.

What are your reasons for wanting to start your business?

What is your vision for your business?

What do you intend to create in your new life as a business owner?

_____
_____
_____
_____
_____
_____
_____
_____
_____
_____
_____
_____

What does your business bring you and/or your community?_____

_____
_____
_____
_____
_____
_____
_____
_____
_____
_____
_____
_____
_____
_____

The Vision and Intentions of Nest

Rebecca Kousky is the owner of the nonprofit Nest (www.buildanest.com). Below she shares how her values came together to form her business.

"Three years ago, at age 24, and just out of graduate school in St. Louis (where I received my masters in social work from Washington University) I started a nonprofit called Nest. It came to being at a wine bar in my neighborhood. I was sipping a glass of red and thinking about what I wanted to do with my life. I was fresh out of school and unsure of my next move. I was tired of job searching and feeling discouraged about not finding something that felt right. I decided to start by making a list of all the things I loved. When I looked at the list, though, it was full of contradictions: a passion for social work and a love of design, a yearning to effect social change and desire to own my own business. There was an undeniable compulsion to travel, but also a love of the comforts of home.

"I stared at the strange list and wondered how I could find a way to bring together these passions. How could I combine my urge to nest with my urge to explore? How could my call to social work mix with my love of art and design? After many talks with my parents, I figured out a way to make it work.

"Nest is an unusual combination of shopping, social change, and celebrating artistic traditions. We give interest-free microfinance loans to women artists in developing countries to begin or maintain art or craft-based businesses. But we also give them mentoring, support, education about business and finance, and, most important, an online venue to sell the traditional crafts they create.

"Nest provided a new way to solve global poverty by fully supporting women, their craft, and their communities, while also allowing me to bring together a passion for design, social work, and entrepreneurship. It was also a conscious choice to focus on art-based businesses. Women have been artists through the centuries. Whether they're creating utilitarian household objects, clothes for the family, or decorative objects for themselves, the female artistic tradition is a way of defining and maintaining the community. By providing entrepreneurial loans to craftswomen and artisans, their life can become their livelihood."

Know Your Strengths, Know Your Kryptonite

Being your own boss means having a handle on what you're capable of and what you're not. Are you a Type A bookkeeper who gets excited by Excel spreadsheets? Or will you be shoving receipts into dark crevices of your apartment and frantically trying to round them up come tax time? Maybe you're excellent at networking. You love talking to new people, you have no qualms handing out business cards, and while charming a prospective client you've been compared to Lucille Ball. Or maybe you're a total wallflower who balks at the idea of selling yourself.

There are some weaknesses you have to work on improving, and others you can manage by farming out to professionals (like an accountant, bookkeeper, or website designer). You just have to know which ones are which. Usually, the social ones—like networking, public relations, and the ability to sell—are qualities you'd be wise to work on improving. Of course, with the right amount of money, you can hire anyone to do anything. You can always hire a PR person, but PR comes with a hefty price tag—usually, several thousand per month—and you may need to do it yourself for the first few years. It's okay to delegate—especially because it gives you more time to focus on the creative side of the business—but the more aspects of your business you have a handle on, the better.

For now, list the strengths that will make you an excellent business owner, followed by your weaknesses. For the weaknesses, put a check next to the ones you can dole out to either a business partner or a professional. Put a star next to the weaknesses you plan to actively work to improve.

Earlier, we discussed the value of your transferable skills for any career transition. Recall those skills here, too. Draw from all your life experience; these aren't strengths and weaknesses you've only displayed in a job environment. If you have a natural flair for organizing fundraisers from your days as a sorority girl, that strength may prove vital to your success as a small business owner. Continue to look back at this list to be sure you're working on your starred weaknesses and capitalizing on your strengths. Once you enter the planning stages of opening your business, you can look for professionals to pick up the slack.

If you're stuck, consider qualities like leadership, analytical thinking, forward visionary thinking, and innovation. Think about skills like marketing, financial planning, communication, conflict resolution, problem solving, bookkeeping, organization, and sales.

Business Strengths:

From this list of strengths, go further to define your **Core Competencies.** BNet Business Dictionary (dictionary.bnet.com) defines a core competency as "a key ability or strength that an organization has acquired that differentiates it from others, gives it competitive advantage, and contributes to its long-term success." Meaning, what will your business do better than the competition? This might come straight from your **Business Strengths** above, or it might be a strength that occurs to you when you compare your abilities to others in the same field. You're at a great advantage when your core competencies are unique and not easily imitated by competitors.

Core Competencies: _____

_____

_____

_____

_____

_____

_____

_____

_____

_____

_____

You're not going to be perfect at everything. List the areas you need to improve.

Business Weaknesses: _____

_____

_____

_____

_____

_____

_____

_____

_____

_____

_____

_____

_____

_____

_____

If you're concerned about your weaknesses or lack of expertise in key areas, you can attend low-cost business classes through score.org or continuing education programs in your area. Sharpen your business knowledge by studying online resources like www.womanowned.com and www.entrepreneur.com.

You can also consider teaming up with a business partner.

Business Partner 101

Deciding whether or not to partner up is one of the biggest decisions you'll make. Sometimes, financial reasons may point to a partner as the best option. Often, partners arise when a CG has a fantastic talent or idea, but lacks certain skills on the practical side. Maybe you're

Whittemore House

CG-in-action Victoria Hunter opened the salon Whittemore House with her business partner, Larry Raspanti. She says, "Larry and I are both creative types, so there are business aspects we farm out to an accountant and a lawyer. Creative and social aspects, like PR and customer relations, are my strengths, whereas my eyes start to glaze during a meeting with our accountant. Still, I have to know every single thing about my business and how it operates. Just because you have an accountant doesn't mean you can fool yourself into thinking someone else can manage your financials. That's how you lose a business. Excelling at both the creative and the business side is a challenge. If it wasn't, everyone would own their own business. You have to find your inner business woman. If it's not natural, it can be learned—as long as you're willing to put in the time and effort."

✻ CREATIVE TIP ✻

Sample Documents

To see examples of partnership agreements (or any other documents you have questions about) visit www.docstoc.com to check out samples and templates.

a tremendous chef who needs a business partner to run the restaurant so you can focus on the culinary aspects. Same goes for an introverted shoe designer who partners with a public relations maven to launch an indie line of vegan footwear.

A partner shares the workload (and, of course, the profits). Many CGs prefer a joint venture; it comforts them to bounce ideas off a trusted partner and share the risk and reward. It can be a built-in support system to have someone to commiserate with when times are tough and to toast champagne with while celebrating a new client or piece of press. It can also mean added stress from personal and creative disagreements. Choose wisely.

You may already have a lucky creative girl (or creative boy) in mind to share the hard work and profits of your joint venture. But you absolutely, positively must sign a partnership agreement. I don't care if she's your blood relation or your best friend since summer camp. Your life and your vision may change in five years; there needs to be an agreement on paper to help you proceed if your partnership needs to dissolve.

A partnership agreement is a legal document that delineates how the work, rewards, and liabilities of a partnership will be divvied among the partners. It details what happens in the event that one of you wants to leave the business, or can no longer work due to an injury, postpartum depression, or any other event that might be hard to foresee now, but would leave you devastated (financially and emotionally) if you haven't properly planned. Have the agreement reviewed by a lawyer and signed by both of you in the presence of a notary public. File the agreement with the county clerk to be sure a copy is always accessible.

Ask Yourself The Important Questions

The remainder of this chapter is the *who what where why* and *how* of your new business (we'll deal with the *when* in the following chapter). Get your pencils ready.

What's the Big Idea?

Just like in your high school English class, you should be able to summarize your main business idea in one sentence. Be succinct so that when you go to gather feedback, you have a concise and to-the-point summary of your business.

Example:

> *A hair salon in a business-heavy district that provides affordable cuts quickly; customers can come in on their lunch break and leave 30 minutes later with a fresh cut.*

In one sentence (you can use a semi-colon, too, if it helps you fit in more details) lay out the idea and how it will serve its target market.

Your Business Idea: _____

_____

_____

_____

_____

_____

_____

Get to the Point

Being able to provide a concise explanation of what you do applies to all sorts of creative ideas. When an editor asks me what my novel is about, I have to have a precise explanation ready—something longer than, "It's a paranormal romance," and something shorter than "Well, there's this girl. And she lives in New York City and she has dark hair and she meets this guy. . . ."

Be able to summarize both your business and your current projects in a lucid, concise way that imparts necessary information and keeps your audience intrigued.

Now that you've got your business idea narrowed down, how confident are you that your idea or creative service has a place in today's market? Run your business idea by everyone you know and anyone who will listen, including your mom, other business owners, creative thinkers, and your target audience (say, teens, dog-lovers, or teenage dog-lovers). While you ask for feedback and ideas, keep your mind wide open. You can't go into this thinking, "I know my idea is great, so it hardly matters what so and so says because they don't know the product as well as I do." Certainly you won't let a cranky naysayer stop you from starting your business with broad comments like, "That's too much of a risk," when it's a risk you're willing to take. Filter the feedback you receive and embrace constructive criticism. Reexamine your business plans with that constructive feedback in mind.

Why?

Why does this idea warrant a business? Answer this question by stating what problem your business solves. What need does your product or service fulfill?

_____

_____

_____

_____

_____

_____

_____

_____

_____

_____

_____

_____

_____

_____

_____

_____

What are you selling?

If you're selling a product, say, antiques, you might be thinking, "Duh. Antiques." But there's always more to what you're selling than just the actual product or service. Are you a hole-in-the-wall antique store with great finds for under twenty dollars? Or are you selling luxury and exclusivity along with the antiques—items with a documented history that sell for thousands?

There's an experience and a vibe you sell along with your product or service. You may sell handmade baby quilts that incorporate heirloom fabrics from your client's family (a swatch of a wedding dress worn by a beloved grandmother in 1949). Here, you're selling nostalgia, history, and personalized craftsmanship along with the quilt. If you're launching a freelance wedding photography business, you're selling photos, but also the experience of a couple on one of their biggest days. Will your company sell photography for hip, artsy brides and grooms who prefer a photojournalistic look to traditional footage? Think about how you're different from other photographers. If you open up a showroom for clothing designers, are you selling an intimate, hands-on experience meant to grow small designers? Or are you hoping to compete with the elite showrooms in New York City and Paris to attract big name design talent? Does your dog-grooming salon trim Fifi the poodle on Fifth Avenue or hose down mutts on cement floors? You get the idea.

In the next chapter, we'll go into further detail about your product line and the services your business will offer. For now, journal below on the experience, product, or service your business sells. _____

_____

_____

_____

_____

_____

_____

_____

_____

_____

_____

_____

_____

_____

_____

_____

_____

_____

_____

Who are You as a Business Owner?

Are you the next Kimora Lee Simmons or a stay-at-home mom who runs the show at her kitchen table? Whether you fantasize about being a mogul or dream of a cozy existence behind the cash register at your own bookstore with your golden retriever snuggled at your feet, use the space below to describe your desired business persona.

Attention, Carrie Bradshaw: if you're feeling stuck, brainstorm characters in movies or television shows that embody your ideal. _____

_____

_____

_____

_____

_____

_____

_____

_____

A Hole in the Market

When hand model Ellen Sirot closely examined the hand care market, she found a real shortage of performance-driven, anti-aging hand care treatments. Ellen says, "I surveyed more than 100 women over thirty and found the majority of them believed their hands were aging faster than any other part of their body."

Ellen saw a hole in the market and created Hand Perfection, a comprehensive range of treatment products for hands with clinically-proven results which has become a runaway success.

Petite or Plus-Sized

How big do you want your company to be? How many clients or vendors will you ideally serve? Will you serve your neighborhood, your city, or is the entire world your oyster? Will you have employees or are you a one-woman show? If you're not thinking about a massive empire, take heart that the solopreneur trend has gained huge momentum over the past decade. Petite businesses offer flexibility, strong customer relationships, and targeted specialties, a must in today's marketplace. And you can always grow once you're sure of the viability of your business.

What size do you want to be? Are you going solo or hoping to create an empire? _____

Your Customer:
Who's Buying What You're Selling?

Who calls you in a pinch for your services or shows up at your shop once a month? Is she a teenaged hoodie-sweatshirt-wearing skateboarder looking for a limited edition comic book you stock? A twentysomething fashionista decked in skinny jeans and a fedora who raids your vintage store for bargain prices? Or a thirtysomething organic-soy-milk-drinking academic who wants her manuscript edited?

Knowing your customer informs everything from how you decorate your place of business to how you advertise. When profiling your target audience, think about demographics (social and economic factors like gender, marital status, and household income), geographics (where your customer lives) and psychographics (consumer characteristics like attitudes and political beliefs). If you have vastly different types of customers, use the ideas below to create several customer profiles. After opening your business, continue to create profiles as your market expands or narrows.

Gender: male, female or either: _____

Age range: _____

Ethnic background: _____

Marital status: _____

Socioeconomic status: _____

Where do your customers live? In your neighborhood? Across the U.S.? All over the world? Is there a specific climate where your customer lives? _____

_____
_____
_____
_____
_____
_____

Are your customers city dwellers, suburban types, or both? _____

_____
_____
_____
_____
_____

Why are they buying your product? Remember, it's about the experience, too. What experience are they hoping to have by visiting your business, buying your product, or using your service? _____

_____
_____
_____
_____
_____

Will they use your product or service once, or will they become repeat customers if they're satisfied with your work? _____

_____
_____
_____
_____

Are your customers college graduates? What level of education do they have? _____

_____

_____

_____

_____

_____

What are they interested in? _____

_____

_____

_____

DailyCandy

You met CG-in-action Dany Levy in Chapter 10. Dany created the phenomenon DailyCandy as a one-woman enterprise. Now, DailyCandy reaches 3 million subscribers daily and employs 75 people.

Dany says, "When I started, I wasn't thinking about dollar signs. I was just doing something I loved. I loved finding new things and the show-and-tell of sharing. I realized there wasn't anything like DailyCandy out there, and I knew I could create compelling content that was relevant to my demographic: New Yorkers. It was a gut instinct for me. DailyCandy's passion was infectious to subscribers and the staff I began to employ, and the company kept growing."

Know that starting small has big potential. Dany says, "Start doing one thing, and do it well."

What other products/services do they buy? _____

_____
_____
_____
_____
_____

What problems and challenges do your customers face? _____

_____
_____
_____
_____
_____

What recent milestones have they experienced and how might that milestone affect their priorities? (i.e. graduation, marriage, or the birth of a child) _____

_____
_____
_____
_____
_____
_____

How Will You Sell
Your Products or Services?

Let's say you're hand making scarves and handbags. Are you selling them from your own boutique or wholesaling to other boutiques, or both? (If you're not sure yet whether you're a wholesaler, retailer, or both, we'll talk more about these structures in Chapter 16.) Are you also selling on the Internet? If yes, are you selling from your own website, or do you wholesale to other online retailers who then mark up your wholesale cost? Do you utilize e-commerce on your own website, or does a client call you to place an order with a credit card or by sending a check? How choosy will you be about the stores that sell your wares? For me, it isn't practical to visit every boutique from the U.S. to Tokyo to make sure my jewelry fits with their style. So when a new shop places an order, I ask for a list of the designers they currently carry to get a feel for their aesthetic.

If you're providing a service instead of goods (say, freelance still-life photography), the above questions still apply. Are you a freelance photographer who runs the business aspect from home, creates the project on-site and in a studio, and ships the final product after your client chooses which photos they'd like over the Internet? Describe how you'll get your creative product or service into the world. _____

Where Are You Running Your Venture?

You may start at home or by leasing a month-to-month office space or artist's studio. If you plan to lease a storefront, this is quite a big commitment, both financially and in terms of time. Are you ready to sign a five-year lease? Is your product/service ready for it?

Just like we talked about gauging interest and demand for your product in the previous chapter, it's often a great first step to sell your product on the web to see if your product or service merits a storefront. Of course, online businesses have plenty of costs, like hosting fees, website designer fees, and payment processing fees. But those are still usually less costly than a storefront.

As you expand, you may find a symbiotic relationship between a storefront and an online store. In 2002, CGs-in-action Catherine Chow and Corina Nurimba opened Azalea Boutique in San Francisco. Catherine says, "We always had online retail in mind, so we launched our website, www.tobi.com six months after opening our storefront. The storefront drives traffic to our online store, and the online store creates a new channel of distribution and gives others visibility to our store and our products."

❋ CREATIVE TIP ❋

Cut Online Fees

If you choose to sell online and need to save costs, you can start out with PayPal or Google Checkout. Instead of being charged a processing fee, you'll be charged a percentage of your sales. The same goes for selling your product on sites like Etsy.com. You can partner with Shopify.com to integrate an online store with your current website, allowing you to keep your own domain name. This is a great way to test the water without making the financial commitment to the costly fees of an online account or a tricked out e-commerce website.

Home is Where the Sales Are

If feasible, you can try selling out of your home, but first check to see if your city and county zoning laws allow home-based businesses. Do this before applying for a business license or you could have a sticky situation on your hands.

Finding the right brick and mortar location may take some time. You'll want your business to vibe with the neighborhood. You'll need to find a spot where the foot traffic will serve you well. Certainly, you'll have to balance your ideal location with an affordable rent—I'm not saying you have to open in the most expensive area of town. Sometimes it involves a sixth sense on what neighborhoods are up-and-coming. When Stacia Valle opened her New York City boutique in the Meatpacking District, there was only one other clothing store in the neighborhood.

Fast forward six years, and her neighbors include Alexander McQueen Helmut Lang, and Stella McCartney. Rents in the now trendy neighborhood sky-rocketed to over ten times the rate she locked down.

If you don't have a strong sense of the real estate market, ask around for trustworthy realtor contacts. Of course, when someone's trying to sell you on a property, you have to take what he or she says with a grain of salt. So get outside opinions on a neighborhood's viability, and be sure to talk to other local business owners.

Pay By the Hour

If you need a professional space to meet with clients, but aren't quite ready to commit to a lease, check out www.regus.com for reasonable hourly fees.

Your Core Values:
The Soul of Your Business

Certain qualities will remain at the core to your company no matter how much you grow. I still make custom pieces—a client can talk with me in detail about specifications for a jewelry piece she'd like to order. This is how I started, and it's important to me to always offer this service no matter how many retail stores carry my jewelry. It was also important for me not to have e-commerce on my website. For me, though I knew it would result in increased profit, I felt it devalued the artistry of the design. Many business owners would shake their heads and call that crazy-talk. But I started my own business so that I could create something that lived up to my standards and reflected my values. Take the time to pay attention to these details now. You'll grow and change, but setting your core values will keep you clear-headed and focused on making your vision a reality.

To uncover your core values, think about what inspires and motivates you to create and sell your product or service. Those baby quilts might be a way for you to commemorate a special occasion and offer a product that has great sentimental value to a young family. Knowing this now means that if your business is to wildly expand—say, a quilt section in Barneys with your name on it—you'll still be sure to keep intact the part of the business that originally inspired you. This is how you avoid a high-profit-low-satisfaction situation five years from now. It *is* possible to have artistic fulfillment and financial fulfillment as long as you actively prioritize both aspects of your business.

Core Values: What matters most to you? _____

_____

_____

_____

_____

_____

The Core Values of Lipstick Queen

At 18, CG-in-action Poppy King started a cosmetics empire from her love of all-things lipstick. Poppy is one of the most introspective and thoughtful business owners I've ever met. Here, she reflects on the core values of her company and how they influence the way it is run.

"*Motivation*. The word itself sounds so positive that we tend to think our motivations have to be positive too. Not true. Some of the most effective motivations for my business and my brand are negative. Meaning that a lot of what drives my business and my passion for it comes from what I *don't* want it to be. Through knowing what I *don't* want, I can understand more clearly what I *do*.

"Here is a specific example of how this works. The biggest motivation that keeps me inspired is that *I don't want to do anything the way a corporation would do it*. When I ask myself why is this so motivating to me the answer that comes back is: people. I hate the way that corporations treat people, both their own workers and their customers. They often treat their customers like sheep and their workers like robots and I refuse to do either.

"So this tells me that interaction, dignity, communication, respect, and individuality are core values for me. Individuality is something lost to many women facing makeup counters as they are bamboozled with images of standardized beauty and airbrushed über-human perfection. I have never used models to sell my products or any notions of standardized beauty as a way to pique customer interest. Instead, I only use graphic art, color, and language to inspire my customer to look at my products rather than intimidate her into thinking that she has to look a certain way and that I will help her to look this one standardized way. I like to appeal to her mind through my concepts and her sense of color and exuberance through my graphic art, and leave physical appearance out of it as each one of us is entitled to our own notion of physical beauty.

"Finally, strong communication and interaction with the people that work with me and with my customer is a core value. The way in which I communicate my products, myself and my direction in business is something I take very seriously. I am inspired by the idea that if you give people a sense of ownership in what they are doing and buying they will give that back to you tenfold in commitment. Then, in turn, their commitment motivates me to keep going on my darker days, so it is a win-win scenario. I try to listen as much as I talk. This is something that so few businesses attempt, and even though I never claim to do it perfectly the fact that I even try is appreciated by my market, my customers, and the workers who are dedicated to staying with me.

"So what does all of this tell you? Well, it tells you I will never be a mega multi-million-dollar corporation because my core values are not conducive to huge structures and huge profit seeking machines. But I'm fine with that because I know what motivates and inspires me to love what I do. It doesn't mean I can make my business a charity, it is a business after all and needs to be effective financially. But I have an unwavering passion to make it effective without making it corporate. If that means it will always be a smaller business, so be it. I would rather have a small business supporting my values than a big business where my values are compromised. The more aligned with your values you are, the more successful you will be at endeavors that reflect them. Some of us may value wealth, some of us may value security, or discipline or difference or power or fun or ease or whatever, but the most important thing is to establish what it is you do value to find your most motivating forces. There is no one right way; there is just *your* way, and that is all you need know."

Name the Baby

Now that you've got all of this information down on paper, it's time to name your business. Take your business's core values and personality into consideration along with your customer (you'll find more on business personality and branding in Chapter 17). If your business is sophisticated and classic, you won't want to name it "Jewelry 4 U." If your customers are teenagers, you'll need something more tantalizing than "Goldstein and Associates."

First, to which types of business names are you drawn? Do you like a message within the name that sounds like it could have come from the one-sentence business idea summary? Say, "Eco-friendly Products for Tots." Or do you prefer something more imprecise, like, "Natural Baby." Maybe you'd like your name to appear, like "L. Harrison's Organic Baby."

Brainstorm a list of possibilities. Think about what makes your business different from competitors. You may find a detail from your Core Competencies list to riff from and expand. Don't edit your ideas just yet. Keep going until you have at least a dozen possibilities.

Look over your list. Which names stand out to you? Put a star next to your six or seven favorites. Your name is a very public part of your new company, and this is one of those decisions where you do need a second, third, and twelfth opinion. Ask anyone and everyone, and then ask target customers. Your target market reigns here, so listen closely to their feedback. Once you've got two or three clear winners, pick your favorite.

The name will be yours for years to come, so make sure you've picked a name that you're proud to say over and over. From personal experience, I advise you to pick something very easy to spell. In hindsight, I should have named my company Katie Sise Design, because the second "a" in Katharine Sise trips up customers and fashion editors more often than not. Within months of opening my company, someone poached my web address spelled with the more traditional spelling. They offered to sell it back at the bargain price of several thousand dollars. It took five years before the poacher relinquished the domain and allowed me to buy it so that my web traffic could be redirected to the proper site. Pick a name that is both easy to spell and pronounce.

Make sure your business name doesn't pigeonhole you as a one-trick wonder. You never know when your product line or range of services will change. I chose Katharine Sise Design instead of Katharine Sise Jewelry so that I'm free to design handbags, clothes, shoes, or beer cozies somewhere down the line.

CHAPTER 13

The Small Business Game Plan

You need a business plan.
Write it with a purple marker on flowered stationery
or oil on canvas—but get to it.

Write Your Own Plan: Set Financial, Career, and Personal Goals

I know, I know. You don't want to write a business plan. But I urge you to do it and here's why: a business plan is your roadmap for the creative journey ahead. It's the best way to clarify your ambitions and maneuver your course. Business plans are not only for those starting a business; if you currently own a business or have started a freelance career, it's never too late to reap the benefits of a well-thought-out plan.

Most business plans are created to secure financing from banks or investors. From my interviews, it became clear that the majority of CGs either write the traditional lengthy business plan to secure this financing or, if they're starting small, they write nothing at all because the process sounds too intimidating.

So let's take the scary out of the business plan. Unless you're looking to get a loan or investors, your business plan can have all sorts of unconventional goals. Write it in a way that feels right for your business, but take it seriously, and get to it.

The Whole She-Bang

In this chapter we'll create a smaller scale version of a full business plan—think of it as a thorough warm-up, like jumping jacks. If you decide to write the full-scale version, your local bookstore will have numerous options for guidance. Try *Anatomy of a Business Plan* by Linda Pinson, *Write a Business Plan in No Time* by Frank F. Fiore, or *The Complete Idiot's Guide to Business Plans.* You can download free plans at http://office.microsoft.com/en-us/templates/default.aspx or www.score.org. Also check out www.bplans.com, where business plans are customized for different businesses, from restaurants and cafés to beauty salons and pet services.

BizPlanIt is a business plan consulting firm that works with companies to create investor-grade business plans. If you're looking for financing from private equity firms, venture capitalists, angel investors, corporate investors, banks, or SBA lenders, give this service some serious consideration. Visit www.bizplanit.com.

Still wary? Don't be. You've already done much of the work by brainstorming in the previous chapter. We're simply going to take it a step further with more detailed exercises. Remember, no matter what career you're in or transitioning into, when you define what a successful life, career, or business means for you, your ultimate goals become clearer. When you know specifically what your objectives are, it's easier to follow a step-by-step path to achieve them. This is your career, and you're the one who sets the goals and moves forward. You need to always be moving in the direction of your goals, not just grabbing any gig, client, or project. It's absolutely up to you to decide what those goals are. Maybe you want to sell enough records to make Carrie Underwood jealous, or maybe you want more time to raise your family. In the latter case, if it's all about having more time, you'll start saying no to the jobs that are fluffy and fun but don't pay well. On the contrary, if you've already been meeting your financial goals but want to start taking on more high profile jobs that move you forward (whether or not they pay well) you'll do the opposite.

Last month, my agent called to see if I wanted to go on-air as a spokesperson for a beauty product. It involved a ten-week time commitment and a ton of travel. It paid very well, and my first instinct was to grab it. Five years ago, I would have. But it didn't make sense for me now, because I was meeting my financial goals with my jewelry, writing, and other on-air television work, and this job wasn't in line with where I want to go careerwise. That, added to the fact that I'd be away from my husband and living in hotels for ten weeks, made it not worth it. Having a business plan helps you know which gigs to take and which ones to say no to if they're not in line with your career plans. As your work becomes more advanced and you become more established, you can say no to some of the projects you would have jumped on when you were younger. It's your career, so keep it on track.

Write this plan however you feel comfortable. You can cull from the brainstorming you did in the previous chapter and organize it into bullet points to get your

The Power of a Plan

Katherine Power and Hillary Kerr cofounded www.WhoWhatWear.com in 2006. Their company has enjoyed tremendous success. Katherine says, "Have a plan and an overall vision of where you want to go. It's not the lack of ideas or thoughts that stops a business from taking off, it's the lack of strategy and prioritizing. Know the first five steps of what you need to do to get where you want to be. Really think about this, prioritize and begin to tackle each step. Hillary and I knew we wanted to start with a fashion newsletter, and that our newsletter would always be the anchor for our brand. The next step was adding a video component to the website. We followed that with a book on style. We mapped each big step out in a thoughtful way that meant we were working on our priorities, and not spreading ourselves too thin with miscellaneous details not in our plan."

document started. You can answer the questions below (feel free to skip the ones that don't apply to your freelance or small business idea). Just remember, this plan is flexible. Don't be afraid to jot down ideas; they don't have to be perfectly formed concepts. Brainstorming isn't set in stone, and you can always revisit and revise. You'll make adjustments along the way, but getting your ambitions down on paper means more focus, direction, and planning, and less flip-flopping and confusion.

The Plan, Stan

Microsoft describes the following nine criteria as the information you'll need for your business plan.

1) An executive summary outlining goals and objectives.

2) A brief account of how the company began.

3) Your company's goals.

4) Biographies of the management team.

5) The service or product you plan to offer.

6) The market potential for your service or product.

7) A marketing strategy.

8) A three- to five-year financial projection.

9) An exit strategy.

Easy as pie. We'll cover these topics, plus more, in this chapter. You'll have a working business plan after completing the exercises in these pages.

Start the Plan

Get yourself to a computer or grab a notebook. Write the first draft of your business plan by following the exercises below.

Your Mission Statement

Reread your journal entries from the previous chapter. Do you notice a common theme? Synthesize the material to begin your plan with a mission statement. This statement declares the mission and purpose of your business in a clear and concise manner. A mission statement tells everyone from your Aunt Edna to a customer in Beijing why your business exists, what it offers, and who it serves. Craft your mission statement by providing one-sentence answers to each of the following questions: What are you doing/selling/creating? Who are you selling to? Why are you selling it: what values motivate you? You may want to draw from your Core Competencies to add a line about how your company is doing business uniquely. It may be your actual product or your approach to business that sets you apart from the rest.

Rebecca Kousky from Nest shares her Mission Statement:

Nest is a nonprofit organization that empowers female artists and artisans around the world. Using a unique combination of interest-free microfinance loans, mentoring from established designers, as well as a market in which to sell their crafts, Nest helps its loan recipients create successful small businesses. Nest instills pride of ownership, preserves ancient artistic traditions, and successfully moves women from poverty to self-sufficiency.

Company Overview and Goals

After your mission statement, include a few pages summarizing the type of business you plan to run (see pages 194–196 for legal structures). Include how your business idea was born, along with your nonfinancial goals for the first few years in business. This is a very personal part of your plan, so if you need more clarity on your business objectives, finish the exercises in this chapter and come back to this section to draft your overview.

The Players: Who Does What?

In this section, describe everyone involved in running your company. Do you have partners? Store managers? Employees? What roles do they play? What are their responsibilities? What key people will you bring on board to make up for the skills you lack?

If you're a one-woman show, describe your responsibilities, along with the ones you'll need to farm out to a bookkeeper, publicist, or accountant.

Financial Projections

List realistic projections for your first three years in business. I know this part is tricky; if you haven't gotten your business off the ground, it's hard to come up with numbers and you might feel like you're conjuring them from Magic 8-Ball. At the very least, write a list of goal projects and what they might bring in for revenue. If you're selling a product, set a goal for how many units, at a determined price, you'd like to move the first, second, and third year. (We'll cover pricing in Chapter 16.) You'll have to toe the line between being polite and nosy, but if you can talk to other CGs with businesses like yours, you may be able to get a better sense of what you can expect financially during your first years. Or, at the very least, how business owners in your line of work went about gauging their financial projections.

Of course, if you're looking to secure financing, your numbers have to be backed up to the letter. Find out more about balance sheets, income and expense statements and cash flow statements at www. score.org and www. inc.com. Check out the templates provided at office.microsoft.com. You can plug in numbers for your start-up and monthly costs and create balance sheets and cash flow spreadsheets. Even if you're not looking to secure outside financing, understanding your cash flow is vital to your business's health. You need to manage cash flow properly to pay your bills, pay your vendors, fund your expenses and purchase the raw materials needed to create your product.

Costs: From Hair Dye to Health Insurance

Detail your start-up costs. List every single thing you'll need to start from raw materials and a Mac computer to legal and business license fees. Then, include monthly costs for your first three years in business. Include your rent, utilities, equipment, office supplies, bank charges, insurance, marketing materials, website hosting fees, professional service fees (like an accountant or bookkeeper) and every other expense you can imagine your particular business may incur in the first years of operation.

Financing Your Business

Most of you are likely starting your business with your own hard-earned cash (I did). Some of you may be borrowing from friends or relatives. In that case, make sure there's an agreement on paper. Clarify what the lender is looking for in return from the money; does the loan accrue interest, or is he or she expecting a stake in your venture with a return on the investment? Check out www.virginmoneyus.com to set up friends and family financing in a professional way through the Social Loans service.

It's okay to pay for office supplies or certification courses with a credit card. It's *not* okay to finance your small business with credit cards. Think about how long it may take you to turn a profit: do you really want high-interest debt piling up around you? If your business has major cash needs, talk to a financial planner about getting a loan from a bank, getting a loan from the federal government's Small Business Administration, or looking for investors.

Detail your plans for financing your enterprise.

Legally Speaking, What Type of Business Are You?

Check out the definitions below to get a feel for legal structures. To find out which structure makes the most sense for your individual situation, consult a lawyer or an accountant.

Sole proprietorship: A sole proprietorship is the most common form of business ownership. It's the business model you'll likely open if your business will be run by you, the sole owner. Sole proprietorships are easy to start up (there's no formal paperwork), easy to discontinue, and subject to fewer regulations. One disadvantage to this structure is that all assets of the business are owned by the individual; there is no legal separation between the individual and the business. This means there's no distinction between the assets of the business and the assets of the business owner, so you're liable for all debts if your business tanks. It also means you're liable for any personal damages your business causes. In other words, if you open a decorating business and accidentally set the client's house on fire with your new line of aromatic candles, the client can come after your car, your house, and your vinyl record collection.

Because a sole proprietor isn't a corporation, there are no corporate taxes; the sole proprietor pays self-employment taxes on her profits. (See Chapter 15 for an overview on paying taxes for your small business.)

If you start out as a sole proprietor and experience massive growth (accruing greater risk, as well), you can always switch your model to a corporation or an LLC.

When at least two individuals share the profit and liability, the structure is referred to as a general partnership.

Corporations: A corporation is a legally defined form of business ownership with limited liability granted to the owners. Most corporations have more than one owner (called shareholders or stockholders), but it is possible to form a corporation with one individual. Most states require a corporation to have a board of directors responsible for making decisions regarding the operation of the business. The majority of corporations formed are C Corporations. A C Corp offers limited liability—meaning, if the company is sued, your assets are protected. It's subject to double taxation, which means that the company's profits are taxed, as is the money each shareholder takes from those profits. An S Corporation offers limited liability, but without the double taxation of a C Corporation. An S Corp may provide tax benefits for your situation, but are still subject to more regulations and are pricier to set up than a sole proprietorship. If you decide to form a C or S corporation, you must have an attorney or an accountant get your paperwork in order.

❋ CREATIVE TIP ❋

Visit www.nolo.com

Nolo.com is a fantastic resource for every legal issue from forming a corporation to finding a lawyer to fill your business needs.

Limited Liability Company: An LLC is a hybrid of a corporation and a sole proprietorship. It's become an increasingly popular ownership option because it combines the protection and liability benefits of a corporation, but with the tax benefits of a sole proprietorship. This is an option to consider if you'd like more legal protection than that provided by a sole proprietorship but less regulation and more flexibility than a C or S corporation.

A limited partnership is formed when at least one partner has limited liability for the debts of the business.

Check out irs.gov and sba.gov for more information on business structures and taxation regulations.

Your Timeline

After providing a summary of your business (including legal structure), your objectives, and your financial needs, include a timeline for the execution of those objectives and your financial goals. Remember, the timeline (and the proposal) aren't set in stone. This is your plan, for your benefit. So don't paralyze yourself by trying to get it down to the exact date and time you want to make your first sale to Nordstrom.

Start with when you'd like the business to be up and running, and expand to include any business goal you want to achieve within a given time frame. For example, maybe you plan to work six days a week for the first year, with the goal of hiring an employee to help you at the twelve-month mark. If you're borrowing five Gs from your twin sister to cover start-up costs, when is your goal date to pay her back?

Having a timeline for achieving financial and professional milestones will keep you moving in the right direction. Refer back to your timeline on a monthly basis to see if you're on track.

Industry Overview

Write a summary—like an old-fashioned book report—of your industry. Include everything from historic growth rate to recent trends. Check out resources from Wikipedia to The Bureau of Labor Statistics and research topics applicable to your field. If you're stuck, the following questions are a good place to start.

1) Who are the major players in the industry right now? Ten years ago?

2) What might be hard for a newcomer to this industry, and how will your business overcome this?

3) What are the industry's estimated sales during the past five years?

4) What economic trends have influenced the industry during the past five years, and how might these trends affect the next three years?

5) What is the market and customer base for this industry?

Your Target Market: Do Your Research and Know Your Customer

A target market refers to the section of the market you feel is most likely to buy your product or use your service.

You must be willing to narrow your definition of your target market to understand your target customer. Often, new business owners are so afraid of turning customers away that they kid themselves into thinking their product is for everyone. This results in misspent advertising dollars, missed marketing opportunities, and an unclear brand. We'll talk more about branding in Chapter 17. Your brand is, quite simply, your message. It's how you're perceived by the world and—most importantly—your customer.

Synthesize your customer profiles from the previous chapter to define your target market. Ask yourself: what does my customer want? What kind of experience is he or she looking for? Is he or she finding my product or service elsewhere? What would my customer find remarkable and how can I cater to her needs?

As you define your market, understand that there is depth and strength to a niche. These are the customers who will come back again and again because you're speaking their language and understanding their needs. Ask yourself: Where is my niche? Who belongs there?

If I thought my jewelry was for every woman out there, I'd be misunderstanding my market. My jewelry is for fashion-forward (likely urban) fashion-magazine-reading women in their twenties and thirties who make enough money to afford it.

Does this mean that I don't get the occasional seventy-year-old customer? Of course I do. She's a CG named Betty from Okatie, South Carolina. And she's loyal as can be. I can guarantee you she's reading this book right now.

But if I marketed to the over-fifty set, I'd be missing the point. It doesn't mean that you close your doors to these customers. It means that you cater to your target market at every turn, from your product line to the advertising they'll respond to best.

Do not be afraid to specialize. Sure, you may not want to open an interior design business that only serves two-bedroom bungalows owned by women in their forties, but maybe your interior design business can cater to redesigning office spaces. Narrowing your business or service down to its most potent form will help carve your place in a niche market. If you try to market to everyone, you end up with a seriously lame and watered-down message and product. And that's a surefire way to appeal to no one.

Take this, for example. An art director from Saks shot the first jewelry collection on my website. It involved hair—actual human hair—draped over antiques and vintage books. My mother was horrified. So were my aunts. But—as much as I love them—they're not my target audience. So I thanked them for their opinions, but chose to focus on the enthusiastic responses from my twentysomething and thirtysomething fashionista friends.

Here's where you get to be imaginative with your research. How is your customer currently being marketed to? What kinds of graphics are used in the ads? What publications reach this market? What kind of music is your customer listening to, and is there a local radio station that might be perfect for your ads? What about alumni or other group associations? If you're marketing to teens, check out how they're currently being marketed to by companies like yours. How might you use new technology to reach your market?

Often, very smart marketing and PR ideas can come from knowing what blogs and websites your target market reads. Become friendly with bloggers and they may quote you or write a post on your product or service. (We'll cover blogs in depth in Chapter 17.)

Next, list your ideas for how you plan to reach your target market. What will your message be? How will you advertise in a way that makes your customers take notice?

If you're stuck, come back to this section after reading Chapter 17.

The Competition

It's your job to know what your competitors are doing, and what you plan to do differently or better. What can you do to continually stand apart from them? Search everywhere from the World Wide Web to your backyard and find what else is out there.

As part of your market research, talk to other business owners in your area, whether or not they run similar businesses. You can

✿ CREATIVE TIP ✿

A Competition Caveat

It's important to understand the competition as you form your business plan, but don't fall into the trap of becoming obsessed with their every move. You give your power away when you fret over or badmouth your competitors. Competition can even serve you if it makes you focus on making your business stronger. Play up what makes you unique and feel confident that there's room for all types in the creative world.

find contact info for small businesses at your local Chamber of Commerce. You'll gain insider knowledge about the local market from talking to these owners.

When approaching other business owners, keep your manners intact; you'll have to draw the line at asking for trade secrets and private information. Don't walk into your neighborhood craft store and ask how much they pay in rent or grill your local greeting card shop about how much they net in profits each month. Keep your class, creative girl. If your business will be a direct competitor to a business in your area, it's smarter (and more respectful) to go outside of your neighborhood to interview a similar business. You'll be amazed at the information you can gather from similar businesses, whether or not they're direct competitors to your own. You don't want to rip off their ideas, but check out generalities, like their hours of operation and the way they advertise. Ask about their busy seasons, which may differ from yours in terms of what you're selling, but will alert you to the times of year that their increased foot traffic will positively affect your business. They'll be able to tell you about the demographics of the neighborhood and the types of customers they most often see.

Do your research and make sure that in your area, there is a high demand for the service or product that you're providing. You're going to have competitors. That's a natural part of commerce. You have to thoroughly research your competition to determine how you'll provide a unique service or product and distinguish yourself. After you've done your research, you may be inspired to tweak your idea.

What's for Sale and How Will it Stand Up to the Competition?

Use your brainstorming from the previous chapter to form a concise definition of your product or service. Describe the products in your debut line or the initial services you plan to offer. Then, answer the following questions.

1. What makes my product or service viable in today's market?

2. What are the benefits my customer receives from my product or service?

3. In the market, is there another company who dominates my niche?

4. Will I be able to break into the market as a newcomer? How do I plan to do this?

5. How will I market my product or service?

6. What makes my product or service competitive?

7. What's my advantage? (Here, you may want to refer to your Core Competencies to verbalize why your company will do things in a unique way.)

8. What is my pricing structure and strategy? (You can use this section of your business plan to list the prices for your products or services. Feel free to come back to this question and the next one after reading Chapter 16.) How will my prices compare to the competition? It's okay if your price point is higher, you just have to have a fabulous reason. Say you own a bakery: your three-dollar cookies can be justified by your organic, vegan ingredients and family recipes.

9. Is my company a wholesaler, retailer, or both? How will I sell my product?

10. How easy is it for other companies to challenge my prices with a similar product or service? How easy is it for another company to knock off my wares? How would I handle this scenario?

11. As far as my product goes, where do I see my business in five years? Will I expand on a product line or add services to my current business model?

12. What equipment and materials do I need to create my product or service?

13. How will I package my product? Great packaging draws attention to your product sitting on a shelf. It also increases the likelihood of it being bought as a gift. Choose

Package Makes Perfect

You can personalize your packaging by including a slip of paper with the story behind your business and tips for how to wear, use, or take care of the product. Check out www.thedieline.com, a website devoted to new trends in the package design industry.

packaging that suits your brand and matches the aesthetics of your target customer, say, using environmentally friendly packaging for handmade organic soap.

14. **Will I make everything by hand? Will I need employees or hire other freelancers on a need-only basis? Will I outsource?**

15. **How much volume can I handle with my current way of doing business? Having a plan to handle volume helps you say yes when a big offer comes along, instead of hemming and hawing and losing the business to someone who's quicker on her feet. When Target asked me if I could produce a larger quantity of jewelry than I was used to, I immediately said yes, because I'd already had a conversation about the possibility of bulk orders of chains at my current supplier. As a business owner, you have to be prepared for both the worst-case and best-case scenarios. Ask yourself: How will I adapt if my business grows rapidly?**

Your Exit Plan

If your business is funded with investment capital, you need to describe an exit strategy. How will your financial backer get his or her money back with a return on her investment? Search

Sarah Horowitz Parfums

Perfumer Sarah Horowitz was accustomed to shipping orders of $300-$500 to individual boutiques for her line of fragrances. That is, until Nordstrom placed a $105,000 order. Sarah says, "I said yes on the spot. But I would have made my life easier if I'd done the research beforehand. I scrambled to find a filling house, but they didn't have enough workers to finish my order, so my boyfriend, my friends and I drove to the warehouse, put on hairnets, and jumped on the assembly line. And still, that filling house could only produce the first $65,000 of the order. We were stuck completing the final $40,000—that's over 2,600 bottles of perfume— in my 800 square foot house. I ordered pizza and beer for my friends, and we spent days pouring the perfume into each bottle, spraying the pump to be sure it worked, putting each cap on, sticking the ingredients label underneath, sticking the brand label on the front, placing each bottle in a pouch, and tying that pouch into a pretty bow. For 2,600 bottles of perfume! Looking back, I love that story about my first big order. But if I had done my research on factories and filling houses in advance, I would have saved myself a lot of trouble."

"exit strategy" on bizplanit.com to educate yourself on the options.

If your business is funded by you, use this section for long-term business planning. Do you envision running this business for a few years, or a few decades? How much money are you willing to spend before seeing a profit or signs of a blooming business on the horizon? How much time will you give your venture to succeed? Will you attempt to sell your business? Do you have a plan for restarting life as an employee if your business tanks?

In this part of your plan, you can also list ideas for generating additional income through side jobs so that you don't have to jump ship if your startup is slow-going.

The Power of Intention:
Your Big Picture To-Do Lists

A great way to round out your plan is with big-picture goals. Because they're ever evolving, leave plenty of space at the end of your business plan for these lists. You'll continue to set intentions and goals as your business grows. Tack them to your wall or say them out loud. Notice the impact of intention—putting your mind, thoughts, and energy into achieving a goal—on your business and your life.

For me, this section works as a big-picture to-do list. I encourage you to divide your list into financial goals, career goals, and lifestyle goals. If it feels natural for you, divide your goals into timeframes; list how you plan to achieve them during the next three months, six months, one year, and five years. Be as detailed as possible. Certainly, you'll have to revise as new opportunities and goals arise, but for now, you're setting intentions. They may be flexible, but if you don't have goals, how will you reach them?

Dividing my plans into timeframes works well for me, so I've excerpted that part of my business plan below. You'll see that I listed a few career and lifestyle goals for my one-month, three-month, and one-year business plan.

In my one-month plan, I have things like:

- **Finish making the necklaces for Target.com and have them to Target's warehouse ahead of June 24 deadline.**
- **Formulate a game plan for the press surrounding the collaboration with Target.**
- **Finish making jewelry pieces for the *Lucky* Magazine fall trends story**
- **Contact the Home Shopping Network and talk about upcoming jewelry shows.**

My three-month plan looks like this:

- **Finish one chapter per month for *Creative Girl*.**
- **Rough schedule: Start each day with three hours of writing on *Creative Girl*, then two hours on fiction project, three hours on jewelry. Go to gym before Brian (my husband) gets home.**

- **Try to cook dinner for once in your life.**
- **Enroll in a writing class to workshop the chapters.**
- **Meet with my editor to make sure the chapters are going in the right direction.**

In my one-year plan, I have things like:
- **Finish this book (if it's in your hands right now, I've accomplished this goal).**
- **Finish fiction manuscript and deliver to Dan (my literary agent) by April.**
- **Continue hosting television show and meet with Tracy (my television agent) to discuss future TV projects. Schedule Los Angeles trip to meet with the Style Network and E! casting directors.**
- **Maintain jewelry press and store orders each month, even though writing books is taking over my life (albeit in a good way . . .).**

For me, this big-picture-thinking part of my plan works best when written in a conversational tone meant for my eyes only. I include a combination of how I plan to schedule my day, broad goals for the longer term, and actual to-do's. Experiment with what style works best for you. If it feels right, include your lifestyle goals, too (like I've included going to the gym and cooking). This is about having the life and career you want for yourself, so really delve into what this looks like. On my list, having a baby and finding a part-time babysitter I trust is in the section for the next five years. You create your life, so get clear on everything you've ever dreamed of, and get started.

CHAPTER 14

Set Up Shop

*From websites and interns to tips
for the organizationally challenged*

Create Your Space

You get to create your own work environment. How cool is that? It doesn't matter if you're renting a 3,000-square-foot loft in a trendy business district or creating a workspace in the corner of your studio apartment. This is your space. Make it shine.

If you're working from home and have the extra square footage, try to set up shop in a quiet room that isn't your bedroom or living room. I'm writing this sentence from my living room, so know that it's doable to work from your coffee table. Some pretty big ideas have come from small spaces. But if possible, a room with a door makes it easier to leave work when you leave your home office. If this isn't realistic, try a curtain or strands of beads—anything to divide your workspace from your living space.

Finding a spot with natural light is a bonus; you may find it stimulates your natural energy even better than espresso. If you can't find natural light, be sure to use enough artificial light so that you're not squinting or having trouble seeing colors and textures properly.

Make a list of everything you'll need to outfit your space. Choose wisely where you'll splurge and where you'll save. You may find an ergonomic chair is well worth the price to avoid screaming back pain, but that you can do without a $200 futurist lamp that doubles as an

alarm clock. If you'll be on the phone talking to clients and vendors, a headset helps you avoid the neck pain caused by crunching the phone against your shoulder.

If you're transitioning from a corporate office to a home office, shared studio space, or your own shop, what did you like about your previous workspace? Bring those elements into your new situation. A bulletin board is great for tacking up to-do lists and loose papers. Grab a whiteboard if you're the type to get inspired and scrawl big ideas. Fill your space with whatever inspires you. When I was little, I loved *The Wizard of Oz*. So I have a framed photograph of the characters to remind me how lucky I am to use my imagination each day. When I'm writing fiction, I tear pages from magazines that remind me of my characters and settings. Create your own version of an inspiration board—set aside a space where you tack up language or images that inspire you. If you're stimulated by sound rather than visuals, make a playlist of songs that keeps you energized and ready to conquer your work.

What are your necessary supplies? If you're on a tight budget, everything from pottery wheels to mannequins can be bought secondhand.

What about electronics? You may be able to start with a computer and printer and hold off on buying a scanner and fax machine. What software will your computer need? A backup system is a must; try back-

✳ CREATIVE TIP ✳

Renovations

If you're opening a restaurant, salon, boutique or any other public space that requires renovations—and you think the space is too far gone to pull off a dilapidated-chic look—get at least four quotes from contractors. Know that even with a quote, renovations rarely come in on budget (or on time). If one of the quotes is priced way under the others, figure out why before hiring him or her. You don't have to go with the lowest bidder. Check that the contractor has the proper certifications and insurance. You should ask for a client list and references and check in with other clients to be sure you're hiring the right contractor.

Hairstylist and salon owner Victoria Hunter says, "Securing building permits for our salon and completing renovations took so much longer than expected that we paid six months of rent before the space was ready to take paying customers. I kept waiting for Ashton Kutcher to jump out and tell us we'd been punked."

up software with compression technology and features that match your level of tech-savvy so that you'll actually use it. You may want to try an external hard drive or USB flash drive. If you and technology don't mix, ask a tech-friendly sibling or friend for advice, or check out user reviews on Amazon to choose products that are a good fit for your needs.

Depending on your budget, see what you can borrow or find on www.craigslist.com or at a trusty IKEA. There are ways to get around certain start-up costs. If you can't afford a fax or copy machine, use your neighborhood Kinko's or a similar outpost. You'll learn to be resourceful and thrifty in those first months (or years) as a self-employed wonder-girl.

Keep Great Records: Find the Method That Suits You

Get ready to get organized. You can hire an administrative assistant (or just answer your phone in a British accent and ask the caller to "Hold please while I transfer you to the CEO"), but not even the best administrative assistant or accountant can keep track of your records, due dates, or finances unless you keep diligent records. This applies to every aspect of your creative career. Actors should keep track of each and every casting director they've met and their corresponding mailing addresses for headshots. Travel writers must keep lists of editors and story ideas they've pitched, along with a detailed list of expenses particular to each project. And business owners need to keep track of every invoice and receipt.

Many CGs prefer programs like Quicken or QuickBooks. Research the most current options by quizzing fellow CGs and local business owners to find a system that works for you. Check out *Keeping the Books: Basic Recordkeeping and Accounting for the Successful Small Business* by Linda Pinson.

Disorganization is Bad for Business

Disorganization can leave you feeling chaotic. It's overwhelming when work is piled up and your agenda and to-dos aren't organized properly. If you're fishing around for misplaced papers and memos on a consistent basis, it's time to implement office management strategies before your profits and reputation suffer (in addition to your well-being). Enforce the following strategies to get organized.

File Away

Filing is about as fun as picking up your dog's poop. But you absolutely have to do it. You should only look at a piece of paper once before dealing with it. There are three categories any piece of paper falls into: 1) It belongs in the paper shredder or recycling bin. 2) It needs to be or can be dealt with immediately. 3) It should be dealt with later and needs to be filed in the proper place. Move as many items from the third category into the second as possible. If a task can be completed in less than five minutes, do it and get it over with.

Grab yourself some color-coded folders and create the filing system that makes the most sense to you. Some business owners use monthly folders; they store projects, invoices, and receipts monthly and enter the information at the end of each month into a software program like Quicken. Many freelancers prefer a folder per project; they store pertinent information on a project-by-project basis. You can create broad divisions and file alphabetically under each (say, vendor information and Fed Ex tracking numbers). You may also want to create a filing system on your computer for easy access—just be sure you have a backup system in place so that you don't lose valuable records.

The important thing is that you have a filing system, and that the system makes sense to you. No matter how you choose to organize your paperwork, maintaining up-to-date business records is vital to your company's wellbeing.

Manage Your staff

When you put one person in charge of certain aspects of day-to-day office management, it's incredible just how much more efficiently the office operates. Delegating allows you to streamline your workload and leaves you able to better focus on creative work and big picture thinking. You might ask an intern to be in charge of replenishing office supplies and another employee to be in charge of entering new client information into a database. Communication is key; take ownership of your role as the leader and be very clear about what will be required of each of your employees. Make sure everyone knows his or her responsibilities.

Set Up Shop

Set your office up to make your life easier. Items that you use every day should be within easy reach to make you as efficient as possible. Knick knacks shouldn't get in the way of these items. Your filing system should be very close to the desk (if not actually inside the desk) so that you aren't tempted to leave papers strewn across your workspace. Furniture shouldn't create an obstacle course; you need to be able to get from the desk to the printer without feeling like a high-school hurdle champion.

❋ CREATIVE TIP ❋

Technology On the Fritz

You and your employees must know who to call and what to do when technology fails. Keep those numbers handy in an address book or anywhere other than on your currently kaput computer.

Become a List-maker and Daily Business Planner

Each morning, set aside twenty minutes to jot down your to-dos and goals for the day. It's best to keep these lists in a computer document, notebook, or day planner so that you can refer to the previous day's goals and tasks to be sure you've met them. At the top of the list, jot down the three most important things you'd like to accomplish.

Naturally, there will be the grunt work you'd rather never do. But scheduling time for that work is vital. Often, it's the nitty-gritty aspects of business management that pile up and leave us feeling overwhelmed. So plan to tackle grunt work along with the fun stuff. Many CGs find it best to undertake the toughest work in the morning, so it doesn't weigh on them throughout the day. Try it: identify which item on your list you least want to do, and tackle it first.

Have a broad idea of your agenda. Set blocks of time for each goal. Having a plan for your day ensures that you'll be far more in charge of your progress instead of just acting in response to the day's events. Of course, business matters will pop up unplanned and you'll have to navigate these changes to your schedule. But there's just something about a plan of action that makes a CG far more efficient.

Business Cards

If you can afford it, business cards are a nice place to splurge; a great one makes for

CG Anonymous

Maybe I've watched too many scary movies, but I'm not a fan of putting one's home address on the business card. Play it safe with your name, job title, website, and business phone number. If you want to list an address, investigate fees to open a P.O. box at your local Post Office.

If you don't want to open a separate business phone line, try a voicemail service to avoid listing your home number. I pay sixty-five dollars per year for a business voicemail service through Aerobeep. Check out aerobeep.skyweb.net.

a stellar first impression. If you're on a budget, sites like moo.com, zazzle.com, and overnightprints.com make it easy and affordable to get creative. Fonts and graphics should match your business's aesthetic.

Your Website

Your website is one of the most important business investments you can make. Scrimp elsewhere, splurge here. For creative girls, your website is your calling card. It's your way to attract potential clients from all over the globe without even having to wash your hair. Done poorly, a website is also the easiest way to turn off potential clients even if your creative service, product, or talent is top notch.

Having an online portfolio saves time and money. Clients can view your work without any time commitment on your end, thereby avoiding the dreaded, "Why don't you come by and show me your portfolio?" Instead of trudging to their workspace without having agreed on the promise of payment, you can direct potential employers to your online home.

So do it right. It doesn't need to be a $6,000 investment. You can often find a friend or design student who does incredible work and will listen to exactly what you need and want. My web designer, Code and Theory, now designs websites for companies like Dr. Pepper and The Daily Beast. Seven years ago, when they did my site, they were a younger company and within my price range. Those designers are out there now for you to uncover: the ones who will eventually end up charging tens of thousands of dollars for their work a decade from now, or are currently students or start-ups themselves. If your budget matches mine when I first started, you have to do some homework and find a web designer who is innovative and talented and willing to work within your budget.

Before you meet with designers, know what you want. Check out the websites of creative professionals you admire. Take note of what you like and dislike about their online domains. What can you create to make your site original and representative of your unique work? Take care to create a site that embodies who you are. Once you have design ideas, scour web designers who understand your aesthetic. Start by comparing portfolios of designers within your price range. Check out students at design programs who need to take on work to add to their portfolio. You can meet them by posting your website-needs on a bulletin board at a local design school. Take the student to coffee to discuss what you're looking for in a website and see if they fit the bill.

It's critical that you can run and update your own site. Communicate your level of tech-savvy to your web designer. You don't want to have to rely on his or her expertise every time you want to add a piece of press or upload new product photos, and consistently updating your website keeps customers coming back to see what's new.

If you're providing a creative product, finding a photographer to shoot photos of your collection is key. The same principles apply to finding the right artistic fit; if your budget is tight, scour local arts schools for up-and-coming photography talents. You may be able to do a full or partial trade. When my photographer shot photos of my collection, we agreed to a half-jewelry, half-monetary payment.

Website Basics

It's crucial to display your information and products in a clear and concise manner. Each section of your site should be easy to navigate and easy to open. The following headings will get you started, but exercise your creative freedom and tailor your site for your unique skill set.

Your Bio: Depending on the clients you're looking to attract, you can be as serious or spunky as you like in these few paragraphs. Let people know who you are. You can list anything from awards and work history to your astrological sign. This is entirely based on what rings true to you and how you'd like your business personality to come across to potential clients. Check out how other CGs in your field handle the Bio sections of their websites. Depending on the type of creative service you offer, clients may also want to see your professional résumé.

Your Work: Here's where you provide a web portfolio of your creative product, service, or talent. This can be pictures of your design work or samples of your music.

Sara Mann is the singer/songwriter we met in Chapter 6. She recently released an album and tours with Miley Cyrus. Her website, www.saramann.com, showcases her talent—samples of songs and vocals—along with her bio, recent news, press, contact information, and a fabulously well-written blog about her life as a singer. She includes stories about her own songwriting and stories about singing backup for Miley Cyrus and Billy Ray Cyrus. It's a great example of a site that's both personal and professional. Sara told me, "My voice is my calling card. With a website, a producer or casting director can listen to my music from

a studio halfway across the world."

In Sara's case, she needed a designer who could post videos and demo tracks of her vocals. Be sure that the web designer you choose knows how to provide what you need to showcase your goods.

Press: Scan items of publicity you've received, and continue to update this page as you make your way to creative superstar status. With online press, it's best to create a hard copy to upload onto your site, instead of linking to blogs and interviews as those links tend to eventually expire.

What Other People Say About You: Depending on your work, you may want to include testimonials. Especially if you're short on sample work, having clients write short blurbs about your business can be helpful. For some creative services, it's harder to display samples of work on a website; the work may be copyrighted or a client may feel uncomfortable having you post the work on your site. In this case, client testimonials are key. Regarding her work as a ghostwriter and editorial consultant, CG-in-action Philana Marie Boles says, "Endorsements from past customers are one of the most powerful ways to strengthen your credibility and ensure steady growth. The roadblock, in most new business ventures, is that you are a complete stranger to the person you want to do a great job for. People want to feel they can trust the person to whom they are giving their hard earned money. The toughest sale should only be your first one. After that, you should be equipped with written proof from others that you've got the skills to accomplish the goal. When asking your customer for testimonials, you can use standard forms, or ask your client to send you a sentence or two summarizing their experience with you. If the feedback is negative it may help you better conduct yourself during your next experience. If it is positive, though, it just may help you acquire your next experience."

Contact Info: I wouldn't put your home address here, either. A business phone number and an email address will do (and not hotpants@yahoo, please). Keep it professional. Your best bet is YourName@Your WebsiteAddress.com

Extras: If you sell your wares through retailers, a store locator is helpful. Include a list of shops and their telephone numbers. If you'd like to send customers email updates with newsworthy items, provide a place for them to sign up for your mailing list.

Protect Your Work: Copyrights, Trademarks, and Patents

On each page of your website or any creative work you do, add the copyright symbol, ©, along with your name and the year you created the work. As soon as you create something, you own the copyright. But placing this symbol underscores your copyright and can help keep imitators at bay. Clear and concise answers to copyright questions can be found at www.copyright.gov. Find information about trademarks and patents at www.uspto.gov.

A general differentiation between the three goes like this: a copyright protects original works of which you're the author, like a drawing, folk song, or short story. A copyright gives you the exclusive right to perform, display or distribute your work. Ideas are not copyrightable, but the way you execute and present them is. A patent protects a discovery or an invention and provides the exclusive right to create, use, or sell a product or process. A trademark protects words (like your company name), symbols, and designs (like logos) that identify the creator of the goods or services. You'll want to consider a trademark if your name is a big part of your brand identity. If you don't trademark your company's name, someone else can decide to up and use it.

Who's the Boss?

If you're opening a creative business and employing other CGs, remember all of things you wanted as someone else's employee. Be self-aware and catch yourself when, as a boss, you repeat the crummy behavior your old boss did while you fumed in your cubicle. Your fellow CGs crave a partnership relationship; no one flourishes in a top-down hierarchy. If you want to create a successful creative business, encourage every employee's creativity and leadership qualities. Empower those you employ.

A good company is founded on solid values: love, honesty, integrity. As you build your company, you're building a direct representation of your character. Keep this in mind when you become someone else's boss. A boss can be a teacher, guide, and

❋ CREATIVE TIP ❋

Spectrum of Rights

If you want to keep your copyright but allow the public to copy and distribute your work—while still crediting you—check out the licenses provide at www.creativecommons.org. Debra, lead singer/guitarist of the rock band DEVI, explains, "My band got a Creative Commons BY-NC-SA license that allows people to use the music from our album, *Get Free*, for their own creations as long as they attribute the music to us (BY), do not sell it (NC-non commercial) and allow other people to use their creations in the same fashion (SA-share alike.) This is to our band's benefit because it will expose more people to the album."

Nine Inch Nails frontman Trent Reznor made waves in the music industry when he used a CC license to release Grammy nominated *Ghosts I-IV*. Google and Wikipedia use these licenses as well.

Now That You've Set Up Shop, Venture Outside of It: Proactive Networking

If you skipped over the networking section in Chapter 8, refer back to it now. It's absolutely imperative that you network with other freelancers and business owners; they'll be one of your biggest sources of guidance and referrals. Especially if you're just getting started, your rate may be lower than theirs, and the next time a gig comes their way that doesn't pay their full rate, they can pass it along to you. If they're overbooked, they'll do the same. You'll hear about jobs to which you otherwise wouldn't have had access.

Freelancers in all fields have their own distinct specialties, so if a job comes around for someone with your specific qualifications, your freelance contacts will pass them your way. This kind of networking makes everyone look good. Last month, my agent called me about a television spot looking for a jeweler who solders metals. I don't have these qualifications—the safety goggles are ungainly and the fire scares me—so I passed along the information for a CG I knew with the proper metalworking skills. This is how freelancing and business networking works all the time. Think about it: if you were a hiring manager, and a freelancer couldn't fit your job into her schedule, would you rather sort through 60 new résumés or ask that freelancer if she knows someone else right for the gig?

Get out there, meet people, and soak up the warm fuzzies when it's your time to return the referral favor. Check out www.entrepreneur.meetup.com to find networking groups in your neck of the woods.

In addition to meeting new freelancers and entrepreneurs, it's important to open your mouth and tell everyone you already know—your aunts, cousins, friends, babysitter, former coworkers and bosses, alumni network, volunteer or religious organizations—about your new life as a self-employed CG. It's highly likely that someone in your current network will introduce you to your next client.

Befriend local business owners and think up creative ways to work together. D.J. Clarissa Steed approached a neighborhood boutique and offered to D.J. a shopping event for a reduced fee as long as she could leave her business card on the table for interested party-goers.

Do some recon and find out whether CGs in your field work through creative agencies. If so, search for contacts within your network to get you in the door. Cold call and write cover letters following the same advice in Chapter 8.

If You Can't Afford Creative Staff, Hire an Intern

They're optimistic, idealistic, and creative. They'll work for college credit. The beauty of hiring an intern is the chance you have to mentor a young woman. And I bet you'll find her gumption and creativity will inspire you, too. Approach collegiate programs in your area to find an intern for your business. The college's career center is a good place to start.

source of encouragement. Be all of these things and more for the people you employ. Your own humility and ability to learn from others will allow you to grow and evolve.

One new boss told me, "Without a doubt, managing a creative staff—with their egos and personalities—has been the biggest challenge of owning a business. Sometimes, I feel as though I've just birthed fourteen children—I'm part mother and part therapist."

If you're having a hard time stepping into your new role as the boss, check out Caitlin Friedman and Kimberly Yorio's book, *The Girl's Guide to Being a Boss (Without Being a Bitch)*.

Can I Get Some Service?

My dad owns a golf course in upstate New York. When I started my jewelry business, he told me, "Realize that every small business is in the service industry, and you'll be just fine."

Great customer service makes for happy clients, and happy clients make for a successful business. Start at the very first point of contact. When a customer enters your place of business or calls your business phone, how is he or she greeted? Whether it's by you, a receptionist, a salesgirl, a barista, or a bartender, what general feeling does a customer get when first contacting your business? Boutique owner Kerrilyn Pamer says, "I choose salespeople who are kind, helpful, and never pushy. They have to understand the clothing and be knowledgeable about designers, but more importantly, they have to make the store a welcoming place where customers want to shop."

Think about the way we talk about or recommend small businesses to each other. We love a local coffee shop because the owners are interesting and kind and we walk a block out of the way to drink their coffee instead of stopping at a large coffee chain. We love a restaurant because the food's great but the service is better. We love our hairdresser and think she's just the coolest CG and we wouldn't go to anyone else. Do we actually think no one else can cut our hair? No. We go because we feel loyalty and have formed a professional friendship. Forming a relationship with your customers will keep them coming back. Newcomers are great, too, but you want to ensure that new customers become returning customers. Growing and maintaining a customer base is how you'll keep your business moving forward. The only way to do this is with a solid service or product, and excellent customer service.

Businesses spend many hard-earned dollars advertising. But when it comes down to it, customer service creates the face of your business. Put your best face forward.

Customer Service Tips for CGs

Manage Expectations: Remain realistic about what you can deliver and the timeframe in which you can deliver it. If you think you can edit a manuscript, build a website, or have a dozen organic soaps ready in ten days, tell the customer two weeks. Don't fall into the trap of setting expectations you can't meet because you think it will somehow motivate you to work harder.

If, even after your greatest effort, you find yourself unable to meet a deadline, contact your client immediately. Don't avoid emails or save the bad news for the morning of your deadline. Your straightforwardness will make an awkward situation less problematic for your client.

Treat Your Customer as a Partner in Your Creative Process: Sure, you know more about your industry and business than your customer. But make the experience a collaborative partnership. Make her feel at ease and able to ask questions and express opinions. When I create a piece of jewelry for a client, I make sure I know exactly what she envisions and encourage her input. I don't just assume my ideas are the best ones because I'm the designer and she's the customer. The more comfortable your customer is with the creative process, the more likely he or she is to come back with more business or recommend you to his or her network.

Insider Deals: People feel special when you treat them like an insider. Boutique owner Stacia Valle keeps a select list of customers who profess themselves to be fans of certain designers she carries. When a shipment of clothing arrives at her boutique, Stacia calls the customers on the designer's fan list and offers a 10 percent discount. Without fail, the customers flock to the store, excited to be the first ones to know about an inside deal.

Gifts: You may want to send tokens of appreciation—good old fashion presents—to clients who bring you serious revenue. You can choose a traditional gifting day—their birthday or the holidays—or, a day that marks a significant event for your business partnership. If you wrote the press release for a restaurant's opening or helped launch a new product, you could send the owner a gift on her one-year-anniversary of being in business.

If doable, it's smart to send holiday cards to everyone you've done business with each year. Boutique owner Kerrilyn Pamer keeps track of her customers' birthdays and sends a 10 percent off coupon each year, good for the entire month of their birthday.

Be Responsive: The amount of work client communication creates can be overwhelming for new business owners. You do need to stay on top of phone calls and emails. Always return messages within 48 hours. When you let too much time lapse, you come off as either above-it-all, inconsiderate, or incompetent.

Stay in Touch: To encourage repeat business, check in with your clients every few months. Toe the line between pushy and helpful. A casual, "I really enjoyed working with you on X project, do let me know if you'd like help in the future," every three months is okay. Writing weekly and inquiring about work will annoy any client, even one who adores you and your work.

Hire Wisely: No more bored or too-cool-for-school employees. Unless you're running a dominatrix business, your employees should be polite and helpful. Remember, they're the face of your business. Check out *(Great) Employees Only: How Gifted Bosses Hire and De-Hire Their Way to Success by Dale Dauten.*

Conduct Yourself Like a Pro

Always remain professional in a disagreement with a client. It's business. There's no room to get hysterical. Keep your voice calm and use reason to sort out the matter. Take the blame and apologize if it's your fault. There will be times when a client is completely in the wrong. Like the time a customer tried to return a top with sweat stains to Stacia Valle's boutique. The customer bought the top the morning of New Year's Eve, and tried to return it with said stains and reeking of cigarettes on January 2nd. You know when someone is trying to take you for a ride. Stand firm. But if the lines are blurry, see what you can do to resolve the matter with kindness and a level head.

Stay clear of disclosing too much information with your clients. It's okay to let people in on your personal life to a certain degree—the new world of creative business means many of you will form relationships with your customers. It can be tempting to share the dirty details of your breakup. Don't do it. And *definitely* do not gripe about any aspect of your business to your clients.

The same goes for your staff. You're going to employ some seriously great people. You'll have laughs together, create great work together, and bond. But make sure there's a line you don't cross. Confide your deepest, darkest secrets to your best friends, not your employees.

And speaking of your best friends, don't hire them. It's one thing—though still sticky—to go into business with your college roommate. You'll still have to learn to keep your working environment professional. But employing a friend creates a boss/employee dynamic your friendship isn't accustomed to and may not be able to handle. Support her while she continues her job search and let her know your friendship is too important to jeopardize.

Finally, tame your inner Luddite and get up-to-date with technology. If art portfolios are being teleported by some sort of crazy iPhone app by the time this book hits shelves, get on board. Becoming tech-savvy is part of conducting yourself like the pro you really are.

CHAPTER 15

Too Legit
to Quit

*Small business licenses, insurance,
and paying Uncle Sam and Aunt Retirement*

Mind Your Own Business

The IRS defines a business as anything you do that makes a profit. Guess what that means? If you've made twenty dollars off a sale of a hand-knit scarf, you're officially a business in their eyes. Check out sba.gov and http://www.business.gov/register/licenses-and-permits/to investigate your individual business license requirements. If you'll be charging sales tax, you'll need a sales tax license (also called a certificate of resale). Check with your local government office to find out your state's regulations and instructions for obtaining these licenses.

To be extra safe, check out zoning regulations. Depending on what type of business you run, you may need a health permit (especially if there's food or bodily contact involved), a sign permit, and a fire department permit.

Doing Business As (DBA)

Any time you operate under a business name other than your own legal name, you need to file a DBA. You can operate under Jane Doe without filing, but if you choose Doe Designs, you're required to file a DBA. Do this before you apply for your business license or start working on your company logo to make sure the name isn't already in use.

Check out http://www.business.gov/register/business-name/dba.html to find out about your state's regulations regarding registering.

Open a Business Account

This is the easiest way to keep track of your finances as a small business owner, freelancer, or all around self-employed-wonder-girl. Almost all major banks will allow you to set up a small business checking account free of charge. This account should be separate from your personal checking and savings accounts and will have its own debit or credit card. Use this card for all business expenses and deposit all income into this account. On April 14 when you're scrambling to finish your tax return, this will make matters much easier. You won't be trying to remember which purchases you made from your personal account were actually business expenses. When you see that eighty-dollar charge on your Amex for a karaoke bar, your memory will be jogged about the night you took those non-English speaking Japanese buyers out to dinner. The evening was a little fuzzy after all of those sake bombs. (Was that you onstage belting out Marvin Gaye's "Let's Get It On"?) Miraculously, the buyers ordered your entire spring collection. The dinner is deductible. Ibuprofen tablets for your sake hangover are not.

Don't Piss Off the IRS

On the majority of creative career paths (even for those employed by someone else) there will likely be some self-employment or independent contractor work. If you're employed as a music director at a performing arts program, you still may teach a few private voice lessons on the side for extra money.

Don't blow off the IRS with an idea like: "I'm just conducting a few extra hours of business in addition to my full-time creative job. And I already pay taxes there. So what's a few commissioned paintings on the side? Who'll ever find out?" The IRS, that's who. Don't even think about it, CG.

Register your business and file taxes.

Paying Taxes: Get Thee to an Accountant

You absolutely, positively need an accountant if you are self-employed. I pay mine $360 to do my small-business taxes at the end of the year, and it's the best $360 I spend. Finding an accountant who deals with self-employed CGs like you will assuage your headaches and answer your individual tax questions: like, "Do I *really* have to pay quarterly taxes?" There are so many unique situations with small business and freelancers that the best advice I can give you (besides getting an accountant) is to put aside the appropriate percent of every dollar you earn for Uncle Sam right as you earn it. I know it's painful, and if it's too tempting sitting in your bank account, create a separate bank account for tax money and freeze the debit card.

An accountant can answer your questions about everything from payroll taxes for your employees to what expenses are tax deductible. It can be thrilling to realize your monthly *Vogue* is a tax write-off, but even the most excitable creative girl must refrain from getting carried away with what she claims as a business expense. As a jewelry designer, it's tempting to write off manicures because making jewelry makes my nails look shabby, but unless you want to raise governmental red flags, you'll have to be reasonable.

Don't fret: your trusty accountant will show you the way. Ask your self-employed and small-business-owning pals for recommendations. Find an accountant with plenty of experience dealing with businesses like yours. You can also check out www.AccountantsWorld.com or www.CPADirectory.com.

❊ CREATIVE TIP ❊

Can I Write This Off?

To get clear on what you can claim as business expenses on your tax return, go to www.irs.gov and search "Schedule C." Part II of this form lists the expenses considered a-okay for sole proprietors to write off.

Retirement Planning

Once you start making money, you need to start putting money away for retirement. Now, before you slam this book shut, visualize your little old lady self (I like to picture myself as a dark haired version of Rose from the *Golden Girls*) sitting by the pool and sipping a martini. Don't let your Golden Girl self down. Talk to a financial planner. Saving for retirement is easier than you think.

Individual Retirement Account (IRA)

IRAs are available at many banks and very easy to set up. There are eleven types of IRAs, but for most creative types and entrepreneurs, a traditional IRA, Roth IRA, or a SEP-IRA is sufficient.

At present, you can invest up to $5,000 tax-deductible per year into a traditional IRA. I know you'd rather go on vacation with this amount, but remember that retirement planning is one of the best ways to invest tax-free income into your future. You get to save what you would have paid to the government in tax dollars, and this money will earn interest that compounds. When you do go to take your money out (which you can do without penalties as

✺ CREATIVE TIP ✺

Keoghs

If you're overflowing with extra income, ask your financial planner if a Keogh retirement plan is right for you. Keoghs are the Chanel gown of retirement planning for self-employed workers and small businesses—a way to provide a pension for you and your employees if you are highly compensated—and they present a great savings opportunity.

soon as you blow out the candles on your 59 ½ birthday cake) you'll most likely be in a lower tax bracket. In other words, Golden Girl, you'll pay far less in tax dollars than you would have in your thirties.

You qualify for an IRA as long as you aren't involved in any other tax-deferred retirement plans.

With a Roth-IRA, your yearly contribution is taxed, and there's no taxation when you go to take your money out after retirement. There are also fewer withdrawal restrictions. Check with an accountant or financial planner to determine which setup is right for your situation.

Simplified Employee Pension Plans/ Individual Retirement Accounts (SEP-IRAs)

SEP-IRAs are the next level of retirement planning as far as the amount you can save. Currently, SEP-IRAs allow you to contribute up to 25 percent of your income, or a yearly amount not exceeding $49,000. The big difference between traditional IRAs and SEP-IRAs (besides the amount you can contribute) is that if you have employees working for your business, SEP-IRAs require you to set up and contribute to employee retirement accounts.

Business Insurance

If you open up shop and Suzy Tourist trips over your Zen rock garden, you need to make sure your butt is covered. Talk to a legal advisor. Business liability insurance protects your business if a customer hurts herself at your place of work or sustains an injury from one of your products.

If you're freelancing or run your business from home and business liability insurance sounds like overkill, do some research on what other freelancers in your line of work have for coverage. Graphic designers and writers may have an Errors and Omissions Policy for mistakes made—like writing a 10,000 copy press release that omitted the launch date of a new product and requires another printing run.

Home-business insurance can be a life-saver if your home stores valuable work equipment. Your homeowners insurance won't cover everything. Anything from a burglar to a pipe bursting could set you back thousands of dollars. You'll also want to look into property/casualty insurance for coverage from fire, flood, and other dangers.

If you have employees, check out worker's compensation.

Disability Insurance

If you're working for yourself, what will happen to your income if something happens to you? In the unforeseen event that you're unable to work for months, this coverage can keep you from losing your shirt.

Health Insurance

You need it. I know it's expensive for self-employed CGs. But there's no easier way to wipe out your hard-earned cash than wiping out on a crooked sidewalk slab and breaking your leg. If you suffer an injury or unforeseen illness, your hospital bills could take years to pay off—or worse—put you out of business permanently.

Check out the health insurance supplied by national organizations like mediabistro.com and the freelancers union. You can find your state's health plan choices at www.ahirc.org.

CHAPTER 16

The ~~Starving~~ Thriving Artist

*Pricing creativity and
getting your product into stores*

Let's get over this idea of the starving artist.

If you want to survive in the creative world, you have to see yourself as both an artist and a businesswoman. As inspired as I am by the musical *RENT*, when I hear the ensemble belt the title track, there's a little part of me that thinks, "What do you mean you're *not gonna pay rent?*" Everybody has to pay rent. If your creative talent is such that you can offer something valuable, you're going to be able to afford your rent and the down payment on your first home.

Making your living in the arts is the best way to show the world—and the younger gen-eration of artists—that creative people have an integral place in our society. Making money certainly doesn't need to be the first priority for you and your creative career. If money was my first priority, I would have chosen a field that had a step-by-step path to making a six-figure salary instead of trying to get there making jewelry on my coffee table. But like it or not, being financially solvent is a valued part of any successful career, creative or otherwise.

Almost as damaging as the romanticism of art and madness is the romanticized cliché of art and poverty. Financial security means you have less worry, which allows you to spend more time peacefully creating. And here's the great news, if you start making way too much money with your rock star creative talent, there are many, many charities that will gladly relieve you of your burden.

The world is ready for creative types more than ever before, so let's figure out how this impacts you.

Art and Commerce

There will be jobs you take to pay the bills. Sometimes, I design jewelry for bridal parties. Do you think I'm artistically inspired by designing ten of the same necklaces to match the pea green sash on an orange taffeta dress? Not likely. But here's the trade-off: I don't get paid for my editorial work. Meaning, when you visit my website and see a necklace dangling between Beyoncé's cleavage in a three-page shoot for *Elle* magazine, I didn't make squat off that. The full page shot of Miley Cyrus wearing one of my pieces got me a ton of street cred with my younger cousins, but cash? Think again. Of course, editorial work attracts potential buyers and boutique orders (essentially it's free advertising), but I've had plenty of magazine press that resulted in zero cash reward. (Calls from excited relatives: priceless.)

Some high-profile gigs, like chiming in my two cents on Sarah Palin's eyewear choice on *Good Morning America* or showing how to design a jewelry piece on The Oxygen Network, also pay zero dollars. But they're great exposure and good for beefing up my résumé. I balance the free gigs by hosting the monthly television show on The Home Shopping Network that pays brilliantly. I have to haul to Tampa to film it, but I love doing the show *and* it pays my bills.

Bottom line: you have to pay attention to and pursue what's sellable about your creativity if you want to make a living. You'll balance more commercial jobs (your personal version of bridesmaid's jewelry) with the ones that fulfill you artistically. And of course, someday you may choose all of your own projects and do exactly what you want to do. But let's get real about what making your living means: your creativity-as-business means you need to treat it as such.

Let's get to it.

Pricing Your Creativity

Pricing is tricky. You'll have to experiment to find what works best for you. Just keep in mind that if you don't make a profit doing what you love, then you don't have a career, you have a hobby. Hobbies are wonderful, but if you want a career, you'll have to charge accordingly.

Creative Mogulista

CG-in-action Shelly Sabel is a lighting designer who specializes in sculptural lighting for retail and domestic spaces. Her clients include Ralph Lauren, Diane von Furstenberg and Levi's. Shelly teaches a course called, "How to Succeed: Prostituting Yourself Without Becoming a Whore," geared to NYU theatrical design students. She says, "The biggest problem my students have is understanding how to charge for their creative services. Without fail, they underestimate their worth. I teach them to empower themselves by remembering that though it's art, they're doing a job for people. If what you're doing is particular and specialized, and you're good at it, you should charge accordingly."

After this chapter, CG, you'll be ready to get down and dirty with your inner mogulista.

Your market, your level of experience, the cost of goods sold (we'll define this further in the next section), your pricing strategy and the perceived value of your product or service determine your pricing. For our purposes, we'll divide the pricing conversation into pricing for services (like web design, writing, yoga lessons, or coaching) and pricing for a creative product.

Coming Up with an Hourly Rate for Your Service

Hourly rates vary wildly in creative professions. Are you a beginner, intermediate, or high-profile and in-demand creative talent? Your first step is to research what professionals with comparable experience, products, or services are charging. CGs like you don't keep their rates secret; it's information available just by asking or visiting their website. A violin teacher told me, "It was simple. I spent one day thumbing through the Yellow Pages and called every single violin teacher listed in my hometown. I asked each about her training and her experience in addition to her pricing. I found that I had more experience than most—I studied at Julliard and performed professionally. So I priced my services twenty percent higher than the average price for local violin teachers."

When coming up with your hourly rate, don't fall into the trap of multiplying a rate by forty hours to come up with a weekly salary—as a self-employed CG, it's nearly impossible to make forty hours a week *billable* hours. Especially during the first few years, you'll spend many hours marketing to clients, making phone calls, and searching for work—none of which are paid.

You can also try working backward to come up with an hourly rate. First, go back to your business plan and add your start-up and first-year business costs to your yearly living expenses (refer back to Chapter 9 for a refresher in tallying living expenses). Once you have an estimate, what will you need to earn above your living and working expenses to feel you've had a successful first year? What number do you realistically think you can earn your first year in business? Don't forget to deduct at least 30 percent of your profit to pay your taxes.

Once you have a financial goal for your first year of business, estimate the number of hours you think you'll work that year. Remember to account for vacation weeks and the fact that you just won't work every day during your first year as a freelancer. Say you work forty-five weeks per year.

And let's estimate that during that first year, you're really only able to bill twenty hours per week. (The rest of the time will be spent hunting down clients, marketing, etc.) That means you'll be working about 900 hours that first year. Now, say you'd like to earn $60,000 during your first year to cover your business and personal budget. Divide $60,000 by 900 and your hourly rate becomes $67.00. Let's round that number to $70.00

If you balk at a rate like $70 per hour and think, "I couldn't possibly charge that much," realize that as a self-employed CG, no one is covering your health insurance, sick time, business expenses, or retirement fund. Now the question is: can you get it?

Check in with the research you did on similar CGs in your market. Is the hourly number you came up with a comparable rate for freelancers with your qualifications? Check out pricing structures. Do they charge per project, or by the hour?

If you choose to charge per project, be wary of blurting out a number when a potential client asks about your project rate. Find out exactly what kind of work and time commitment the project entails. When you've ascertained the amount of hours you think the project will take (including every single thing from initial brainstorming phone chats to the trip to the post office to mail the final product) multiply that number by your hourly rate. Pad that number by 15 percent so you're covered if your original estimate didn't account for

Get on the Same Page as Your Client

It's vital to communicate what your price involves. Confusion arises when you quote a price to a client without explaining what specific services your rate includes. If you write a press release for a company, be clear whether a third round of edits is included in your initial price. If not, a job that seemed like reasonable money per hour dwindles when a client has demands you didn't foresee or discuss.

a high-maintenance client with unforeseen demands. It's up to you whether you want to add an additional percentage onto that amount so you have wiggle room if the client wants to negotiate. As you begin to work per project, check out myhours.com or toggl.com for a free time management and time tracking solution. You'll be able to track how many hours you're spending on each project and have a better grasp on what you're making per hour. If you see that a $1,000 freelance project took ninety hours to complete, you'll likely raise your project rates or work significantly faster.

If you're unsure about your pricing, get support from other freelancers and small business owners. Let your colleagues weigh in on the pricing structure you've created. Check out www.freelanceswitch.com for help calculating rates and expenses.

As you work with clients, get their feed-back on your pricing. Ask them, "What would you like to accomplish together so that you feel your money was well spent?"

Pricing a Product

Pricing a product takes into account your cost of goods sold, overhead, inventory management costs, your market and pricing strategy, and profit margins. This is a very detailed and complex process. We'll have a general conversation about pricing a product, but I urge you to check out www.toolkit.com and www.entrepreneur. com, (search "pricing your product" on both sites). Also search "pricing strategies" on Wikipedia.org and Netmba.com. Here's why: setting a price often has more to do with what kind of business you're looking to start. If you're a jeweler looking to sell

---

✻ CREATIVE TIP ✻

Get it in Writing

There are many different creative contracts out there and not all are created equal. Know your rights. Check out www.keepyourcopyrights.org. This site provides sample contracts (the good, the bad, and the ugly) and detailed, need-to-know information for all kinds of creative contracts.

mass quantities, your profit margin per unit will be less than a jewelry designer looking to create a feeling of exclusivity and high fashion. So you'll need to research this topic further depending on what type of creative business you're establishing.

First, let's take into account your cost of goods sold. As the creator of a product, the cost of goods sold is the amount it costs you in raw materials to make your product and the direct labor cost. (A direct labor cost can be paying yourself or an employee twenty dollars an hour to create the product, *not* the cost of time spent soliciting sales or drumming up publicity.) A *very* general pricing formula is to double your cost of goods sold to get your wholesale price. Multiply that price by 2.2 to come up with a retail price. This means, at the *very* least, your retail price should be four times the amount of your cost of goods sold (see more on wholesale and retail pricing in the next section).

How long will it take you to make each unit of your product? (A unit can mean one individual handbag or one bar of soap.) You'll likely fall anywhere between a mass-manufacturing plant in China and an artist who labors weeks over an original painting. Knowing how long it takes to make each unit and the cost of materials means that you can

start to play around with sales projections and profit margins. Your profit margin is the difference between the price you sell your product and your cost of goods sold. A sales projection is as simple as how many items you think you'll sell in a given timeframe. Your gross sales is the total dollar amount you make in that given timeframe (say you sell 20 handbags for $200.00 dollars each, your gross sales is $4,000). Your profit on sales is your profit margin multiplied by the number of units you've sold.

Test your pricing: multiple the profit margin per unit by the amount of units you think you'll sell that first year and see where you stand financially.

In my experience, as important as any formula, is to refer back to your research and see if that pricing is congruent with your market. Whether you sell tea cozies, jewelry, or greeting cards, you need to do some research to find out how products like yours are priced. It's crucial to know what your market will bear in terms of pricing. Who's creating a product similar to yours and what are they charging? Research your market through magazines, websites, retail stores, and craft fairs. Attending trade shows is a great way to see what else is out there, and what kind of pricing structures your competition utilizes.

Wholesale and Retail Pricing

If you plan to sell your product through retail shops or online vendors, you'll sell to these buyers at a wholesale price. Under normal circumstances, the retailer takes that wholesale price and marks it up by at least 100 percent. Generally, to derive a retail price from a wholesale price, multiply your wholesale price by 2.2. The number can vary by vendor and location.

Your retail price must be high enough that when divided by 2.2, it covers your cost of materials and still provides you with your goal profit margin. This pricing information is important for you to understand even if you're currently only selling your product from your home-based business or your own retail shop or website. As you and your product line gain visibility, it's very likely that another store will want to carry your wares. Increasing your vendors is how you'll grow your business.

Say your hand-blown glass vases sell for $395. When you sell your first order to Barneys, you'll wholesale to the store at around $175 so that Barneys can mark the vases up to the $395 retail price.

Make sure you have your wholesale and retail pricing structure in place before Saks Fifth Avenue comes calling. If your current website advertises your felt hats for $88 and a store decides to place an order, you'll piss them off by realizing too late that the hats need to be marked up to $195 so that you can take home $88. The store won't want to anger customers who may have previously seen your product retailing for $88.

❄ CREATIVE TIP ❄

Perceived Value

Pricing your product creates a perceived value. Of course, you have to have the product to back it up. You can't use fake fabric and price it like cashmere. But understand that pricing creates prestige. If you're making something incredible, your pricing should reflect this. You shouldn't be trying to compete with retail prices at Urban Outfitters if you're making everything by hand.

Shopkeepers

If you're the storeowner and you're selling products by other artists, you'll be the one marking up the product's price from wholesale to retail. You'll likely markup the goods by multiplying the wholesale price by a number anywhere from 2 to 2.8 depending on the cost it took you to get the product to your shop. If it's a local designer who dropped the goods off on her walk to class, you may choose to multiply by 2. If it's a Japanese designer and you were charged some serious customs tax and shipping fees, you might multiply by 2.8. Of course, you need to check out other stores who carry your designers and make sure your products are priced similarly.

For this same reason, be prudent about dropping your prices for a sale. If you've just sold to bigtimeonlineretailer.com, you don't want to send out a promotion for a sale on the same items through your website. Of course, if you're creating new lines every season, end-of-season sales are fair game. Just make sure your vendors have ample time to sell your wares at full price. Shoppers get very angry when they see a product they've just bought elsewhere now discounted 50 percent.

You're Ready to Get Your Product into Stores

Before we get into price negotiations, let's take a detour into the world of retail. Now that you've got your pricing structure down, you're ready to approach stores.

Besides local shops in your neighborhood or cities you've personally explored, the best way to find stores for your product is to scour magazines and search the Web. You can also scope out the retail stores listed on websites of CGs who design a product like yours. You're looking for an aesthetic, so check out pictures of the shop's interior and the product lines it carries. You're searching for a store where your product will compliment—not mimic—the merchandise. There can be a few similar designers, but if there are six or seven designers that make you wonder if you were separated at birth, move on.

Your retail price should be within the store's range. Don't waste your time approaching a shop where retail prices are under $100 if your goods retail at $250. The prospect of having your product in stores is thrilling, but do respect your time and the buyer's time by doing as much research as you can to ensure your product is a potential fit.

If you start locally, do not, under any circumstance, trot into your dream boutique with your wares or introduce yourself as a new business owner who'd like to sell your product at said boutique. You will look like an amateur. Instead, call any shop you're interested in selling to, introduce yourself, and ask for the name of the buyer. If you have a catalog and line sheets, tell him or her that you'll be sending these materials along for consideration.

If you don't have a catalog or line sheets yet, ask for the buyer's email address and send a link to your website. You don't need to send samples. Unsolicited samples can be annoying—if a buyer has no interest in

Catalogs, Lookbooks and Line Sheets

A catalog typically refers to the book of product photos (including the size, color options, style numbers and price) that you send to customers. There's crossover, but lookbooks generally refer to images of a collection sent to editors, storeowners and others within your industry. When it's time for you to construct yours, research photographers, stylists, and production studios in your area. Get creative to save money: scout locations that are free to shoot product images and capture the mood and feel of your product.

A line sheet generally contains sketches of your product, and includes the materials used in construction, item numbers, and wholesale or suggested retail price of your product.

carrying your line, he or she may feel obligated to mail the samples back to you.

If possible, strike your dream stores when you've got company news. Maybe your product was featured on a sitcom or just received a hot piece of press. Or perhaps you've expanded your product line to include candles and you're throwing a launch party.

If you don't hear back within a month, follow up by email. You can continue to follow up until you hear something, whether that's a *no, thank you,* or a *let's set up an appointment.*

When a store calls you in for an appointment or arranges a phone chat, they're already interested in carrying your product. So don't feel as though you have to impress them by making sure they know every reason why it's the best thing out there. This part is less hard-core-sales-pitch and more first-date-getting-to-know-you.

The buyer will ask if you have an order minimum. An order minimum is set by you and is the minimum dollar amount (or per item amount) required for a store to be able to place an order for your product (usually, anywhere between $1,000 and $3,000). I'd advise against implementing an order minimum if you're just starting out. If you choose to set one, keep it low (less than

$500.) Small boutiques may not have the budget for a bigger order. Other retailers may want to try out a few of your products to make sure their customers respond well before placing a large order.

A buyer may have advice on your product line. Take it in stride. She may request that you change a specific detail for her order. If you're flexible and it feels authentic to make the change, go for it.

Bring any relevant paperwork to your meeting, including order forms and line sheets. An order form should include your company name, a space for the name and contact information of the company placing the order, the purchase order number, goods ordered, and payment terms. If you like, you can combine the order form and line sheets into one cohesive document.

While placing an order, a buyer will ask about your lead time. He or she is asking how long it will take you to complete the order and ship. A lead time of two to six weeks is normal.

Bring your product in a professional carrying case. At my first appointment at a chi-chi boutique, my cheap-o jewelry display case broke and my pieces spilled out across the counter. Not exactly the first impression I was looking to make.

Payment Structure:
Consignment, COD and Net 30

When you're first starting out, you may approach a tiny boutique in your neighborhood to sell your handmade wallets, journals, or greeting cards. Often, the boutique's owner will offer to take on a few of your creations on consignment.

Payment on consignment means that you get paid when your product sells. Consignment is also the likely payment structure for an artist or sculptor who sells work through a gallery.

A word to the wise: stay on top of your vendors. Get a signed invoice when you leave merchandise. Do not be so thrilled to sell to your first shop that you coo, "Oh, just call me when it sells!" I'm not teasing you; I say this because it's exactly what I did in the second boutique to which I sold. I was really excited to have a hip boutique sell my jewelry and the owner was lovely so I figured it was kind of like the honor system. It wasn't. Years later, she still owes me $700.

Leave an invoice with both yours and the owner's signature at the store, and keep one for your records. Have a written agreement outlining when you get paid. Try for a monthly

❋ CREATIVE TIP ❋

Mark Your Territory

Know that within a city, shops get territorial over their product lines. It's not okay to sell similar products to shops within the same neighborhood. And it's your responsibility to know what shops are within competing distance (don't wait until the buyer walks past a neighboring store and see the same bracelets she ordered twined around a mannequin's wrist). You can print out a map of the city, or you can ask the buyers directly whether it's okay for you to retail to the same-city shop you're considering.

Invoice Like You Mean It

Your invoices should look professional, but don't agonize over making a fancy spreadsheet unless Excel documents are your thing. Include the date, your company's name and mailing address. Include the total to be paid, the terms of payment on which you've agreed and when payment is due. If the buyer supplied a purchase order number, include that at the top.

Include an invoice number. I won't tell anyone if you start numbering at 101. (I did.) Wherever you start, continue in sequence so you can easily keep track of your records.

agreement rather than quarterly. To be safe, ask for a list of designers the boutique currently carries on consignment. Call several of these designers for a reference to be sure the shop pays in a timely manner and takes good care of merchandise. When consigning your goods, many shops expect you to cover the shipping costs to get your product to their store.

You'll likely get to a point where you'll stop offering consignment as an option for payment. I don't offer consignment unless it's a very special exception, like a close friend opening a boutique who's tight on cash. But in the beginning, it can be a great way to find new shops. Once you've proven your product sells well or you've gotten great press, you're on your way to bigger stores who will pay upfront for your goods. Usually, to get paid upfront, you'll select COD—cash on delivery; the vendor gives a check to the delivery person, who then sends it to you. Or you may agree on Net 30—the vendor remits payment to you within 30 days of receiving goods. Sometimes, you won't have the choice of payment terms, especially when dealing with larger retailers who have their own accounting department. They may offer Net 60 or even Net 90. You'll have to choose whether or not to accept their terms.

Trade Shows

Check out the trade shows where CGs like you exhibit their products. In addition to being the perfect place to research your market in terms of pricing, trade shows are a great place to find vendors who sell supplies you need. When you're ready, you can pay a fee to exhibit at your chosen trade show to get yourself in front of vendors placing orders for their shops. The prestigious trade shows are pricey—usually around $5,000. But if 20 new vendors place orders for your handmade rugs, it will be well worth your cash.

Trade shows are also a great place to find overseas manufacturing if your business eventually needs this. Do visit the across-the-world plant to make sure it's legit and that you're not funding something unethical, like ten-year-olds stitching your swimsuit line in the tropics without air conditioning.

No Fear Tactics: Negotiate Like a Pro

If you're in an industry where negotiations are part of doing business, you'll have to get in touch with your inner tough-girl. But just like we talked about with salary negotiations, a negotiation is not an argument. For CGs, our work is closely related to who we are, and we can feel affronted when someone doesn't think our service or product is worth the price. Don't let things get personal.

Before negotiating price, you have to know the rock-bottom-drop-dead price you'll accept. First, set your desired price. This can usually be calculated by adding 30 to 40 percent on to your rock bottom price, but tweak the number until it feels right to you. When you've ascertained the base number, you can creatively negotiate with confidence, knowing you won't accept anything lower than your rock bottom price.

When negotiating, instead of immediately lowering your price, first try adding something to sweeten the deal. You can offer to do the project more quickly, or add an extra service onto the package. An artist could offer an original painting at full price and an additional print for no extra cost.

If you quote $3,800 and the client says she can't go higher than $2,500, but you still want the gig, you can say, "This is what I can do for $2,500," and trim a few particulars from the project. Maybe you'll submit three possible illustrations instead of five.

There will be limitations on both sides; your client will have a maximum amount she can spend and you will have a minimum amount you can accept. But in the most successful negotiations, both parties are able to communicate their positions and leave the negotiation feeling good about the outcome.

There are certain contracts—film, television, book—that are extremely detailed and you'll most likely need an agent to negotiate these for you.

On Your Way to Prada Prices

Depending on what creative industry you're in, there are massive price discrepancies. Sometimes, consumers simply decide a person, brand, or service is highly valuable. Of course there are other factors, like exclusivity and handmade work, limited editions, materials, etc. But painters use the exact same materials for oil on canvas and we've all seen the differences in their pricing.

It would be remiss not to mention that sometimes this elusive consumer love just happens and those artists, designers, actors, writers, chefs, and motivational speakers who receive it can charge more for their work. You'll know if your pricing is working by how your business is doing; if you're overflowing with clientele *and* you're making a comfortable profit without having to work sixty hours a week, then you're right on track. Unless you're a mass retailer, not everyone should be able to afford you. But if too many people are complaining about how pricey you are and not buying, you have to go back to the drawing board.

If your prices are fair and you're delivering excellent work, you're on your way. Do remember to give yourself a raise. Raising your hourly rate or product price by 5 percent per year is a general starting point.

Pricing and Negotiation Tips from a Pro

Tracy Weiss, my television agent extraordinaire, lends her expert guidance to CGs.

CG: Why do you think women in general have a harder time setting a price for their creative service or product?

TW: From a young age, many of us are taught that a lady never discusses money. We're taught that it's tacky, it's gauche, and it's not what nice girls do. But, in reality, it's not "nice" to ignore your expertise and contributions, rendering it impossible to make a living doing what you love. If you can create a service or product the world is screaming for, you should profit from it.

Tracy's tips:

1) **Do your homework. Before going into any negotiation, make sure you know what and with whom you're dealing.** Google-stalk the company and know the position of the person you're meeting with, along with specifics about the clients and projects. If you're a freelance writer, you should know the tone and scope of the magazine you're pitching. If you're in retail, you should know if your product would be a seamless fit on Barneys high-end shelves. You should know the going rate for the project you're discussing. Online research or past experiences can help you guide your quote. If the Public Theatre in Manhattan paid their costume designer X amount of dollars to design costumes, you know you can ask for a rate in the same range in the same city and same size production.

2) **Never fear the no.** "No" is a scary word for many people. But it's harmless. What is the worst possible thing that can happen by asking for something and getting shut down? We use "no" in the non-business world every day: "No, I would not like to go on a date to the Olive Garden."

3) **Don't act bitchy.** There's truth to the saying, "You catch more bees with honey." Don't walk into a negotiation acting aggressive or entitled. It's perfectly fine to stand up for yourself and state your case. However, if you're only focused on the win you won't really be listening to what the other person is saying. You'll miss out on an opportunity to turn a stalemate into a mutually beneficial partnership.

Always be sure to recognize concessions being made on your behalf. Zero in on the one or two points you really care about. The person you're dealing with will shut down very quickly if they don't think the two of you are on the same page. People who feel you're respectful of their position will want to give you a better deal.

4) **It's okay to ask questions.** If you're really stumped for a starting point, it's okay to ask, "What do you think is fair?" Just recognize that if someone is throwing a number your way, they're almost always going to come in low. If you're backed into a corner, do not start with your bottom line dollar amount. You have to be sure to give yourself some wiggle room.

Ask everything you can think of that's relevant to the job. It's imperative to know all of the details up front. As obvious as this sounds, the time spent on a project should directly affect how much money you're making. You'd be surprised how many people lock in a rate before finding out how many days they're working or how many words their article should be. When you have all the information you can get creative to make the deal sweeter for yourself. Will they reimburse you for travel costs? Can your name appear anywhere on signage or in the marketing materials?

5) **Make sure you know what you bring the table and do not sell yourself short.** Generally, *you* are the commodity. The contents of your brain as a consultant, the thoughtful restaurant reviews you write, or the hand mirrors you whimsically découpage… they are all *you*. So when discussing possible employment or a partnership, you'd be crazy not to work your strengths into the conversation. Select areas from your skill set and make sure they're mentioned. Discuss prior examples of success and apply them to the situation at hand. In my line of business, this is vital. Knowing you've already succeeded at the same sort of initiative will garner confidence and a higher price tag.

6) **Take some time to reflect.** When it looks like negotiations can't go any further, you're allowed to take a night to think over the final offer. Anyone who demands an answer on the spot isn't worth being in business with. So take time to mull it over or bounce it off your sounding board. It's possible you'll come up with a compromise that neither side saw while negotiating. Either way, be prepared with an answer after proposing your last ditch effort. No one likes to be strung along.

The more comfortable you get with putting a price tag on your creativity, the easier it will become. State your case and make sure to believe in yourself. Because if you don't believe what you're saying, no one will.

When It's Okay to Do a Few Freebies and Cheapies

Sometimes pricing is out of your control—budget restraints may make your regular rate impossible—and you need to make the decision whether or not to accept the price and the project. If you're just starting out in a creative field, you'll be eager to get as much résumé-building experience under your belt as possible. Jobs that are high-profile with great exposure are often worth doing for a reduced rate when getting experience in your field is necessary to procure well-paying jobs.

First, consider visibility. Is this a project that will get your name into the market and lead to future business? Is there prestige to having your work showcased in this venue? Second, consider whether there's a likelihood of referrals from this particular client for a job well done. Finally, it comes down to whether you can afford to take on a low-paying gig.

As you begin work as a freelancer, do pay attention to what you're actually getting paid for; this can be an indication of your strengths and how they fit into the current market. It doesn't mean you shouldn't take on your passion projects too, but use this information to balance your passion with what you're compensated for so that you're both fulfilled *and* able to pay rent. Even within a particular creative field, there are

❋ CREATIVE TIP ❋

Be Ready to Supply Information About Your Price

A client may ask detailed questions about your hourly rate or how you price each project or product. It's within a client's right to ask not only what your prices are, but also how you come up with them. You don't want to hide how your pricing works; this can be a red flag for potential clients. Sometimes it's an awkward conversation and you feel like you have to defend your pricing. You don't. Just explain how you got there.

A clear explanation of pricing will be helpful for your customers, but don't let yourself be bullied. It's your price. If they don't like it, they don't have to buy it.

Spec

You may be asked to submit work on spec (short for speculative). This means doing work without the promise of payment. When you create on spec, you only get paid if the client sees your completed work and decides it's what he or she wants. There are some industries in which this is standard. First-time fiction writers need to complete an entire book before submitting it to publishers in the hope that an editor will buy it. But for most creative industries, this is complete baloney and you should run for the hills if asked to submit on spec. So do your homework. Talk to CGs in your field and find out whether submitting work on spec is par for the course or foul play. Check out www.no-spec.com for more information.

aspects of your talent that you'll have an easier time making money with than others. There are writers who love writing poetry, but can't make a living off of poetry alone. They may support themselves writing freelance food columns or celebrity profiles.

Of course, if you're passionate about the project and your schedule allows you to take it, go right ahead. But be wary of doing too many jobs for free just because they sound interesting. Lowering your prices isn't a sustainable financial plan, and worse, it devalues your talent. Your creativity is worth compensation. Believing and understanding your worth is a crucial step toward charging appropriately for your talent.

Bring Back the Barter System

Definitely consider a trade when you offer to do a service for reduced compensation. If you're designing a website for a new hair salon, trade your services for a few haircuts. Do note that Uncle Sam requires that you report goods and services exchanged as income.

CHAPTER 17

Grab a Headset and Act Important: You Are Your Own Best Publicist

Publicity, branding, celebrity clientele, digital marketing and social media

Smart marketing and public relations (PR) are the most effective ways to build your platform and take your career to the next level. When done correctly, branding is a powerful tool to reach your audience and establish yourself as an expert in your field.

What's the Difference Between Marketing, Advertising, and Publicity?

Think of marketing as the umbrella term for an overall game plan; you're focusing on your intended demographic (that oh-so-important target market) and how to reach them. Marketing includes everything you do to get your name and brand out to the world, including advertising and publicity. Advertising costs money, while publicity is free. Marketing is how you communicate to your customer. It's your pricing, your packaging, your promotion, your website, and your blog. It's the night you wear your new line of opera gloves to a black-tie event and a dozen fashion editors and socialites ask for your business card.

Advertising can mean putting up posters or buying an ad on the Internet, radio, TV, or in a magazine or newspaper. Where and how you choose to advertise is based on the research you did about your target market in Chapters 12 and 13. Pay attention to whether or not people in your industry actually advertise. In some industries, it comes off as desperate, and your efforts might be better spent garnering publicity. But if you've researched the competition and creative businesses like yours do advertise, decide whether you want to advertise locally or spend money on a national publication. If you go national, you'll likely want to hire an advertising agency to ensure you're advertising in the right venue, and you'll want the ad itself to be perfect. (When meeting with ad agencies, be sure to ask for a client list and references.) If you're going to take out an ad in the local newspaper, do it yourself. Just remember, with both advertising and PR you have to keep at it to see results.

Publicity is golden and exponentially more credible than advertising. It's what a person from a respectable media outlet says about you or your product. A trusted source—a celebrity client, a magazine editor—giving a glowing review about your product or service is far more effective than you taking an ad out to say it about yourself.

Before we get into PR strategies, let's create a clear picture of your brand.

Have a Handle on Your Brand

The word *brand* has a bit of a slimy connotation and some CGs are resistant to the idea. But really, a brand is as simple as your message and your company's personality. It's how people perceive you or the words they would use to describe your image. So you can either get on board and create your own brand, or let your customers piece together information by themselves.

Think about the adjectives you'd use to describe your business's personality. Is your business artsy? Modern? Edgy? Sassy? Urban? Academic? Classic? Romantic? Luxurious? Minimalist? Environmentally and socially conscious? Ask yourself how you'd like to be perceived by your clients, your target market, or the general public. How would you like them to describe you? How do you think they'd describe you now? You can learn quite a bit from the feedback you get when you ask people how they perceive you or your creative product. Is their view of your brand in line with the image you want to create?

The more you know about your business's vibe, the better equipped you'll be to make decisions from product design to marketing to your target demographic.

Personal Branding

Decades ago, branding was more about a product. Personal branding is really just about being yourself and delivering a clear, consistent message. It's easier than corporate branding because you already know who you are and what you stand for. Have a handle on your story and how you landed in your creative field. There are all kinds of ways to put yourself out into the world, so find your comfort level. Your goal doesn't have to be fame. In fact, for branding to work well, the only people who need to recognize your name are the people in your market.

Unintentional branding can happen very, *very* quickly. Look how fast Omarosa was crowned the Queen of Mean after a season on *The Apprentice.* So take heed, budding reality stars. You better know what you're all about before you reach millions of Americans.

Ereka Vetrini shared the stage with Omarosa on the first season of *The Apprentice.* She went on to work as Tony Danza's sidekick and now hosts her own television show on HGTV. Ereka told me, "After my first few jobs in television, people saw me as the girl next door. That wasn't how I saw myself, so I had to do some thinking about my brand. I realized that, more

Jane Lauder

You met Jane Lauder, the Senior Vice President and General Manager of Origins in Chapter 9. When I asked Jane what CGs should take into account when creating a brand, she said, "Every successful brand has a consistent message and a clearly defined position. Know your message, and be sure that every single thing you create reinforces that message. As a creative person, it can be hard to be consistent because you have so many ideas, but the discipline comes in knowing what isn't in line with your brand and what you have to say no to.

"Creating a brand is like creating a story, and there's value in telling your story over and over again. Sometimes, you're too close to your product and what you may think is repetitive hasn't even scratched the surface of becoming clear to your customer. It's vital to get feedback so that you're sure your message is shining through. Go beyond traditional consumer research and utilize feedback from your sales people and circle of friends. And remember, consumers buy products for emotional and psychological reasons, too, so be sure to pay attention to the climate and what your customer might be feeling. There are times when you'll want to talk about value and times when you'll want to create a feeling of luxury. Great brand strategy balances intuition with facts and research. Find the place in the market where you resonate and capitalize on it with a consistent message to your customer."

than the girl next door, I was a new mom who cared tremendously about balance, health, and fitness. And I wanted to do television work that supported this new era of moms who want more balance in their lives." Ereka's current televison show, *Kid-Space*, is a hit on HGTV and caters to the exact mom-market Ereka described.

Building your brand is a way to become the go-to girl for certain areas of expertise on a local or national level. Magazine beauty editors call on makeup artists like Gucci Westman and Pat McGrath when they want an expert opinion on how to achieve runway makeup looks. Television programs like *The Today Show* call on cosmetics queen Poppy King to appear as the on-air guest when they want to run a segment about how women can look and feel their best with cosmetics.

If you're a beauty guru like Gucci, Pat, or Poppy, what's your hook? Maybe it's your knowledge of organic beauty products or anti-aging techniques. What can you put out there to make someone want to learn more about you and your product? What puts you on the map in your individual industry? Branding and PR expert Lori Diamond says, "There's a lot of room to play in the same space. Identify your brand's point of difference and capitalize on it." Take the brainstorming you've done

---

❋ CREATIVE TIP ❋

Get Comfortable on Camera

For most people, being on camera feels unnatural and worthy of a major freak-out. But if you're going to be interviewed about your product or your expertise, it's worth it to get as comfortable as you possibly can. Take an on-camera class offered at a local acting studio, or have a friend tape you and review the tape closely. Look at yourself with fresh eyes; what do you notice? If you were viewing your on-camera appearance, what kind of impression would you take away?

If nerves are taking over, refer back to the relaxation pep talk in Chapter 9.

If you have some extra dough, you can book a few sessions with an on-camera coach.

---

so far about the ways your company stands out among the competition, and make sure that message shines through to your customer. That means considering your brand in every way you communicate: from your logo and website design to your product packaging and advertising.

Once you know what you're all about, you'll bring focus to your marketing and PR strategies. As you build brand recognition, continually check in to be sure you're delivering a consistent message. You'll build brand loyalty by educating your client about your product and giving them a good reason to seek out your work in a crowded marketplace.

Now that you've got a handle on what you're all about, let's get you out into the world.

Hiring a Publicist

Publicists work on retainer (i.e., when you need them) and charge anywhere from $500 to $10,000 per month. The $500 to $2000 range would likely be for a freelance publicist just starting out, or for a small firm. The average price is between $3,000 and $5,000. There are a handful of publicists who charge per placement, say, $1,000 every time they place you or your product in a national magazine. But for the most part, if you decide to employ a publicist, plan on forking over thousands of dollars per month.

A publicist will work with you to strategize and come up with a marketing plan. He or she will pitch your product to their editorial (newspaper and magazine), radio, and television contacts. Most publicists will help with everything from writing press releases to shaping your brand.

Ask fellow CGs and business owners for PR contacts in your area. Interview several publicists until you find one who understands

Agents, Managers, Publicists, and Sales Reps

When you employ someone who represents you or your work, choose wisely. This person is going to be speaking on your behalf and collaborating on business and artistic decisions. Make sure he or she is trustworthy and comes with sterling references. Your agent, manager, showroom rep, publicist, or anyone else who represents you doesn't need to be your best friend. Don't choose this person based on who'd be the most fun to go out for drinks with on a Friday night. The people you work with should be well-respected in the industry for their professionalism and ability to get the job done. Save the shopping trips for your sister and the coddling and hand-holding duties for your therapist.

This extends to everyone who works for you and interacts with clients on your behalf. Certainly, your agents, managers, showroom reps, and publicists will be aggressive while negotiating on your behalf. But are they respectful and fair? The representation you choose is just that: a representation of you, so choose wisely. Every PR person, sales rep and employee you hire becomes the first point of contact for you and your business. Be sure your clients have a great first impression.

Don't jump at the first PR person or agent who's interested in representing you. Remember, just as you want to make sure the job is right for you in an interview, finding representation is about finding the right fit.

See Appendix A for more information about meeting with an agent or manager.

your business, artistic vision, and goals, and will consistently represent your company well. Because they want your business, the president of the PR firm may meet with you at first. Make sure you know who will be working directly on your account and get to know that person before signing on with the agency. Do be sure you're on the exact same page as far as what you expect from each other. Ask for references and talk to the firm's clients. If you already have media contacts, ask those contacts if they've had a good experience working with this agency.

Be Your Own Publicist

It is absolutely possible for you to get glowing, national press on your own. I'll let you in on the PR secrets I've learned during the past six years, and with a little gumption, you'll be on your way to a publicity strategy that makes sense for your business.

The first step to getting in the press game is knowing who to contact and how to contact them. If you're the next Cyndi Lauper, do you know which music magazines and blogs to approach when you're performing a gig? Or maybe you've created a very special line of handmade throw rugs or home products. Which lifestyle magazines cover these products? What food and wine magazines cover local pastry chefs and chocolate shop owners? Let's say you've decided your line of beaded handbags is perfect for a spot in *Lucky* magazine. Pick up a copy of the magazine and check out the masthead. Find the accessories editor's contact information and email her.

Write a concise email with a link to your website or photos of your product. Refer to the section below on press releases. For an introductory email, summarize your press release into four or five key sentences introducing yourself and your product. *Elle* magazine's Annie Ladino says, "I find the best way for a designer to approach an editor is when they reach out to you personally and outline how their product fits into your magazine." Publicist Lori Diamond says, "You have to do your homework. I make sure that the email I write is written in the most appealing way to the editor who is best suited to receive it. That means knowing how that editor covers stories, including her writing style and the products she's drawn to." Think about it: if an editor receives a blurb about you that sounds like something she herself might have written, you've already made it easier for her to imagine covering your work and how you might fit into her magazine/newspaper column/blog.

Know the voice and personality of each magazine or blog before you write an email. Some magazines, like *InStyle* and *People*, will respond to a celebrity angle. Others, like *Lucky*, care more about a unique shop to which you've just sold your first collection. Know the magazine's market. Don't email *Teen Vogue* about Diane Keaton buying a pair of your sunglasses.

✤ CREATIVE TIP ✤

Email Addresses Aren't National Secrets

Uncover which publisher (likely, Conde Nast or Hearst) publishes the magazine you want to target by visiting their websites at condenast.com and hearst.com.

Check out the masthead at the front of each magazine (the masthead is the page that lists the magazine's editors and directors). Decide whether you should email the market editor, the fashion editor, the accessories editor, the food and wine editor, the beauty editor, or whoever fits your business. This takes research on your part: every time you read a magazine, notice which sections cover CGs like you and take note of which editors work on which subjects.

This information is available by a Google search, but to make your life easier, here it is: depending on the publisher, follow this formula for contacting the editor you want to target: firstname_lastname@condenast.com, or firstinitiallastname@hearst.com.

In *The Fashion Designer Survival Guide*, Mary Gehlhar writes, "The September and March issues of the fashion magazines are the biggest because they introduce fall and summer respectively and new designers have a better chance of being included." Find out what months are best for your industry. Remember that national magazines work on stories several months in advance, so if you've got a story specific to a date—like the opening of your gallery or restaurant—be sure to pitch the idea at least four months in advance. Of course, blogs and weekly magazines have a fraction of that turn-around time, and you can pitch whenever you're ready.

Do email *Teen Vogue, Seventeen*, and the weekly celebrity magazines about Miley Cyrus registering for your closet-organizing services or purchasing a product from your line of homeopathic pet care.

Press is exciting. But don't get so ahead of yourself that you send an email to a very busy editor saying, "I've been working on some really crafty hair pins, and here are some pictures of the first attempts." Your first contact should take place when you have a fully developed product line and the means to produce enough for the publication's customer base should the editor choose to feature you. You're going to disappoint *Lucky* magazine if you can only make five of those beaded handbags. Don't do it. Wait until you've got professional-looking photos and have worked through any production kinks.

Email once, with product information and photos. You can follow up by snail mailing a press release. If you haven't heard anything, follow up with one more email after four to six weeks. Unless you have a reason for calling—say, your sister's college roommate is now an editor at *Bazaar* and she's okayed the phone call—leave it to email or regular mail.

If you send emails to multiple editors and more than one would like to write a story, be honest about the other interest. You don't want to mislead any editor into thinking they have an exclusive scoop. Often, editors want to be the one who discovers you. So be up front, and offer an exclusive to the magazine or newspaper in which you're most interested. Another media outlet can still do a story, but they may spin it differently. They may showcase your product instead of writing a half-page blurb about you and your product. Always be clear so that your PR efforts don't backfire.

If you've got an amazing product, you *will* get press coverage. It's the media's job to

seek out the great stuff in the marketplace and display it in print or on television.

As you continue to hone your skills, it's possible to develop a symbiotic relationship with the media. Years after I got my first piece of press, editors will call with specific story ideas. An editor at *Lucky* recently emailed to ask if I could make necklaces to fit into a bondage story (at first I thought, "What the . . . ?"). But I found some leather, went to work, and the magazine showcased those pieces in a three-page spread. Make yourself available to editors and other media and when they do ask for something, show how no-fuss it is to work with you. If you make their lives easier by doing a stellar job, they'll keep coming back with story ideas and requests for your products.

When stylists and editors call in your products for a magazine shoot, it's not appropriate to charge any money. There's an understanding that loaning your pieces means they may end up in the magazine, resulting in sales for your company. But you should absolutely expect the products to be returned in the same condition you lent them and in a timely fashion.

The exception to the *don't charge* rule is for boutique owners, who may choose to charge an editor or stylist because items are being removed from a potential sales situation. It's up to you whether or not to charge a rental fee. It varies, but a rental fee usually runs around 20 percent of the retail cost of the product borrowed, per day. Editorial budgets can be tight, and if you'd

Local Yokel

Get to know local reporters. Approach news stations and papers or send a press release whenever you have a story. A story is anything from the opening of your restaurant to your band playing a new venue. People love human-interest stories, and you and your business are likely one of those stories. Rachel Ray started by hosting her "30-Minute Meal" cooking classes on a weekly local news show in Albany, New York. Getting local press is a great precursor to national press.

Create Your Own Big Break

Put yourself places where media and industry bigwigs frequent. Clothing designer Asli Filinta chose to work part-time at a hip boutique known for attracting magazine editors. Smart creative girl that she is, Asli wore her designs while working in the boutique. Her work appeared in magazines like *Self* and *Nylon* because of the visibility she created for herself by working there. Now, she's got a cult following as an international design talent.

CGs, if you tear out one creative tip from this book and stick it on your wall, let it be this one. If you want creative superstardom, work your fingers to the bone, then put yourself and your work where the world can find you.

be psyched to have your store credited in *Vogue*, you might not want to complicate matters with a rental fee.

Many CGs charge a rental fee to lend products for an ad campaign, especially because you won't likely be credited. I've charged when lending jewelry to companies like Vera Wang and Gap. If there was exposure involved—like when a magazine credits your product on the page—that would be different. But unless you work out a different arrangement, it's very unlikely a big company would link your website to theirs or credit your name in their ads. You can create a simple rental agreement to be signed by the stylist borrowing the merchandise. Include the date the goods should be returned, the rental fee per day, and a line stating that anything lost or broken will be paid for at wholesale cost.

If you're serious about getting national magazine coverage, make a solid effort to get your product into New York City stores. Of course, editors look around the globe for great finds. But the vast majority live or work in New York City. When they're strolling around their neighborhood boutiques, they'll be able to see your product up close and personal. When they want more details, they'll ask the salesperson or boutique owner for your name, website, or contact information.

Write Your Own Press Release

A press release announces something newsworthy: a story, an event, a new line of products, or the merging of two businesses. You're enticing the media with details so they can decide whether they want to cover the story. Keep your press release to one page. Tell your reader who you are and what you're doing. Let them know where and when this big thing is happening. Then, tell them why this is such big news and what's unique about your business. You've already brainstormed these answers in your business plan. Now, find a punchy way to make your reader sit up and take notice. Run your press release by several readers to be sure it's as polished as possible.

Narrow in on the people who should receive this release. Send it to the appropriate media, from national magazine editors to local reporters.

See the next page for an example of a stellar press release written by a pro.

Become the Go-To Girl

Gain visibility by giving free advice on your area of expertise. You can offer to teach a free workshop and invite the media. You can call a local news or radio station, let them know your area of expertise and that you're available to talk about it. If you're nervous about making a cold call, remind yourself that this is part of the business and that you're making their lives easier. If there's a story and you're the right expert to interview, they've got your information handy and can pick up the phone to get a quick quote.

Connect With Your Customers

Sign up for the online mailing lists to which your customers subscribe. If you're a budding wardrobe stylist and you find a style blog that shares advice from guest bloggers, offer to do a post on next season's footwear trends. A personal chef could offer to share a recipe. An event

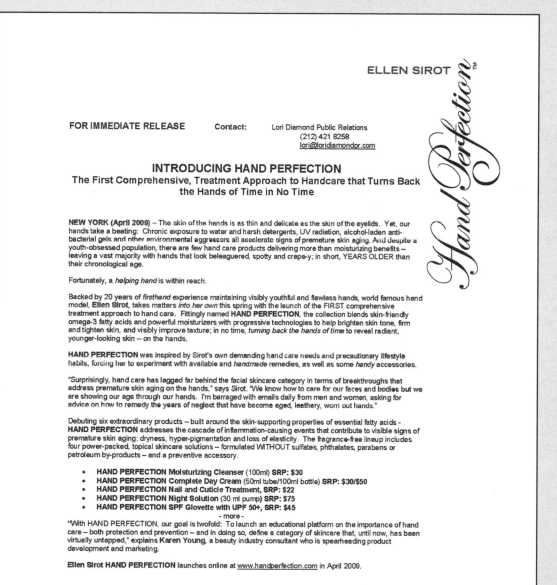

ELLEN SIROT

Hand Perfection™

FOR IMMEDIATE RELEASE   Contact: Lori Diamond Public Relations
(212) 421 8258
lori@loridiamondpr.com

INTRODUCING HAND PERFECTION
The First Comprehensive, Treatment Approach to Handcare that Turns Back
the Hands of Time in No Time

NEW YORK (April 2009) – The skin of the hands is as thin and delicate as the skin of the eyelids. Yet, our hands take a beating: Chronic exposure to water and harsh detergents, UV radiation, alcohol-laden anti-bacterial gels and other environmental aggressors all accelerate signs of premature skin aging. And despite a youth-obsessed population, there are few hand care products delivering more than moisturizing benefits – leaving a vast majority with hands that look beleaguered, spotty and crepe-y; in short, YEARS OLDER than their chronological age.

Fortunately, a *helping hand* is within reach.

Backed by 20 years of *firsthand* experience maintaining visibly youthful and flawless hands, world famous hand model, **Ellen Sirot**, takes matters *into her own* this spring with the launch of the FIRST comprehensive treatment approach to hand care. Fittingly named **HAND PERFECTION**, the collection blends skin-friendly omega-3 fatty acids and powerful moisturizers with progressive technologies to help brighten skin tone, firm and tighten skin, and visibly improve texture; in no time, *turning back the hands of time* to reveal radiant, younger-looking skin – on the hands.

HAND PERFECTION was inspired by Sirot's own demanding hand care needs and precautionary lifestyle habits, forcing her to experiment with available and *handmade* remedies, as well as some *handy* accessories.

"Surprisingly, hand care has lagged far behind the facial skincare category in terms of breakthroughs that address premature skin aging on the hands," says Sirot. "We know how to care for our faces and bodies but we are showing our age through our hands. I'm barraged with emails daily from men and women, asking for advice on how to remedy the years of neglect that have become aged, leathery, worn out hands."

Debuting six extraordinary products – built around the skin-supporting properties of essential fatty acids - **HAND PERFECTION** addresses the cascade of inflammation-causing events that contribute to visible signs of premature skin aging: dryness, hyper-pigmentation and loss of elasticity. The fragrance-free lineup includes four power-packed, topical skincare solutions – formulated WITHOUT sulfates, phthalates, parabens or petroleum by-products – and a preventive accessory.

- **HAND PERFECTION Moisturizing Cleanser** (100ml) **SRP: $30**
- **HAND PERFECTION Complete Day Cream** (50ml tube/100ml bottle) **SRP: $30/$50**
- **HAND PERFECTION Nail and Cuticle Treatment, SRP: $22**
- **HAND PERFECTION Night Solution** (30 ml pump) **SRP: $75**
- **HAND PERFECTION SPF Glovette with UPF 50+, SRP: $45**

- more -

"With HAND PERFECTION, our goal is twofold: To launch an educational platform on the importance of hand care – both protection and prevention – and in doing so, define a category of skincare that, until now, has been virtually untapped," explains **Karen Young**, a beauty industry consultant who is spearheading product development and marketing.

Ellen Sirot HAND PERFECTION launches online at www.handperfection.com in April 2009.

planner could share her top five tips for a successful party and a hairstylist (or dog groomer) could give tips for a shiny mane. Remember, the more your name is associated with your area of expertise, the more recognizable your brand is.

Don't post a message that's clearly an ad for your services in the comment section of a blog. Comment if you have something related and valuable to add. If there's an article about a designer and you happen to carry that designer at your boutique, go ahead and link to your boutique's website.

Promotions

You can send mailings about product promotions, just be very careful not to do this too often because it can look a little desperate. If you're continually mailing a 30 percent off coupon, it looks like you overpriced your product or service or you're making a last-ditch attempt to get rid of it. Plus, it's tricky to get anyone to pay full price if you always have a promotion going.

Promotions are great to announce something newsworthy: say, the addition of a new line of scented oils to your perfume collection. You can announce a sample sale or seasonal sale. You can partner up with another CG and offer a combined service for a discounted rate.

Your Game Plan for Getting That First Celebrity Client

Celebrity clientele has catapulted creative businesses to a whole new level. CG-in-action Carolyn Davis, a staff writer at *Us Weekly Magazine*, says, "Because cosumers

Party Animal

If all else fails, throw a party and invite the press along with the rest of your guests. If you're just starting, call it a launch party. If you've been in business for a while, call it an anniversary party or come up with another creative title. Press people flock to events where people are having a good time. Provide free booze and showcase your products or talents. Have a fancy book for guests to print their names and email addresses so you can contact them with future company news.

admire and take notice of celebrities, there's real potential for celebrity clientele to bring awareness to a product, charity, restaurant, shop, or any small company in a big way. And with forms of social media like Twitter, it's easier than ever for celebrities to expose something they like."

If you decide you'd like celebrity clients, there are five main ways to get your product into their hands. You can do each of the following on your own and without the help of a publicist:

1) **Gift your product through the celebrity's publicist.**

2) **Gift through gift lounges at celebrity events.**

3) **Connect with celebrities through their wardrobe stylists.**

4) **Work on building strong editorial connections so your product is used in magazine shoots with celebrities.**

5) **Sell your product at shops that have celebrity clientele: hello, Rodeo Drive.**

Personally, I'm not crazy about the first two options, but other CGs have gone this route with successful outcomes, so I included them for you to decide.

Target the Celebrity's Publicist

A celebrity's publicist's information and mailing address are easily found on the Internet by googling the celebrity's name and "publicist." Once you have an address for a PR firm, you can send a gift to a celebrity through their publicist—anything from your latest book to dark chocolates from your newly opened pastry shop. There is absolutely a chance that your product could be a hit and really connect with the celebrity's tastes. But gifting through a publicist can also be a waste of time and money. You have no way of knowing if your product will actually get to the celebrity, or if the celebrity will like it. What if Gwen Stefani is allergic to the rosemary in your line of scented candles? The celebrity may pass it along to their dentist or housekeeper.

I've only attempted the gifting method once. Five years ago, I went on-air for a segment during which I designed a new-mom bracelet with baby charms for *The View* co-host Elizabeth Hasselbeck. Afterwards, a PR-savvy friend of mine was convinced these new-mom bracelets could be the Next Big Thing in Hollywood. She did the legwork and found contact information for each publicist, and we targeted moms like Sarah Jessica Parker and Kate Hudson and gifted the bracelets through their PR firms. It was a flop, and no one wore them. We did, however, end up with a handwritten thank-you note from Britney Spears.

If your product is easy to make and relatively inexpensive to manufacture, go for it. You could get lucky. (Or, receive a thank-you to show to your friends. XOXO, Britney.)

Send your product with a cover letter and/or press release. Keep it simple. Don't gush about the celebrity or the reasons why you think they'll love the product. Keep your cover letter focused on the actual product and give a few sentences about the background of your company.

Gift Lounges

Gifting suites or gift lounges are set up by PR firms and take place before star-studded events like film festivals and awards shows. You pay to have your product given away to the celebrity. This could lead to a picture taken with a celebrity wearing or holding your product, which you could then use on your website, or, best-case scenario, would be featured in a magazine. But there are absolutely no guarantees. And sometimes celebrities send their stylists, so you might not get a photo.

Certainly, these events increase your exposure. And your favorite celebrity could become a huge fan of your product. You could meet Madonna, give her one of your custom yoga mats, and be featured in *Us Weekly*. If you have the extra income, go for it. But if you're on a tight budget, I'm not convinced this is where your money should go. I've been approached by several of these PR firms and it costs around $5,000 to participate. Plus, you have to give away somewhere between 75 and 150 units of your product. If you're going to be manning your own booth, there are also the airline and hotel expenses to travel to the event. If you do choose to participate in a gifting suite, be sure that the suite is legitimate and has a proven track record of attracting A-listers. Publicist Liz Auerbach says, "Selecting the proper celebrity gifting suite for a brand takes research. Be aware of the caliber of talent the suite is promising will attend the event, along with the other brands that are participating. You want to ensure your brand is going to get the best possible exposure while drawing in as many A-listers as possible. It helps if the suite has a charitable angle. Nowadays, brands and celebrities alike want to shake the notion that they are just gifting or receiving free swag. That isn't good press for anyone involved."

Liz recommends choosing a gifting lounge or event by considering your market. She says, "If your product is something that would be geared more toward a red carpet event, look into gifting suites at the Emmy's, Golden Globes, or Oscars. If you

CREATIVE TIP

Get in the Referral Game

Another way to get your business or service out there is to befriend business owners in a related field. Party planners and floral designers should get to know wedding photographers. If you develop a great relationship, you may choose to offer promotions together. When a bride chooses to hire both of you, she gets 10 percent off the combined price.

are creating something that you see appealing to a more indie or artsy crowd, look into major music events and festivals like Coachella, the South by SouthWest Music Conference or the Sundance Film Festival. If your product is appropriate for younger audiences, check out the Teen Choice Awards or the MTV Video Music Awards. There are endless options and opportunities to consider when choosing the right venue, just be sure to do the legwork."

Develop a Relationship with a Celebrity Stylist

Besides my lame attempt at new-mom charm bracelets, I've never actively tried to get a celebrity client. Every single one of them has come through retail stores, magazine shoots or stylists. If you choose to target a stylist, you know that the stylist will show your product to a celebrity only if she thinks it matches the celebrity's aesthetic. Stylists are not in the business of wasting their clients' time. Developing a professional relationship with a stylist means she'll keep your product in mind as her client roster grows, giving you a greater chance of having your product worn or used by a celebrity.

Usually, a Google search will lead you to a celebrity's stylist. If you're unsure, call the celebrity's PR firm and ask. Once you have a name of the stylist, Google the name along with "contact information" or "address." You can start by mailing a stylist your catalog. You can send samples as well, as long as you're okay with them not being returned. If you can find an email address

❋ CREATIVE TIP ❋

Gift Smartly

CGs wanting to learn more about participating in a celebrity gifting suite should check HBO Luxury Lounges, Hollywood Life Magazine events, Silverspoon Events at thesilverspoon.com/events.html, Kari Feinstein at www.fmpr.tv, and On 3 Productions at www.on3productions.com.

online, you can email photos of your goods. It's a small industry; stylists usually style both celebs and magazine spreads (or have stylist-friends who do). Once they're familiar with your line, you're on your way to getting both magazine coverage and celebrity clientele.

If a stylist is interested in finding more about you or your product, she'll get in touch. Be sure to provide your contact information and your company's website.

Strengthen Your Editorial Relationships

As you build editorial relationships using the strategies discussed earlier, you increase your chances for an editor to call in your clothing or accessories to be worn by a star for a photo shoot. Let's say you lend six items of clothing for the shoot. You can let the editor or stylist know that you're a-okay with Beyoncé taking home one of your pieces, if she's so inclined. I've also had it happen that a stylist or editor calls wanting to know the price of a piece for a celebrity to buy off of a magazine shoot. In this case, you can gift it or stand firm and name a price. I've done both. It's up to you to decide what makes you comfortable. Do know that

a celebrity wearing your pieces out on the town can garner loads of sales and PR for your business, so it's often worth gifting. And the celebrity is more likely to wear it if she's chosen it, verses you sending out tons of gift bags to random movie stars and not knowing who will even see the contents.

Product Placement in Retail Stores

In my experience, celebrities best connect with a product the same way the rest of your customers do: through retail stores. So if you're looking for celebrity clientele, be strategic about what boutiques you approach to sell your home goods, handbags, or all-natural body lotion. It can happen anywhere, but your chances of exposure greatly increase by selling through Los Angeles and New York City shops. And remember, if a star buys something for herself in a retail store, you know she actually wants to wear or use it. So cozy up the store's buyer and sales staff, and if you hear the news of a celebrity buying your product, be on the lookout for a photo of her wearing or using your product in the weekly celeb magazines. (Yes, this is the best excuse you'll ever find for reading trashy magazines.)

If you own a shop, salon, restaurant, or a line of products, you'll find that when the media wants to cover it, they'll often ask you who your celebrity clients are. It's up to you if you want to reveal them. If it makes you feel sleazy, you don't have to share the information. I don't list two clients of mine who've since become pals. It wouldn't be unprofessional—it just doesn't feel right. But since the only personal connection I have with Kate Winslet is the twelve times I saw *Titanic* in the theater, I go ahead and list her as a customer. Plus, I can't imagine she'd mind—unless your product is something more intimate, like holistic therapy, lace thongs, or eco-friendly tampons—it's not scandalous to tell people a celebrity bought a piece of jewelry or a bottle of perfume. Just use your good judgment.

Going Digital and Utilizing Social Media

It would be nutty to outline a publicity and marketing plan based on the Internet; by the time this book hits shelves, Twitter and Facebook might be *so* 2010.

Instead, I interviewed several different creative types and social media entrepreneurs so you could get a feel for their approaches to digital marketing and social media. Currently, these forward thinkers do use outlets like Facebook and Twitter. When you read this book, they'll also be on top of whatever trend is currently making waves.

Keeping up with technology makes some CGs shudder. But you do need to embrace the ever-changing digital market. There are very few CGs or creative businesses that thrive while

✳ CREATIVE TIP ✳

Transparency

We all look for transparency: the true story and full disclosure of information. We crave sincerity and a relationship with the brands we believe in. Use the Internet to give your customer an honest, candid glimpse of your creative world.

Get Up to Speed

Founded in 2005, mashable.com is an invaluable guide to social media. If you're wondering how to utilize social media and web-based marketing, you cannot miss this resource.

Chris Brogan's book, *Social Media 101: Tactics and Tips to Develop Your Business Online*, has excellent ideas, and you can find the most up-to-date advice on his blog, www.chrisbrogan.com.

Also check out *Inbound Marketing: Get Found Using Google, Social Media and Blogs*, by Brian Halligan and Dharmesh Shah.

holed up in a cabin and cut off from the social world. You don't need to jump on every digital trend, but you do need to be aware of them and make a conscious choice whether or not to utilize them for your business. How are other CGs in your industry using the Internet to stay relevant and connected to their audience? What digital marketing choices—Facebook, Twitter, blogging, web shows—feel right for your brand?

Author Micol Ostow Twitters from the perspective of her fictional characters. Micol says, "The Internet makes marketing and publicizing one's product more affordable than ever. That's why everyone uses it, making it a challenge to promote yourself in any distinguishable way. You can't just shout, 'Hey, look, I've got this creative thing going on.' That's where the need to be imaginative comes in. Twitter is a fantastic tool, but I found that the best way to attract new followers was to Twitter *in character* and offer potential readers a way to connect to my fictional landscape and characters on a personal level."

The Internet has made digital marketing accessible to anyone with a computer and something to show or say. You have instant access to customers all over the world and you can build relationships that wouldn't have been possible ten years ago. Clothing designer Asli Filinta splits her time between New York City and her home in Istanbul. Asli says, "Digital networking is vital for my business. I can be halfway around the world and still tuned in to the New

York fashion scene. I can post pictures of my travels on my website and release Twitter updates so my customers are connected with what I'm doing for my business and my brand."

These relationships build brand loyalty. The fans of your brand create a powerful word-of-mouth marketing device—all for little or no cost to you.

Blogging: Should You Do It?

Blogging can be an excellent way to up your visibility and contribute to your expert factor. It can also be a time-suck and a detriment to you and your career if you do it the wrong way.

Anica Rissi is an editor at Simon & Schuster. She says, "I look for prospective writers to be available to their readers. This can mean a blog, a social-networking page, or a website. But you have to be careful about blogging. I don't want to consider making an offer on your manuscript, but then stumble upon your blog and find out that your ideal publisher is actually HarperCollins."

Under no circumstance should you bad-mouth anyone in the industry in which you're working (or in which you're hoping to work). Nothing is more amateur than posting pictures of yourself weekend binge drinking on your profile page. This isn't high school. Don't give anyone a reason to discount your professionalism.

❋ CREATIVE TIP ❋

You Need Human Contact. The UPS Guy Doesn't Count.

Do be wary of replacing Internet socializing with actual human contact (no, they're not the same thing). Working alone can be isolating. Don't further that problem by only socializing on gchat and Facebook. Too much time on the Internet and not enough face-to-face interaction can leave you feeling lonely and out of touch.

Guest of a Guest

CG-in-action Rachelle Hruska quit her hedge fund job and created the new media website www.guestofaguest.com, a social diary chronicling the lives of young New Yorkers that provides a sneak peek and invite into the city's nightlife. In May 2009, The *New York Post* named Rachelle the "The Queen Bee" of the new wave of web entrepreneurs. Guestofaguest.com receives 2.5 million page views per month.

Rachelle says, "Part of what I love about my job is that it allows me to meet the innovators of these cool new Internet platforms like Twitter, Foursquare, and Facebook, and then to try and figure out how to integrate their products into Guest of a Guest. The exciting part is that I don't think any of us really know what to expect next. Relatively speaking, the Internet is very, very young, and we're still just getting the hang of it. Mobile apps are changing the way we shop, eat, and live. Social media has revolutionized the way we interact within our own communities, and I believe businesses that embrace these new forms of digital marketing will be ahead of ones that don't.

"What social media can do for creative types just starting out is incredible. Say you make unique necklaces in a small town but want to grow your company to be in cities all over the world. You can start by setting up an account on Etsy.com, then get fans from the innovative Tumblr page you created, support from your friends on Facebook, and maybe even a shout-out from a well-known media source on Twitter. Use a company like Foursquare to accept payments. Let your top buyers gain rewards on Foursquare after "checking in" at your store a certain number of times. The possibilities are endless, and many more will arise by the time this book goes to print. I enjoy helping to lead the way we get our social news, which will undoubtedly involve the utilization of all of these platforms, and many more to come."

Over tea, the week before she was leaving to open the Los Angeles branch of Guest of a Guest, I asked Rachelle what her best advice was for creative girls navigating their careers. Rachelle said, "Be open to opportunities, recognize them when they come your way, and take advantage of them. Surround yourself with passionate people who believe in themselves and take care of themselves because it's contagious. And work really, *really* hard. Every woman you see with a great career has put in the time and the work."

CG Interview with Evolvor

To get more outside-of-the-box thinking on digital marketing, I went to Debra, the lead singer/guitarist for the rock band DEVI who you met in Chapter 14. Debra did one better than answering my questions—she got the inside information from her band's secret weapon, Eric Hebert. Eric is the online business consultant and founder of Evolvor.com, which provides digital marketing services to labels and bands.

Debra: When it was time to make our debut album, *Get Free*, my band and I produced it ourselves and then secured a digital distribution deal with Redeye USA. But we still had to figure out how to promote the album. How do you choose from a gazillion social networks and blogs?

CG: What's the best advice you can give to a creative girl starting her own business?

EH: Start blogging, not later today or tomorrow but right now. As you learn about your skill set or trade, share that knowledge with your audience and become an educator. Continue to provide resources and facilitate conversation. Social networking, from a business standpoint, is all about getting your message out there. The message needs to start with your blog; it has to be a powerful and resourceful message. The social networks are just a way for you to share that message and drive traffic back to your website. Using tools like RSS, you can easily sync and syndicate your blog content automatically to your Facebook and Twitter to make your life easier. Don't get overwhelmed with social networking. Stick to the major networks and focus on building real communities there.

CG: What's the smartest way to approach bloggers?

EH: If you can pre-format content for a blogger with various media like videos and sound, and offer something in the content that will be resourceful and engaging for the blogger's audience, you'll have a far better chance of getting published.

CGs should also think about ReverbNation's FanReach Pro, which automatically searches out each fan's name, location, and social networks and provides the templates to send a monthly newsletter already loaded with retail links, press, and show dates.

Check out Debra's site at www.devi-rock.com. Find out more about digital marketing at www.evolvor.com.

With the user-warnings out of the way, there are several positives. Blogging is a way for you to write about your life or expertise without needing a writing assignment to do so. It increases your visibility. If you choose to blog about your specific area of expertise, this can increase your expert status in your field.

There are all kinds of ways to incorporate blogging into an industry that doesn't seem token on it. If you own a restaurant, you could entice your blog readers to stop by or place an order by posting pictures and recipes.

Pitching a Blogger

CG-in-action Grace Bonney is the creator of www.designspongeonline.com, a website dedicated to home and product design. Creative types clamor to have their products featured on this popular site. During peak season (design shows, student show season) Grace receives 400 email submissions per day. She answers each one personally.

CG: What's the best way for designers to approach you with products or newsworthy information they'd like you to consider? What should they include as far as company background information, product samples, and press releases?

GB: I always suggest that people keep things short and sweet: a personal email, a few low-res images of your work or shop and then one to three short paragraphs with the basic info. Anything more we can get from a follow up email, but too much and you risk losing our attention. Background info, unless it's really pertinent to the core of the product, isn't necessary up front.

I suggest not sending product samples unless they're specifically requested, or a product can't be explained without them. These days you can send images, video of a product in use, and all sorts of other details digitally, so I'd suggest saving the money and waiting to send those samples until they're requested—because you can't guarantee you'll get the sample back.

Design Sponge

Grace Bonney's blog, www.designspongeonline.com receives 50,000 visitors every day.

Below, she shares advice on growing and keeping an online audience.

CG: What are the best ways for a creative girl to attract readers to her blog or website?

GB: First, give back. I started a local series of business advice meetups that turned national in a few months. I saw that my readers needed this sort of advice, and giving something back to the readership allowed me to meet people who were casual readers and connect with them in a way that turned them into more devoted readers.

Next, team up with other sites and groups. Think about the types of people your content will appeal to. That may not just be a design fan, but perhaps your work crosses over into the environmental scene—try teaming up with a well-known green site to host a contest or event that will expose your site to their readers (and vice versa).

Lastly, become active in your home area. When I started, Brooklyn was just becoming the design hotbed that it is now. There were so many designers working in the area that it really allowed me to get out and meet them, meet store owners, and become active in the local gallery, design, and art school scene. No matter what size city or town you live in, it's always beneficial to become an active member of your local scene. Local "fans" and press can lead to attention outside of your hometown, and it's nice to have a home basethat you can rely on for support, feedback, and great ideas.

CG: Once bloggers attract readers, what's the best way to retain them?

GB: The best way to get readers to come back on a regular basis is to make your content or layout easy to follow. That could mean letting them know what days certain types of content will appear (by using an editorial calendar) or using other avenues (like Twitter, Facebook, or a newsletter) to remind them that you have fresh content each day or week.

These days a lot of readers don't visit the actual home page of a blog, but read via an RSS feed (an email newsletter that your readers subscribe to) or a social media outlet like Facebook. So consider making your blog's RSS feed or social networking page prominent on the site so they can continue to follow in the way that best suits them.

Web Show Star

A web show with great video content is a way to punch up your blog or website and keep visitors coming back for more. Kimberly Rae Miller is the Webby award-winning star of the online talk show *The Daily Special* and the comedy *Pretty Imperfect*. Below, Kim shares her ideas for creating a successful web show.

CGs looking to create web videos should also read *Get Seen: Online Video Secrets to Building Your Business* by David Meerman Scott.

KMR: Web shows are still an evolving form of media and we test drove a lot of different formats. We found the keys to optimizing hits are consistency and brevity—no more than three minutes. That may seem short, but the Internet is full of distractions and attention spans are shorter in the land of click-friendly entertainment.

CG: How should a CG decide on her topic?

KRM: It should be something you're enthusiastic about, something in which you are *the* expert. I suggest sticking to one theme—both my video and writing content online has revolved around one thing: health and body image.

CG: What about format?

KRM: The shows that are successful online are ones that have a solid formula. Whether it's a comic, dramatic, or talk style show, viewers get attached to your genre.

CG: How do you retain your viewers and keep them coming back for more?

KRM: Consistency. Whether you are prepared to put up a new video everyday or perhaps limit it to once a week or month, be consistent in your timing.

CG: It sounds like this is an option for any CG with something interesting to say or show.

KRM: Definitely. Nowadays anyone can produce cheap online content. I've worked on sets with a full film crew, and I've used an inexpensive camcorder the size of my cell phone that I keep in my purse.

There are dozens of sites that will host your content for free—the most famous is, of course, YouTube—but you can also use Metacafe, Vimeo, Yahoo Video, and any number of the other free hosting sites. If you're just starting out, I strongly suggest building an entire platform for yourself so viewers can find you, starting with a blog.

There are free templates out there like blogger.com, blogspot.com, and tumblr.com that make setup easy. Others have software and hosting fees but will likely allow you a free trial; check out wordpress.org, type pad.com and moveabletype.org. You also may want to sign up for a service that tracks the amount of visitors (hits) you get to your blog, like Google analytics.

Successful bloggers post a new entry at least a few times per week. Choose a topic that truly interests you—not just something you think other people will be interested in—so that you keep posting. Of course, if you're interested in S & M and you run a children's clothing store, it's probably best to blog anonymously. But if you can figure out a way to blend your genuine interest

Design For Mankind

In 2006, Erin Loechner was laid off from her advertising job. She created her blog, Design ForMankind.com as an outlet for her creativity. Within a year, her blog became her full-time job. Erin says, "Find your voice, and sometimes instantaneously and sometimes a year later, you'll find your audience. Blog about something you're passionate about, the more niche the better. My blog became an online catalog for what I love."

Design for Mankind focuses on emerging artists. Erin's readers include art enthusiasts, along with art curators and gallery owners who scour her blog to find up-and-coming artists.

To gain readership, Erin advises, "Involve yourself in the online community. Most blog readers read several blogs. Bloggers are a supportive group and link to each other's sites. So if you become involved with high-traffic bloggers, new readers can find you. And be open with your readers. Always respond to comments and emails."

Two years after Erin started blogging, AOL hired her to blog professionally. Erin says, "In addition to ad revenue, blogs help you develop all kinds of business relationships. Bloggers become experts in their niche specialty, and that expertise is sought after."

with content your business audience will love, you've found a great match. Connie Wong and Carolyn Hsu, editors of the online lifestyle guide TheDailyObsession.net say, "Providing your audience with fresh, honest, and interesting content is essential in retaining readership."

As Connie and Carolyn mention, blog readers are looking for authenticity, so don't create a blog full of self-promotion. Don't use corporate-speak. Blogging is like having a candid conversation with your audience, so let your personality come through. Involve and empower your readers—at the very least, respond to their comments. Think about giveaways or ways to share their ideas. If it's a blog about crafting, you may want to allow your readers (and fellow crafters) to share photos of their work or tips of their own. Cooking bloggers could provide a community space to post new recipes.

If you possess the elusive blogging skills to create an addictive blog with thousands of readers coming back each day for more, you may be on your way to garnering enough Internet traffic to procure advertising dollars. CG Kimberly Rae Miller says, "To draw readers, start thinking in terms of key words and Google search terms. Themes, giveaways, top five lists, are all highly searchable ideas that will draw traffic to your site."

To learn more, check out www.blogging basics101.com.

Those of you interested in blogging professionally can check out Appendix D for more information about securing ad revenue and writing for other online networks.

CHAPTER 18

Wellbeing Rocks

Let's end this journey how we started:
by remaining a spiritually and emotionally sound CG.

"Everybody's an artist. Everybody's God.
It's just that they're inhibited."

—Yoko Ono

We've spent these pages figuring out how to make creative fulfillment your career reality. We're going to end our time together with a plan for you to stay happy and fulfilled as you continue on your creative way.

It's exciting and breezy to talk about PR strategies and how to brand and position yourself for creative world domination. Getting your first piece of press makes for a giddy phone call to your best friend from college. But let's get back to the *really* good stuff—the spiritual and emotional parts of the creative process that help you remain peaceful, steady, happy, and balanced. If you're thinking, *Listen, lady, I just want a great career,* you can hear what I have to say in this moment, or you can learn it in ten years, but you're going to have to face it at some point: *Your wellbeing trumps all else. It frees you to create. It frees you, period.* Let's talk about how to get it.

The Psychology of Creative Types

There are entire books devoted to the psychology of creative people and the reasons we are prone to depression, anxiety, and higher instances of substance abuse and suicide. We can't ignore the data, so how can we do our part to end this perilous cycle of the artist as troubled creator? As a creative individual, doing our part to not enable this pattern starts by looking inward, being proactive about our own emotional health, positively changing the things within our control, and getting help when we need it. Once and for all, let's stop glamorizing this assumption that art and madness are inextricably linked. There's nothing shiny, glamorous, or artistically authentic about poor mental health.

After reading this far, you've formulated a plan for intelligently managing your finances, interviewing for a job, or starting a business. It's even more important to formulate a plan for keeping your spiritual and emotional health in top shape. When you ignore your wellbeing it manifests in big ways, from depression and anxiety to procrastination and inertia. Wherever you are on your creative path, assess your wellbeing and recognize the adjustments you need to make.

Creative Freedom

Any creative block is the direct result of fear and nothing else. The words we use to describe being blocked, like *doubt, laziness,* or *procrastination* are caused by fear. When you sit down and cannot focus, create, or allow your own creative force to move through you, it is the result of fear. Fear is the only thing that blocks an artist. The only cure for fear is love.

When you experience any emotion or behavior that does not serve you—doubt, procrastination, resentment—go deeper. What comes up for you when you can't seem to sit down and focus? What are you avoiding? How can you replace that thought, behavior, or feeling with one that has a higher energy? Remember, a *higher energy* is your fancy new way of saying *a more loving thought, behavior, or feeling.*

You are continually connected to a creative force. You can think of it as a higher power, or you can think of it as your own creative flow, but it is always, *always* there for you to tap into. In *The Artist's Way,* Julia Cameron writes, "Every creative person has a myriad ways to block creativity. Each of us favors one or two ways particularly toxic to us because they block us so effectively." She details the ways we block ourselves, like food and alcohol, and writes, "If creativity is like a burst of the universe's breath through the straw that is each of us, we pinch that straw whenever we pick up one of our blocks."

This chapter will give you a set of tricks for combating procrastination and creative blocks and dealing with rejection and criticism, but still, understand that the deep work you owe yourself is to figure out how to love every part of yourself and realize your connection to a creative source.

Because so many CGs complain about problems with procrastination, we'll use that term to describe the fear that surfaces when you sit down to work. Many of you may have found it easy to rationalize procrastination when you disliked your work, but it's a bit more worrisome when you've finally achieved your dream career and you're *still* procrastinating. Work that you love is still work, but if you've been dreaming of being a novelist your entire life and can't seem to get yourself to sit down and actually write, then there's likely more going on. Everything from procrastination to overeating is only a device we use to cope with an emotion that makes us uncomfortable. When we look at our behavior as a symptom of a larger issue—fear, or any fear-based emotion that doesn't serve you, like resentment, anger, or doubt—it's easier to get at the source of the problem.

The next time you find yourself procrastinating, feeling resistance, or engaging in a behavior or thought pattern that stops you from realizing your creative potential, take some time to answer the questions below.

What fears are surfacing as I begin my work?

_____
_____
_____
_____
_____
_____
_____

Are my fears related to failure? Success?

_____
_____
_____
_____
_____
_____
_____

Do I believe I'm worthy of achieving success? _____

_____

_____

_____

_____

Are my fears related to the specific project I'm avoiding, or is it a
general fear? _____

_____

_____

_____

_____

What do I reach for to block my creative force? _____

_____

_____

_____

_____

Let anything and everything come to the surface. It can seem ridiculous and unrelated. Express it anyway. Be truthful with yourself. Then, be gentle. Speak kindly to calm your worries. Reach for a higher thought just like you did in the Fear Chart back in Chapter 7. Replace fear-based thoughts with truth and compassion.

As you answer the questions, you may find it easier to grasp your fear of failure—no one wants to completely flounder at something or embarrass herself. The fear of success is a bit more complex. It may sound counterintuitive, but it's present in many artists. How many of you know your true potential, but attempt to thwart it with self-defeating behavior or doubt? With success comes responsibility and new pressures,

Perfectionism

CG-in-action Anna Carey is the author of the fiction series, *The Sloane Sisters*. Anna says, "I was in my early twenties when I started my first novel, and I had never written more than thirty pages before. The week before I turned in the first draft to my editor, I was plagued with anxiety. I've always been very critical of my writing, and this type of perfectionism was something that I actually prided myself in. But when it came to my new creative career, I was finding it a serious obstacle—to everything. The problem was that I began *judging* instead of *working*, and the two can't co-exist. By the time I finished my first draft I had convinced myself it was nothing more than a compilation of some of the worst sentences ever written. I was paralyzed by all this internal criticism, afraid to make any more (perceived) mistakes.

"What I've learned, three books later, is that any act of creation is a process, and that process can be sabotaged very quickly if your internal critic starts running the show. Now I try to just write, and leave the criticism to the people who are supposed to give feedback: editors, readers, and yes, critics. Now when I hear that judging voice whispering *That's really unoriginal* or *You think that's writing?!?*, I respond with *Enough*. Enough judging, enough beating yourself up because every sentence isn't "perfect," or—God forbid—you aren't "perfect." There will be time to revise, there will be time to get better. Enough, I tell myself, *just get back to work*."

and there's the nerve-wracking idea that once you've achieved success, you have to keep producing and performing at a certain level. While giving a talk at TED about her bestselling novel, *Eat Pray Love*, author Elizabeth Gilbert said, "Unlike any of my previous books, [this book] went out in the world and for some reason became this big mega-sensation international bestseller, the result of which is that everywhere I go now, people treat me like I'm doomed. They say, 'Aren't you afraid you're never going to be able to top that? Aren't you afraid you're going to keep writing for your whole life and you're never again going to create a book that anybody in the world cares about, at all, ever again?'"

Elizabeth admits that yeah, she is afraid of those things.

Many CGs who suffer from perfection-ism often procrastinate and feel paralyzed by the idea of turning something in that they view as less than perfect. That inner critic probably arrived sometime during childhood, so take it easy on your inner kid-artist. What does she need to hear from you to know that she's safe to create freely? Taking the time to heal the inner critic—healing the inner fear that manifests in a voice filled with fear-based, crippling criticism—can set a CG free.

Keep a notebook handy at home or in your office. The next time you find yourself procrastinating, write down the excuses, thoughts, and fears related to your goals. Let your emotions surface, and deal with them.

I wish I could heal all of the stuff that comes up for you with just one chapter in this book. For staggering procrastination, anxiety, or depression that's getting in the way of achieving your creative goals or making healthy choices, find yourself a therapist who can get you on the right track by addressing underlying issues. If you had to move a table, and it was way too big to do on your own, you'd get help, right? Apply that logic here. You don't have to stay stuck. There are all kinds of therapists and energy workers who can help. I encourage you to embark on a path to heal anything that hurts. You're the one with everything to gain by healing whatever's blocking you. So go ahead, free your inner child and your inner creative girl.

Here are tricks and suggestions to get you started on your creative work. Employ these tricks after you've allowed the un-derlying fear to surface and express itself. Remember, if you don't deal with the root of the problem, these tricks and tips are like slapping a Band-Aid over a gaping hole.

Take It Piece by Piece

After my literary agent and I sold this book, I was floating on air. A week after the sale, when the celebratory drinks and dinners were over, I sat down to start writing. I stared at my book proposal (a seventy-five page document with a detailed outline and sample chapter) and felt completely overwhelmed at the realization that I had over two hundred more pages to write. I called my dad, expressed my fears, and he said, "Katie, just take it sentence by sentence, page by page."

When you break down large tasks into teeny tiny manageable ones, life doesn't seem as hard. Go ahead and freak out if that's what you like to do, but limit this self-indulgence to fifteen minutes. Don't allow fear-based, negative thoughts to spiral; they're not productive. Cut them off at the impasse by going for a walk, listening to your favorite music, doing jumping jacks, meditating, or calling a close friend. Then, get back to the drawing board and make a game plan.

When starting a task, keep in mind the following E.L. Doctorow quote about writing. It's applicable to all sorts of creative endeavors. "Writing a book is like driving at night with the headlights. You can only see what's directly in front of you but you can make the whole trip that way."

The Ten-Minute Rule

The next time you find yourself procrastinating, tell yourself you'll work on the task you've been avoiding for just ten minutes. This little trick works for two reasons. First, anyone can do anything for ten minutes. Almost always, you'll find that once you get started, the task isn't so bad after all, and you'll find yourself continuing your work past the allotted time.

The second reason is the more significant of the two; starting a task is almost always the hardest part, so by continually doing this, you're training yourself to get good at simply starting. Within a few weeks, it will become routine.

Enlist a Fellow CG

If your creative work becomes too solitary, it's time to grab a workmate. Having a partner in crime to collaborate with and answer to will automatically make you more accountable. Anyone you know who is also responsible for scheduling her own creative time may want to partner up at a table in your local coffee shop on weekday afternoons. The moral support will keep you buoyed when you're tempted to ditch your creative work and watch soap operas.

Get Out of the House

If the home office is driving you batty, it's time to get out of the house. This can be as simple as a midday break for the gym. Sometimes, just going to grab coffee first thing in the morning—which involves getting out of your pajamas, usually—can set you in the right frame of mind for work.

We've already addressed the importance of factoring in the day-to-day lifestyle that's best for you, whether that be solitary confinement or a community environment that makes Woodstock look anti-social. If there's not a CG in your network who wants to partner, try a shared studio space for artists. You'll meet new friends and reap the social benefits of an office-like setting.

Check out www.workatjelly.com to find a creative, social work environment in your area.

Volunteer: Get Out of Your Head and Put Your CG Plight in Perspective

It's pretty hard to lose sight of what's important in life when you make what's important in life part of your life. While writing this book, I took a week off to go to Lourdes, France, to volunteer through an organization that matches volunteers with people suffering from a myriad of illnesses. I wore a 1940s-esque nurse uniform all week: white skirt, white collared shirt, red cardigan, stockings, black shoes, and a white veil. I was out of my head and using my energy each day to help the five-year-old boy with whom I was paired. It was one of the best weeks of my life.

There's a creative side effect, too. Every time you switch up your surroundings, your creativity is stimulated. So leave your ego at the door and get out there and volunteer. There's no better way in the world to remind yourself that it's only a book, only a show, only a job, than to help people in need.

Bonus points if you can use your creativity while volunteering. Mentoring somone who benefits from your gifts reminds you of the innate goodness of your artistic pursuit.

Check out www.volunteermatch.org to find service work in your area.

Keep to a Schedule

Creative types benefit greatly from a schedule. Of course, ideas will strike at midnight, but the better you become at adhering to a schedule the more practiced you become at buckling down to work. Set an alarm for the same time each day. Try going to bed at the same time every night. These little changes make a big difference. Varying your sleeping schedule too much is like voluntarily giving yourself jetlag.

Pay attention to when you feel the most energetic during the day and schedule your toughest work for those hours. Become protective of those hours. When I started writing, I stopped scheduling afternoonlunches. I found that I can make jewelry whenever— 9 am or 9 pm. But writing took more brainpower; it's an activity that I have to do during the morning and afternoon when my mind is sharpest. Honor the hours when you're feeling your best and get down to work.

Go Offline

If you're not disciplined, the Internet can be a black hole. Email, Facebook, online videos, and links to everything from IQ tests to photos of Golden Globe fashion trends are major time drains. If you're a web programmer or an online video producer, fine. But unless you have a very good reason

✻ CREATIVE TIP ✻

Allow Yourself to Make Garbage

Allow yourself to make mistakes. Not everything you create is going to be perfect or saleable. The CGs I interviewed spoke of how important it is to create every day. Your creative talent is like a muscle that improves when worked out and stretched. Get in the habit of daily creativity.

to be online for several hours each day, you should seriously consider what you *could* be doing with the time you're spending surfing the Net.

When CG-in-action and author Anna Carey is on deadline, she takes her computer to the basement of a coffee shop that doesn't have Internet access. She says, "You wouldn't believe how much you can accomplish in an eight-hour workday without the distraction of the Internet. It's incredible."

In the digital age, it seems we've forgotten what it's like to devote eight hours (with a few breaks for food, water, and coffee, of course) to our projects. If you're serious about accomplishing a creative assignment, unplug the Internet. If you like, devote half an hour to answering emails midday. Depending on your work, you may need to be available by email at all times. But that doesn't mean you need to be on Facebook, Twitter, blogs, and other forms of online procrastination.

If you need to research something on the Web, you may want to save that task for the last part of your workday. That way, if one click leads to another and you find yourself taking an online pop culture trivia quiz, you'll have already accomplished what you needed. Plus, at the end of the day—when you've already finished your work—you're motivated to just get the research done and be finished with your workday, instead of getting lost on the Internet for hours to avoid doing other work.

Try it out. Unplug your Internet during work hours for one week and see the difference it makes to your focus and productivity.

Dip into Your Metaphorical Bag of Tricks and Get Inspired

Pull from your eco-friendly canvas tote of blockbusting tricks. You stock this bag by paying attention to where and when you feel inspired. When are the ideas flowing? For me, when I go to the movies and see the previews, my mind gets supercharged with ideas. Maybe it's the magic of the movies—the popcorn, the dark theater—or maybe it's the movie trailers themselves, each one cut down to the most harrowing and intriguing parts of a story.

Are you visually inspired? Or does music and sound get you going?

Take note of what inspires you, and pull from this supply when you need a boost. The following ideas will help get you started.

Change your scenery. Go for a drive. Take a walk. Go to a museum. Get your hands dirty working in your garden. Try creating in different environments—outdoors, a coffee shop, a campus library—and see what gets you going.

Dive into other artists' work. Either of your own genre, or something different. If it overwhelms you to surround yourself with your type of work, look elsewhere for inspiration. If you're a choreographer, go to an abstract art exhibit.

Ask a colleage for help. Creative people love to collaborate. Casting director Alaine Alldaffer says, "There's something about two minds together that creates synergy and creative flow." If you're stuck on something, run the idea or project by an encouraging peer you trust. Brainstorm ideas with them.

Exercise. Physical activity gets your heart rate going and your blood flowing. Ideas will follow.

Do something related to your business that isn't creative. When I'm just not feeling creative, I tackle a business aspect of my job. This might be calculating sales tax or returning emails. You're not going to feel inspired at every waking moment, but it feels great to be productive in the meanwhile. Usually after a few hours of paperwork, you're ready to get back to the creative stuff.

Have a conversation with yourself. Start a dialogue with yourself by writing back and forth with your left hand and your right hand. I'm not kidding. Try it. You'll activate both hemispheres of your brain and you'll be surprised at what ends up on the paper.

In an article for *O* magazine titled "Creativity Boost: How to Tap into Right Brain Thinking," author Martha Beck writes, "The right side of the brain, which controls the left hand, will say things you don't know that you know. It specializes in assessing your physical and mental feelings, and it often offers solutions . . . You'll find there's a little Zen master in that left hand of yours (not surprisingly, left-handed people are disproportionately represented in creative professions)."

Getting Unstuck

CG-In-action Barbara Barry is an artist who teaches courses in painting and breaking through creative blocks. Here, Barbara shares five tips for moving through creative resistance.

1. Be Curious

Blocks come in all shapes and "guises." A common response is to clutch or panic. The more we fight against them the tighter their hold. What if we approach them with curiosity instead of rigidity? What if we don't take them on face value? Then it becomes possible to create a doorway through the block.

Exchanging the "Oh, no!" response with the "I wonder why…" response is to leave crisis mode and enter into contemplation. We now have options.

2. Listen to the Body

Sometimes we don't realize we are tensing a shoulder or have an ache in the neck. Tune in. Slowly scan your body from head to toe. Locate the sensation. Where blockage exists in the body, flow can't happen. Take a few moments. Stretch. Breathe. And then…

3. Find an Image

Whether the block is a sensation in your body or a strong emotional feeling, it helps to describe it using an image. For example, a burning sensation might suggest a fire, a volcano, or a glass of orange juice. In the painting process we paint it. The image or symbol is the "container" into which we put the ache or the pain. With practice, just holding the image in your mind can have the same effect.

4. Imagine

Why stop there? The more specific we can make the image the more playful it becomes and the looser the block's grip. Take the image another step. What are the visual details? Where is it? If it could talk, what would it say? What would you say back?

5. Repeat a Mantra

In moments of doubt we can "talk" ourselves through crisis by repeating a phrase of support. Speaking positive thoughts out loud can interrupt old inner dialogues. Make it playful. My favorite: "It's only paint and paper."

The tip that works one moment may not in another. What does work is to keep the mind guessing so it doesn't know what to expect. Find playful ways to break through automatic responses. This helps us to stay the course into that unknown place, rich with possibility.

Painting Abroad

CG-in-action Nicole Condon is an American artist living in Beijing. She paints and teaches art at Beijing's Central Academy of Fine Art. Below, she shares her thoughts on getting the creative juices flowing.

CG: When do you find you're most inspired?

NC: I'm often inspired when traveling to other countries or far places, but strangely, I'm even more inspired while in my own city. My brain often freely imagines when I'm on the bus in Beijing or on the subway in New York City. There's something about the white noise in the background. It's nearly impossible for me to sit down and say *I'm going to be creative now*. I'm much more inspired on the go and then can come back to my studio to work the ideas out.

CG: Are you aware of what blocks your creativity?

NC: What hinders my creativity most is the overwhelming feeling of having things to do. I tell myself that I need to do to the dishes, fold laundry, and run errands before I can have time for painting. What usually happens is that I spend all morning cleaning and doing errands and then am exhausted by "painting time."

To resolve this problem, I completely switched my schedule around. I spend my morning being creative, the afternoon teaching, and then do home-based chores—dishes, laundry—at night because they don't take a lot of brain power. It was really about figuring out when I could focus the best.

CG: Any other tips for optimizing creativity?

NC: If there's a specific area in or outside of your home that you can have for your creative space, that's ideal. It's your space. You can close the door or close the curtain and feel that you can be in your creative world. For me it's also important to feel that I can make some really ugly things and unsuccessful paintings without being judged. For every good painting, I will make at least ten bad ones. I close my door and let myself work through the process.

CG: What tricks do you have for getting out of a creative block?

NC: I love to mind map. I started doing this as an undergraduate and find that by brainstorming (not in a list format, but in the round sense where the words can freely expand in any direction) is very helpful. Just by thinking of word associations, new ideas that I hadn't thought about before suddenly emerge.

(Note: A mind map is a diagram that surrounds a central word—ideas and concepts branch out from that word to help you visualize and generate new ideas. You can find more info about mind mapping on the Internet, or check out *The Mind Map Book* by Tony Buzan and Barry Buzan.)

How to Kick Your Butt
When You Don't Have a Boss to Do it For You

Philana Marie Boles is a novelist (her books have been published by Random House, HarperCollins and Viking) and the founder of Ahluve Consulting. Philana is one of the most productive creative girls I know. Below, she shares her tips for optimal productivity.

CG: What are your tried and true methods for upping productivity and nipping procrastination in the bud?

PMB: Three things are key for productivity: My list. My focus. And my schedule. I keep a constant running list of all the things I want to accomplish. Having everything running around in my head overwhelms me; seeing my list on paper makes each item a tangible goal. The next essential for my productivity is focus. When it's time to work I turn the television off and also the ringer on my phone. Because I know how toxic it can be, I avoid the web at all costs.

The final key is my schedule. Depending on the time sensitivity of the project, I might spend a half hour on something or maybe even two hours if a deadline is pending. Once the allotted amount of time is up, I move on to the next project on my agenda and know that *tomorrow* I will pick it up again. It is impossible to be successful if you do not set a schedule for yourself. Otherwise you are constantly spinning your wheels and never moving forward. Who wants that?

CG: Any quick procrastination busters?

PMB: I give myself little incentives: a new movie that I'm dying to see or a new issue of *Vanity Fair* in the mail. I jot down the fun things I *want* to do and tell myself that I can *only* do them once I've accomplished the goal. Another quick cure is going for a walk outdoors. The fresh air gives me a burst of energy.

Discipline

Throughout this book, we've talked to several CGs who've told us they didn't have the discipline to set their own deadlines. These CGs found work at a creative company, where deadlines and limits were set for them. So what if you want to work for yourself but lack discipline? You'll have to take this problem seriously; if you don't have discipline, your business won't be able to stay afloat and your creative potential won't be reached.

You can try incentives like Philana mentioned in her interview: rewarding yourself for a job well done. Or, cultivate your discipline by taking up something that requires, well, discipline. Sign up for a martial arts class or a semester of yoga. Try long distance running or a ballet class.

You can also register for a class related to your creative talent. Try to find a workshop environment that requires you to produce work each week—the deadlines will keep you churning out new work. And when you pay hard-earned cash to do something, you're far less likely to drop it.

Go easy on yourself. Know that you may have a productive day of brilliant work followed by a not-so-inspired one.

Creativity has a childlike quality. I've found that when you keep the sense of adventure in your work, you'll find it's less about being disciplined and more about allowing your creativity to flow.

Balance: Set a Quit Time and Leave the House

You *do* need to stop working at some point. If you're a night owl who loves working in the wee hours of the morning, fine, but make sure there are a few hours around dinnertime when you quit working and reenter the social world. This can be hard when you're working at a job during the day and wanting to work on your own projects at night. It can be exhilarating to work for yourself; there are no limits to what you can accomplish and often, you want to keep going.

While I was writing this book, I thought to myself, *Why not write a fiction novel at the same time?* I worked on the book you're holding during the morning, made jewelry in the afternoon, and worked on the novel

Turning *Aha!* Moments into Creation

Maybe you've never had a creative block in your life. Your imagination makes wild rabbits look infertile. Being creative often means being subject to a barrage of ideas and inspiration. It can help to carry a small notebook so that if you're inspired on the go, you can get your thoughts onto paper.

While brainstorming, don't censor your ideas (that part comes later). Have at it while you brainstorm; one idea usually leads to another. Keep writing until you feel your brainstorming feels complete.

Once your ideas are in front of you, practice boiling down each idea to its most simple and lucid form. Get rid of the superfluous. Examine those ideas and focus on the strongest. As a creative type, you'll have all kinds of ideas and insights, and it can be easy to get distracted by multiple ideas. You'll think, hey, this is a great idea for a novel, but so is this, and this . . .

Focus, and whittle each idea into a core idea.

As you narrow your ideas, get second, third, and tenth opinions. Remember, it's your idea and you have to follow your gut. But outside feedback is helpful, too. After all, your creativity will likely be subject to public opinion at some point.

Once you feel confident that you've narrowed your ideas to the strongest concepts possible, see the ideas through to creation. The point of this strategy is to get inspired, train yourself to narrow down to core ideas, and then *get going*.

in the evening. My husband came home from work and I'd still be working. He'd turn off the TV to go to bed and I'd still be working. I loved writing, so why not do it all the time? But when I got into bed, the computer screen was still flashing and words were swimming around my brain at midnight. After a few months of rotten sleep, I had to curb my own enthusiasm and get some balance. I set a quit time of seven o'clock. The computer goes off—no more writing or emailing. I have dinner with my husband, and then spend twenty minutes convincing him to do a yoga DVD. After yoga, we watch television or read books together.

Pay attention to exactly what you need to achieve balance. The idea is to prepare for a lifetime of creative work, not burn out after six months from stress and exhaustion.

Tough Love

Now that you have a few strategies, get to work. Because in the end, that's how you'll get where you want to go. Planning to work, thinking about work, complaining about work, and daydreaming about work, isn't actually *work*. Buckle down and be the creator you're dreaming of being right now.

Dealing with Rejection and Criticism

You're Not Your Job Title, Your Reviews, Your Awards, or Your Lack Thereof

As creative types, we need to shift our tendency to define who we are by what we *do*. Here's the real story: even if you never act, sing, design, write, dance, or produce creative work again, you're still entirely *you*, and that's enough. Being an actress, a writer, or a designer is just what you do for a living, it's not who you are. I've never heard an accountant say she lived for being an accountant, or that being an accountant is who she is and what defines her as a human being. So quit that kind of thinking. It's only work; it's important, but *it's not who you are*.

Realizing that your career doesn't define you makes it much easier to have your work critiqued by colleagues, bosses, critics, audiences, etc. A review of your latest creative efforts will be just that: a review of your work and how you can improve it. This concept will be tested, over and over again, but when you accept it, you'll gain perspective. The more successful you become, the more you'll open yourself up to criticism and outside opinions of your work; this is part of creativity as a business so it's beneficial to learn this lesson early.

In the digital age, the possibility of someone writing and posting nasty comments about you and your work has increased significantly. Maybe these commentators have an angry boss who yells at them all day, maybe they have inadequacy issues or a deep-seated fear of confrontation, but the bottom line is that the Internet is anonymous and some people get their ya-yas by writing nasty things. Others wish they could do what you're doing or had the courage to try, and it's easier for them to tear down than to build.

The first time I read something negative about my jewelry I cried right into my dog's shoulder. After a glowing article on my work, someone commented, "Oh, please, this designer is so overrated." It was too late at night to call my wise younger sister, but when I told her in the morning she whooped with glee. "Are you *kidding* me, that's practically a compliment, to be *over-rated*, you have to be *rated!*"

The most exciting stuff in fashion, art, entertainment, and literature can also be controversial, and not everyone is going to like what you do. About her final book in the Harry Potter series, J.K. Rowling said, "Some people will hate it. Because in order for some people to love it, others will have to hate it." And even if you have one big hit and fancy yourself a critically acclaimed sensation, you'll still flop from time to time.

Accept that there will be criticism and move forward anyway. I know how personal creative work feels, but understand that it's your work; it's not *you*. You create because it's what you love to do. Take the pressure off by reminding yourself that you'll continue to create as long as it fulfills you and you enjoy your creative process. *What someone else has to say about your work has nothing to do with you.*

Meaningful Work

Your work isn't you, but it's still an important aspect of your big picture. In *The Van Gogh Blues: The Creative Person's Path through Depression*, author Eric Maisel writes, "In order for you to live an authentic, meaningful life, which is the principle remedy for the depression creative people experience, you must feel that the plan of your life is meaningful, the work you do is meaningful, and the way you spend your time is meaningful."

For repressed CGs, not having a creative outlet can lead to depression and dissatisfaction. If you're still in the process of looking for a creative job or collecting clients to go full-time as a freelancer, this means you must pay attention to your creative needs in the meantime. For those of you already in creative jobs or owners of creative businesses, pay attention to the projects you're choosing and the direction your career is taking. Continually assess whether the work is satisfying your creative needs. You must be self-aware. This is *your* lifetime; you create your experience.

As you go forward, have a clear picture of what makes life full of meaning for you. What type of creative work feels authentic? What creative *work* feels more like a creative *force*?

Take some time to articulate your spiritual and creative plan for a meaningful life. You can focus on your relationships, your creative work, and overall intentions for a life well lived. The questions below will get you started.

What work feels genuine and in alignment with what you believe to be meaningful?

_____

_____

_____

_____

_____

Which professional relationships feel authentic?

_____

_____

_____

_____

_____

Which colleagues do you admire and enjoy collaborating with most?

_____

_____

_____

Who do you choose to surround yourself with to feel good about yourself and your work?

_____

_____

_____

_____

_____

What does a life full of meaning look and feel like?

_____

_____

_____

_____

Keep these answers in mind as you take on new projects. Maybe blogging about celebrities for a gossip column leaves you unfulfilled. Maybe it fulfills your every desire. Every CG defines meaningful work in a different way. Pay attention to what feels right for you and choose projects accordingly. Of course you'll balance passion projects with projects that pay the bills. But work toward achieving a comfortable balance between working for a paycheck and performing meaningful, authentic work. As you gain success, this balance will likely shift and you'll be able to consistently choose work that is most meaningful and in alignment with what you choose to create.

Creative Tip: Don't Worry About Keeping Up With the Joneses

Don't waste time measuring your work against friends with more conformist careers. **Many times, their careers have a linear path: law school=lawyer. Our paths tend to be more trial and error. Often, pay is sporadic and unpredictable; we can have a shabby year freelancing followed by a fantastic one.**

It's not productive to compare yourself with other people (creative or non-creative). Return your focus to your individual work. You can never truly know someone else's path. Concentrate on your own.

Gratitude

Gratitude has been a big part of my creative life and spiritual practice. It's a simple concept, and it doesn't mean you have to act like things are perfect when they're not. It means that you focus on what you *do* have, and express gratitude for the things in your life for which you feel grateful.

You met clothing designer Abigail Lorick in Chapter 11. Abigail says, "I continually, consciously, give thanks. Even when I have a bad day, or receive lousy business news, I trust that I always have everything that I need and that nothing is being done to me, it is being done for me."

Gratitude doesn't have to be a fancy offering. You can notice your own gratitude in relation to a creative achievement, or you can say *thank you* quietly to yourself while walking along the sidewalk because the coffee you bought is especially fresh and your entire day is free to create.

Try it.

No Matter What, Keep Doing What You Love

CG-in-action and author Nova Ren Suma writes stories for adults and novels for teens and tweens. Here's what she had to say about her creative journey.

NRS: When you're a creative type and want to make a life doing what you love—when this is your dream above all other dreams, when you dream it so hard, nothing else matters—no one and no thing can tell you to stop. Your first novel could get rejected by the agent you assumed was your "dream agent," and your next novel could get rejected by every agent you query, but that doesn't mean you should stop writing, acting, singing, and creating. I didn't, though I admit I came close.

Before I gave up officially, what I did was take a look at myself and what I was writing. I dug deep and decided to go at it once more. To try harder than I ever have in my life. Again.

I realized I was writing about teenagers all the time—and maybe, just maybe, that even though I got my MFA in writing fiction for adults, maybe I should try to write for young adults instead. And that's how my first published tween novel came to be. And that's how my novel for teens came to be, the one that got me my actual "dream agent" after I'd given up on the idea of agents completely.

If someone had come up to me when I thought it was time to give up—when I was sitting there telling myself it would be nice to give up, that it wouldn't hurt so bad, that I would be a-okay—if someone had said to me, *Wait a couple years, you'll see*, I would have laughed. Or cried.

But that's the thing: I couldn't do it. I absolutely couldn't stop trying. At my lowest points, I wouldn't have wanted to hear this, *but rejection can be the biggest opportunity you can imagine*. It's a chance to show the world—and yourself—what you're really made of.

It could be a matter of reinventing yourself as I did. To keep on trying—but with something new this time. A new idea? A new manuscript? A new outlook? Know that it will take time. It will take more effort than you might think you have in you. It will get your hopes dangerously up, and push you that much closer to perhaps getting your heart stomped on, but the only way to know is to put your all into it. Yes, again.

All I know is that I don't think the person who had almost convinced herself to stop trying would have heard a word I said. I needed to let the rejection run its course. Sometimes I think I needed to get my heart stomped on to gain the strength to start over. Maybe it couldn't have happened any other way.

Rejection: It Happens to Everyone. Keep Going.

Stephenie Meyer, the author of the bestselling *Twilight Saga*, was rejected by every single agent she sent her manuscript to except for one. Stephen King's first three novels were rejected. You will experience rejection. But it's not the rejection that matters. The ability to bounce back from rejection and keep moving forward—even if forward means a slightly different direction—is what sets a creative powerhouse apart from the rest. Go ahead and have a good cry if you like. But know that every single creative success you see has faced rejection. When one avenue closes, others present themselves, so keep your eyes open for your next move.

Welcome to Your New Life

Now you know what's possible for you. Get ready for an adventure. Put this book down, go forth, and conquer. And email me—I'm serious. Find contact information on www.katharinesise.com. I want to hear how you're doing and what you're doing and what it feels like to achieve your wildest creative dreams.

I wish you all the luck, light, and love in the world.

How to Ace an Interview with an Agent or Manager

Agent Tracy Weiss says a meeting with an agent or manager is like a blind date . . . and you'd be silly not to prepare in the same way.

Mints. Check.

Incredibly cute outfit. Check.

Good attitude. Check.

Tracy says, "Agents will have seen what you look like and know some facts about you (think online dating), have gotten the scoop from a mutual acquaintance (think set up), or approached you frantically on the street and swore they could tell by looking at your lovely face that you are very talented (think scary stalker, don't date OR set up business meetings with these people). Every rule you've learned from the dating game applies here. Meeting new representation is like selecting a boyfriend or partner. You need someone you can communicate with, someone you can trust, someone who can support you in good times and in bad, and most importantly, someone you can stand to be around—Treat your first meeting like a date."

WARDROBE
(Dating rule: dress to impress, but not to kill.)

"Potential clients who stand out come into my office looking casually put together. Your best bet is a figure-flattering outfit that looks like you put a little thought into it . . . but aren't trying too hard. Think Thursday night: meeting for one drink. You could choose a casual dress or jeans and an interesting top—something with a bit of your personality infused. The cliché 'dress for the job you want' applies here. For an MTV VJ, I'd expect to see an ensemble with trendy accessories. For a CNN reporter, maybe dark jeans with a bright color layered under a blazer—authoritative but modern. My biggest pet peeve is when a spunky wannabe Alexa Chung comes dressed in a business suit. Makeup and hair should be the icing on the well-dressed cake. And unless you're trying to book the Playboy Channel, leave the over-the-top cleavage at home.

LISTEN
(Dating rule: zip your lip and let your date do the talking.)

"Ever been on a date where the guy talks about himself incessantly? Like you really want to know about his cat's psoriasis? Actors are notorious for being 'that guy' in a meeting. Yes, it's important to be able to sell yourself, but make sure you're having a two-way conversation. Agents pitch their clients all day, every day and live their lives on their cell and Blackberry constantly talking about other people and their projects. If you're the 30-minute meeting where the agent has an opportunity to engage in a conversation about themselves in addition to vetting new talent, you're automatically the bright spot in their day. Agents and managers are people with egos too, and while you don't want to brownnose, it's nice to give them an outlet. Besides, if you have an easy rapport with us, we know you will kill it at an audition.

"An easy opener *(like with stranger you're picking up in a bar)* is to ask where they're from and where they went to college. If you can find a way to tie their answers back to you or to a career opportunity you've had, even better. I still remember a meeting with a twentysome-thing who wanted to be the next Erin Andrews. When I mentioned I went to Michigan State University for undergrad and love college basketball, she immediately named a player from the school's past and referenced a rivalry. Did she Google me and arm herself with the info? It doesn't matter. She sounded sincere, and I remember her for it. You also want to know a little bit about the people sitting on the other side of the desk. This is a partnership. Would you accept an engagement ring from a stranger who got down on one knee in the middle of a busy sidewalk? *(Please say no.)* It has to be a good fit on both sides. You should be as excited about the person you just met as you hope they are about you.

DON'T BE BORING
(Dating Rule: interesting is as sexy as . . . well, sexy.)

"Agents and managers talk to a million people a day, so they're a little proprietary of their time. In this meeting, have something interesting to talk about and know the market and where you fit into it. I specialize in the reality/alternative programming world and every pretty, wholesome girl next store wants to be the next 'lady from the Travel Channel.' If they had done their homework, they'd know that her name is Samantha Brown and that type of programming is on its way out. Instead, they'd know Travel Channel (renamed without the "the" as of 2010) looks for interesting characters with a strong area of expertise they can use to immerse themselves into the situation. Watch television. Be able to say, 'I really see myself in the same vein as _____.' And back up that idea with some facts about why you would work. If you're desperate to do a travel show, tell me about backpacking through India and the time the pilot let you fly the seaplane in New Zealand. You cannot just say 'I like to travel.' So do I, but I don't get to host a show about it.

"We often use this phrase in the industry: 'They just popped.' This means your energy, your look, and your personality jumps off the screen at producers and casting directors . . . and most importantly, will stop viewers from changing the channel. There's no better way to make that impact than to talk about something you're passionate about. Personal stories with some tie-in to your career goals make me feel like I know you and I'd like to get to know you better *(think sought-after second date)*. Regardless of your prior experience in the business, this is how you get noticed. I'll go to bat for a total newcomer who stands out faster than I'll take on someone who's had two series on HGTV who bores me. If I don't believe you're ready for some of the bigger jobs, I'll help you get smaller projects to build on.

"A quick tip: never name drop. We may ask who you've made connections with, but don't gush. For all you know, I hate so and so at that network. What if I call Mr. X at ABC Productions and ask him about you and he doesn't remember meeting? That won't speak well for you. It's always important to be honest and open about the experiences you've had and people you know. But in our tech-savvy age, just because you're Facebook friends with a girl who's a producer at HBO doesn't mean she's about to hire you."

ALWAYS BRING YOUR MARKETING TOOLS
(Dating Rule: leave a lasting impression.)

"Do not take the meeting if you don't have something to leave behind. If you do have some credits, an edited reel is the best possible calling card. It shows what you look like on camera and the kinds of work you've done before. If not? A well-written bio that focuses on your experiences and areas of expertise works fine if you don't have a full résumé. If you're looking for work in the commercial arena, you *must* have a head shot that doesn't look like you're performing the 'Alas, Poor Yorik' speech. And if you think bringing your comp card from when you were a model in the early 90s is a good idea? It's not. Pictures must look like the person who walks into my office.

"It's okay to stand out. If you and the agent decide to work together, they'll help you reel in your sparkling personality if it's 'too much.' However, your stand-out presence is of those things that can help a stranger remember you. I once received a cover letter written by a comedic actor new in town from Denver. Instead of the 'I'm an actor, I'm talented, please meet me' standard, he wrote a skit. A skit where he was harassing me on the subway platform asking for a meeting translated into an actual meeting. Yes, it could have been the cheesiest thing I've ever read and I may have thrown it out. But it was really funny. So take a risk if you can do it well."

DON'T BE DESPERATE
(Dating Rule: don't be a Needy Nancy.)

"We can smell it. It's an automatic turn-off. Being overly earnest and aggressive with follow up emails will make us want to run the other way. It's simple. The meeting starts from when you walk into the office. It ends when you walk out. During the meeting be the best version of the natural you. Have a lovely chat about your accomplishments and any interesting stories that may come up in conversation. From there, you leave your materials and follow up 1 to 2 times over the next few weeks via email. That's it. After a first date, I'd hope you wouldn't stalk the guy wondering when he wants to see you again. The same applies here. If an agent or manager is blasé about you, they're not going to work hard for you. And you'd be better off on your own.

"Just like single ladies who sit home on Saturday nights or scour the Lower East Side for 'Mr. Right' and think the rest of their lives cannot start until they land a man, many people new to show business feel like their career cannot start until they have an agent. Nowadays this isn't true. You can scour the Internet for the first opportunity (though for both dating and show biz, be wary of craigslist.org). Agents can get you bigger and better jobs and will get you more compensation. That being said, there's no need to throw yourself at the first guy/agent you meet. When you're confident and secure with who you are and your talent, that's when someone will fall all over themselves to be on your team."

Creative Moms-in-Action Share Their Tips

Since I'm not a mom yet, I went to the experts for tips on how to balance a creative life with motherhood. Below, they share their Mama-dos and Mama-don'ts.

Moms can also check out www.workingmother.com or www.justformom.com for more advice.

Dina Koutas Poch is a filmmaker and author. Below, she shares her wisdom on juggling mommy duties with a creative schedule.

DKP: Right now I'm typing with one hand as I bounce my 7-week old baby in a sling and my 20-month-old toddler chases our dog singing, "Hello to doggy! So nice to meet you!"—not exactly fertile ground for creativity or space for uninterrupted concentration. So how do you get it done? As a creative mother of two, here are 8 truths to being a creative juggernaut at home while still keeping your kids alive.

1) Let things slide, because they will.

I learned I can't be Julia Child and the world's most fun mom (there is an award for this) *and* a dedicated writer at the same time. It's hard to let dishes pile up and overlook a kitchen pantry that resembles 1940's Stalinist Hungary (read: only canned beets and horseradish). It's usually just for a week (or two) and luckily my husband is a better cook than I am.

2) Invest in personal real estate.

A desk in the bedroom, a folding table in the hallway, a nook in the living room—wherever it is, I try to create a dedicated area for work. Place a plant there, tune in to NPR, and hang a "Kittens on Safari" calendar. Honor your workspace, because a section of the dining room table where your papers get pushed around nightly doesn't exactly read as "important." No more picking couscous off pages the next morning.

3) It takes a village.

Behind most creative moms is a team of baby handlers—grandparents, day cares, nannies, kind neighbors, and husbands that rock. It might seem self-indulgent to find babysitters so you can check out a gallery, because it's not on the direct path to "productivity"; however, as an artist, I have to allow myself be influenced and inspired. If you can't leave them behind, sometimes it's worth the sugar highs and rotten teeth of ice cream bribes to pack up the kids and drag them with you.

4) You're going to be tired: bone tired.
And it's almost impossible to feel creative when you're exhausted. Caffeine and fresh air help but not as much as sleep! It's rough, what can I say?

5) Rome could have been built during your kid's naptime.
It just would have taken longer. If you only have three hours a day, be realistic about what you can accomplish. You are not going to write a new chapter for your book in a week. Give it about three. It only took me a year to figure *that* out.

6) Do-not-disturb sign
Where is baby tiger? How do you get play dough out of the carpet? Does eggplant make her gassy? If you aren't protective of uninterrupted creative time, you'll end up trying to launch your greeting card business in between doing the laundry, shopping online for swimmy diapers, and researching hand-foot-mouth disease. Nothing gets accomplished.

7) The Mommy time tax
When scheduling meetings, interviews, or important phone calls from home, budget at least a ten-minute buffer. Who knows why it happens, but by the time you're fully dressed, with your (not someone else's) car keys, wallet, cell phone, and laptop in hand, ten minutes have vaporized. Sometimes, it's twenty minutes when your toddler places your car keys inside her play veterinary clinic.

8) Not making the dough (at first).
It may take a while before you make money from your creative career. And with kids, money is tighter because kids are lovable, fiscal black holes. Hello, have you read a little book called *Harry*

Potter? J.K. Rowling did it while depressed, impoverished, and with a baby in tow, so get on it.

There will be rejection (you're scheduled to appear on *The Today Show* and you get bumped for a dog trainer) and setbacks (like your kid has the stomach flu *again*). There are always a million reasons to stop; it's important to have a roster of people who bolster you when you feel it's impossible launch a new career with kids at home. No matter the stress, I'm so happy to be able to write *and* have lunchtime mac and cheese with my babies every day. I wouldn't trade it for anything (well, maybe 12 hours of uninterrupted sleep.)

Wendy G. Ramunno is a chef and food writer. Below, she shares the wisdom she gained as a creative mom-in-action.

WGR: Before your new baby arrives, you may be overwhelmed with the logistics of incorporating a little bundle of joy into your very independent life. Or, if you're like me, you'll be more than a bit clueless and assume that you'll get all your work done with no problem, as long as your mom stops over occasionally to babysit. Juggling work and a growing family is a challenge, but there's no question that having a flexible career you're passionate about makes it easier.

1) Maternity leave—take it!

If you can swing it, plan for at least three months off for maternity leave and stick to it. While it may be very tempting to take on a small project or two, keep in mind that a new baby sucks up virtually all of your time and energy in the beginning; you'll be lucky to have fifteen minutes to yourself. If your newborn is a little, let's say, "challenging" like our daughter was, this is especially critical. I vaguely recall editing text in a state of semi-hallucination after consecutive sleepless nights of attempting to pacify a screaming nine-week-old. In the end, I ended up feeling like I was failing at work *and* being a mom. Depending on your field, you may be able to pass a project along to a colleague or ask friends and family members to help you with the most vital tasks needed to keep your business running while you tend to the baby.

2) Breastfeeding bonus

One of the fabulous parts about being a CG is that you likely have flexible work hours and a nontraditional work environment—an ideal setup for a nursing mom. If you decide to breastfeed, rejoice in the fact that you won't be faced with pumping in a bathroom stall or broom closet, which is the awful reality for many women returning from maternity leave. If you're fortunate enough to be able to schedule your work around your newborn's feeding times, you might even decide to skip pumping altogether.

3) Child care options

You'll likely need at least a few weeks of trial and error to determine what works best for arranging child care. Come up with your ideal situation and give it a try, but if it's not working for you or your baby, move to Plan B. Some CGs need a very structured environment to get any work done, while others prefer a more haphazard approach, fitting in a few hours of work during the afternoon nap and then more time in the evening. If you do choose an unstructured plan based on your child's schedule, be aware that a newborn's routine can be very unpredictable (chances are she'll wake up from a nap just as you dial in to an important conference call). Whatever you decide, be realistic about how much work you can get done in the time you have, whether it's two afternoons a week or three full days. If you work part-time, consider joining a babysitting co-op or trading-off with another

mom—both great ways to meet other parents while saving tons on childcare.

4) Home office considerations

If you work at home, assess the size and layout of your house or apartment and your ability to block outside noise. Some CGs find that they're too distracted by the baby playing with the nanny down the hall, but others thrive in an environment that incorporates family time into the workday. At the very least, you'll need an office space with a door you can close for some privacy.

5) Give yourself a break

Remember that a new baby turns your world upside down, so it's not realistic to expect your professional life to chug along without interruption. Even two years after my daughter was born, as soon as I think I have everything all figured out, something throws it all out of whack—an amazing but time-consuming new project comes along when I'm already quite booked with other work, or my sitter cancels and our backup daycare facility is full. That's when I try to remind myself that I'm extremely lucky to do something I love to do and set my own priorities in both family and work life. It's not perfect, but being a CG mom works for me and I wouldn't have it any other way.

Professional Blogging 101

Kimberly Rae Miller blogs professionally for CBS, Yahoo's Women's Network, Shine, and her own blogs, The Kim Challenge www.thekimchallenge.com and Forkful of News www.fork fulofnews.com.

Below she shares her tips for blogging as a livelihood.

CG: What is the first step for readers looking to blog professionally?

KRM: The first step is developing your own blog. Blogger, Wordpress, and Live Journal all have free blog hosting options with design elements for the less HTML friendly among us. If you're looking to go the professional blogging track you can buy rights to your name on any of those sites, or try Drupal or Moveable Type.

CG: When is it time to look for advertisers?

KRM: When your blog starts to have a consistent readership, it's time. Google Ads is the easiest way to integrate ads into your site. Also consider advertising through ad networks, like Adify and BlogHer.

Directly approaching a company to ask for ad revenue can be done with solid statistical data behind you. Track your site statistics through Google Analytics, StatPress, or Site Meter.

CG: Should a CG have a certain amount of hits per month before approaching advertisers?

KRM: There isn't a concrete number. Different ad networks have varying requirements on how many hits per month depending on the demographic they're marketing to and the size of their advertisers, so you'll have to do some research.

CG: What's the best way to solicit work writing for other blogs and online media outlets?

KRM: Sites like www.odesk.com, www.elance.com and media bistro's job board, www.mediabistro.com are great job resources. When you submit for jobs you will need to show clips of your work. If you don't have professional clips, it's okay to present well-edited pieces from your own site. It's your writing style that will land you jobs, so you don't necessarily have to have a big name behind you, just solid writing skills.

Writing, like any other job, has more to do with networking than you'd think, and work leads to more work. Taking classes with other writers (most of them working writers) is a great place to make those sorts of connections.

Once you actually land a job, the technical stuff comes into play. When you blog for a living you want to be very careful about how you get paid, how much, and when. Contracts are important. Having a contract means you are obligated to follow through on a certain number of posts per week, but it also means that the company is required to pay you in a specified timeframe.

Remember that contracts are negotiable; you do have power over what you sign your name to. You can request that sites link to your personal website, what day of the month you are paid, and whether or not you can reuse content elsewhere. Some sites will have you sign a non-compete clause, meaning you won't write for their competitors or on a similar topic. If you write for a sports related site you may still be able to blog elsewhere about the environment, but probably not about health and fitness. That's why it's important to clarify the finer points during contract negotiations. Remember, most things are negotiable, but you have to speak up. You may be able to negotiate down the length of the non-compete clause so that you'll be able to write again on a similar topic in one month instead of three.

If you're paid to write, make sure you invoice on time. Companies usually have a day or two a month they process invoices, so you want yours to be in before that date or you could be looking at an extra month between paychecks.

CG: When starting out, what should a creative girl expect in terms of pay when writing for an online source?

KRM: Average pay for a blog is much smaller than the average pay for a magazine article (even for the exact same amount of words). The average range of pay per blog post is anywhere between $10 to $30. The monetary difference has to do with the site's popularity, advertising income, as well as the length and frequency of the posts.

If you're writing an in-depth look into Elder Law for a legal blog, you may be looking at a higher paid blog, but a short, funny post about a celebrity will probably pay less.

CG: Any last words of wisdom for aspiring professional bloggers?

KRM: Be protective of your brand. Only attach your name to sites you believe in and think are run with integrity. If you need money and have a job lined up you don't necessarily love, use a pseudonym. Become an expert in your field. If you write about food, write about food for as many sites as you can. The more you write about one thing, the more employable you become when it comes to that thing.

CG's looking to blog professionally should also check out www.problogger.net and http://www.kb

For Further Reading

The Small Business Bible by Steven D. Strauss

The Small Business Start-Up Kit by Peri H. Pakroo

The Business Side of Creativity by Cameron S. Foote

My So-Called Freelance Life and *The Anti 9-to-5 Guide* by Michelle Goodman

100 Habits of Successful Freelance Designers by Steve Gordon Jr.

Get a Freelance Life by Margit Feury Ragland

Consultant & Independent Contractor Agreements by Stephen Fishman

What to Charge by Laurie Lewis.

Craft, Inc. by Meg Mateo Ilasco

The Handmade Marketplace by Kari Chapin

Self-Promotion for the Creative Person by Lee Silber

6 Steps to Free Publicity by Marcia Yudkin

The Money Book for the Young, Fabulous and Broke by Suze Orman

A Whole New Mind by Daniel H. Pink

The Artist's Way by Julia Cameron

Free Play by Stephen Nachmanovitch

The War of Art by Steven Pressfield

Visit:

www.artistscommunities.org: find artist's retreats and residencies.

www.fabjob.com: how-to books on specific careers, from art curator to wedding planner.

www.brazencareerist.com and biznik.com: for cutting edge career networking.

www.theswitchboards.com and www.ladieswholaunch.com: find online communities for female entrepreneurs.

www.craftster.org and www.craftmafia.com: for CGs developing crafty projects.

Webworkerdaily.com: filled with articles pertaining to creative types worth reading.

Sethgodin.typepad.com, blog.guykawasaki.com, and www.ducttapemarketing.com/blog: for innovative thinking on work and creativity.

www.score.org, www.inc.com, www.entrepreneur.com, www.nawbo.org, www.nwbc.gov, and www.womanowned.com: for all kinds of small business counsel.

Acknowledgments

Thank you to Dan Mandel, the best literary agent a creative girl could ask for. Your belief in me means more than you know.

To Jennifer Kasius, my wise editor, for your guidance. You embraced this project from the first moment and your support has been unwavering. Thank you.

Thank you to the entire team at Running Press.

Thank you to each reader and every CG who shared her story in these pages.

Thank you to Erika Grevelding for supporting my creativity since we were seven-years-old. Thank you to Claire Noble and Caroline Moore: your friendship is beyond anything words could describe. Thank you to Jamie Greenberg and Wendy Levey: my family in New York. Thank you to Noelle Hancock and Micol Ostow: I'm lucky to have partners in crime like you for this writing adventure. Stacia Canon, there are way too many things to thank you for: a page could not fit them.

Thank you to Liz Auerbach, Brinn Daniels, Jessica Bailey, Megan Mazza, Erin Murphy, Tricia DeFosse, Kim Guy, Stacy Craft, Ali Watts, Carol Look, Maureen Sullivan, Jessica Stanbridge and J.J. Area. Thank you to all of my theater and creative writing professors at Notre Dame.

Thank you Christa Bourg, for being with me from the very start with a sharp editing pencil, guidance and friendship. Thank you to Ryan Fischer-Harbage, Deb DeSalvo, Anna Carey, Allison Yarrow and Corey Binns for making this book stronger.

Thank you to Tracy Weiss for being a superb friend and television agent.

Thank you to my grandparents, and all of my extended family, especially Ray and Carole Sweeney, Christine and Tait Hawes, and Bob and Linda Harrison.

Mostly, thank you to Dad, Mom, Meghan, Jack and Brian for letting me spread my wings and create a life that fits exactly who I am. You are my greatest loves.

Index